THE CHANGING FACE OF
JEWISH AND CHRISTIAN
WORSHIP IN NORTH AMERICA

TWO LITURGICAL TRADITIONS

Volume 2

The Changing Face of Jewish and Christian Worship in North America

Edited by

PAUL F. BRADSHAW
and
LAWRENCE A. HOFFMAN

University of Notre Dame Press
Notre Dame   London

Library of Congress Cataloging-in-Publication Data

The Changing face of Jewish and Christian worship in North America / edited by Paul F. Bradshaw and Lawrence A. Hoffman.
     p.   cm. — (Two liturgical traditions : v. 2)
  Includes bibliographical references and index.
  ISBN 0-268-00784-5
  1. Liturgies—North America. 2. Judaism—North America—Liturgy. 3. North America—Religious life and customs. I. Bradshaw, Paul F. II. Hoffman, Lawrence A., 1942– . III. Series.
BV193.U5C42   1991
264'.00973'09045—dc20   90-50967
                                                      CIP

Contents

Abbreviations

GLS	Grove Liturgical Study
HTR	*Harvard Theological Review*
HUCA	*Hebrew Union College Annual*
JJS	*Journal of Jewish Studies*
JLS	Alcuin/GROW Joint Liturgical Study
JQR	*Jewish Quarterly Review*
RAIL	*Religion and Intellectual Life*
SL	*Studia Liturgica*
TS	*Theological Studies*

Preface

In volume 1 of this series, we surveyed what we know about the origins and growth of Christian and Jewish liturgy from the first century, when both rabbinic Judaism and the nascent church were just defining themselves, until our time. To say that we found no points of contact between the two traditions over the years would be a gross overstatement; but, on the other hand, the relationship between church and synagogue was not, by and large, marked by mutual respect, so that neither Christian nor Jewish worship developed with an overt and conscious sense of common purpose. Living in the same time and place certainly guaranteed that some common cultural concerns determined equally common responses— the penitential character of German Jewish pietists (*Chasidei Ashkenaz*) and the parallel growth of mendicant orders, for example, in twelfth- and thirteenth-century northern Europe. But Europe was far from pluralistic. Even common concerns were shared uncommonly. The age of the Crusades, for example, meant one thing to western Christians and another thing entirely to their Jewish neighbors. Hence, Christian and Jewish liturgical evolution through the centuries has been generated chiefly by internal considerations particular to each of the two communities rather than having emerged as a shared response to environmental or cultural factors that challenged them both in equal ways.

The Enlightenment changed all that—not immediately, perhaps, and not everywhere at the same time, but eventually, perhaps even inevitably. As Jews left the ghettos and entered the body politic, they shared with Christians the need to react to such trends as rationalist attacks on time-honored

ix

theologies, the debunking of clerical authority, and ultimately the growth of secularity alongside a general societal
sense of religion as a private matter in which individuals select a tradition of their choice from among many competing
alternatives in the religious marketplace.

It was World War II that reminded us so forcefully how
much the impact of secular, even demonic, forces can impinge equally on committed Jew and Christian alike. To be
sure, the war was experienced differently for Jews, who
knew it as a Shoah. But one casualty of the war for all of us
was the demise of old-world parochialism. The age of genuine world consciousness was born.

And in precisely these terms Karl Rahner describes the
significance of Vatican II: it symptomizes the movement of
the church into a pluralistic world.[1] And out of Vatican II
came the revolutionary reform of Catholic liturgy. The roots
of change tap into a liturgical movement that traces itself further back than 1963, of course; but what was haphazard, localized, or simply one force among many now became
official, bureaucratized, and lasting. Moreover, liturgical
change was not limited to Catholics. Most Protestant and
Jewish liturgies, too, were thoroughly revised. As one would
expect of a phenomenon sparked by the altered sentiment left
in the wake of a world war, this liturgical revolution is
worldwide. But North America, and especially the United
States, has played its own particular role in experimenting
with liturgical renewal, and so it is that North American liturgies are the subject of this second volume in our series. To
be sure, not *all* of North America is included in this survey.
Much as we should have preferred a comprehensive study encompassing change as far as the Caribbean on one hand and
Alaska on the other, a reasonable compromise seemed to dic-
tate the inclusion only of English-language liturgies likely to
be encountered in churches and synagogues in Canada and
the United States.

In the pluralistic mix of the religious marketplace, with
people moving back and forth across traditions, the very
notion of a stable liturgical tradition passed down through

the generations is thrown into question. We begin this volume, therefore, with an introduction that asks, What is a liturgical tradition?

The introduction is followed by part 1: Liturgical Traditions and Theologies of "the Other," a self-conscious reflection on how Jewish and Christian attitudes toward each other have been expressed in the forms of their worship. Samuel Karff analyzes the Jewish view of Christianity, comparing what the traditional *siddur* (order of prayer) says about Christianity, with parallel assertions in the revised liturgy of the Reform movement in America. John Guerrieri highlights the changing image of Judaism in postconciliar Roman Catholic liturgy by explicating the church's official guidelines for the exposition of scripture in the liturgical context.

With the stage thus set to see the liturgical renewals of church and synagogue today as a common enterprise in which Jews and Christians engage as equal partners in a dialogue with modernity and with each other, we pass in part 2 into the book's essence, American Reform or Second Reformation?

The title of this volume of our series is intended on the one hand to note the obvious: we cannot hope to survey here renewal in worship throughout the world. As already noted, we have therefore limited our efforts to the liturgical changes that a Canadian or American English-speaking church- or synagogue-goer would encounter; and we have asked American writers who are familiar with, and responsible for, those changes to describe them to us. In addition, however, we wish to draw attention to the particular role that North American liturgical reform has played in most of the world's churches and synagogues. This is not to say that any religious phenomenon can remain leashed any more to the accident of national or geographic boundaries; nor is it to claim that American liturgical responses are better or more lasting than those in other countries. Certainly also, the centrality of which we speak varies from church to church; and even where American responses can be documented as having predated—or having been more thorough than—those occurring elsewhere, it may well be that further stages of reform will be initiated in some other quarter and then affect what happens in Canada and the United States.

But we do believe that for better or for worse—sometimes one, sometimes the other—social circumstances in North America during the 1960s and 1970s have tended to lead to a more thoroughgoing and immediate liturgical response to the worldwide phenomenon of liturgical renewal of which it is a part. To some extent, cultural experimentation in the United States has always tended to the virtue and the vice of rapidity; then too, American countercultural forces were particularly strong in the sixties and seventies, so that all forms of traditionalism, the liturgy included, were particularly vulnerable to the advocates of change; finally, economic growth and technological breakthroughs eased the difficulties inherent in institutional experimentation with old forms. Thus American churches and synagogues generally reacted more quickly and more fully to the call for change, even when the call came from across the Atlantic, as it did from Vatican II.

It may even be that future generations will see our efforts in retrospect as having constituted a second Reformation, this one worldwide, cutting equally deeply into Jewish and Christian spheres. And in that context, we may look back on North American efforts at reform, seeing them as having played their own influential role.

All six of the authors in part 2 have been intimately involved with the changes that they describe. They write firsthand recollections of what they believe they and their colleagues accomplished, usually as editors of worship books or as members of editorial committees charged with liturgical renewal. Each author was asked (1) to describe the process by which change occurred; (2) to chronicle the most significant of those changes; (3) to cite significant references that readers may use to delve deeper into these stories of change that are, after all, succinct and highly compressed accounts of complex events; and, (4) above all, to recall the goals that their committees established and the liturgical solutions that mark the work they did. In a book of this size, we were unable to include a study of every denomination. From

Christianity, therefore, we selected representative descriptions of the current state of Roman Catholic, Episcopal, Lutheran, and Methodist worship; from Judaism, we include descriptions of the new Reform and Conservative liturgies.

But the contributors' accounts of their own work are not left unchallenged. The liturgical renaissance of our time has raised critical questions against which the liturgical works themselves must be judged. Three such critiques are offered in part 3, Critiquing Liturgical Reforms. Liturgists now know what we suspect that people worshiping have always intuited: religion is deeply intertwined with other cultural forces that should at least have a vote on, if not a veto over, the process whereby liturgies are adjusted. We have therefore isolated three such cultural domains from which liturgy should be viewed and judged: theology, poetics, and feminism. The claims of each perspective are voiced by prominent thinkers—liturgists all—who have mastery as well in the particular area from which they speak.

The book concludes as it began, with a reconsideration of liturgical traditions in general, but this time against the backdrop of the case studies and their critiques. The conclusion reevaluates the challenges that are posed to Jews and Christians alike as they aspire to reshape, yet retain, the liturgical traditions they have inherited.

Paul F. Bradshaw
Lawrence A. Hoffman

NOTES

1. Karl Rahner, "Towards a Fundamental Theological Interpretation of Vatican II," *TS* 40 (1979): 716–27.

Introduction

The term *liturgical tradition* is frequently used in religious or scholarly discourse as if everyone knew exactly what it means. Christians who belong to so-called liturgical churches often use it to explain how their own worship differs from the Protestant "free church" variety. By that standard, Jews, whose worship is certainly liturgical rather than free, must definitely possess a liturgical tradition. But Jews never use the term, possibly because Judaism knows no free alternative, so that the very dichotomy between free and liturgical is alien to Jewish experience. On the other hand, is it even true that "free" churches have no liturgical tradition? Or is the dichotomy a biased judgment made by one group of Christians against another? Can a religion even exist without a tradition? And insofar as traditions include some form of worship, can there be a tradition that is not in some way liturgical?

Lawrence A. Hoffman, a coeditor of this series, is Professor of Liturgy at the Hebrew Union College–Jewish Institute of Religion in New York. He introduces this volume's concern with liturgical change in our own day by asking, What is a liturgical tradition?

1

What Is a Liturgical Tradition?

LAWRENCE A. HOFFMAN

Some years ago, I was surprised to discover that Christians differentiate between liturgical and nonliturgical traditions, a distinction I had never encountered in my Jewish tradition. That is to say, I knew I had a tradition, and I knew I had a liturgy; but it had never occurred to me that the two words went together. I filed the information away with all the other sundry details of how Christians and Jews organize our particular worlds.

But what, exactly, makes a tradition liturgical? On the face of it, that sounds like a simple question of definition, but when asked to stipulate the point where a liturgical tradition ends and a nonliturgical tradition begins, the experts with whom I spoke could reach no consensus. Catholics and Lutherans are liturgical; Quakers are not: or so they said. But what about Methodists? could it be that some are and some are not? The *United Methodist Hymnal* of 1989 certainly *looks* liturgical enough! Perhaps Wesley's European Methodism was liturgical, but Asbury's American extension was not. Are we really talking about the difference between following a fixed worship book and relying on free extemporaneous outflowing of the spirit?

One problem is that early rabbinic liturgy of the first century C.E., for example, seems not all that unlike the free-spirit variety, in that prayer leaders hewed closely to a thematic order and structure of service but ranged far and wide in their particular expressions of the moment. Yet surely rabbinic Judaism did not become liturgical only when

3

the words became fixed. Moreover, when even the freest of free church traditions meet to worship, not just anything goes. A visiting sociologist would certainly be able to point out some ordering principles. There may be a difference between literary traditions that encode their liturgies in books and nonliterary ones that do not. But is nonliterary the same as nonliturgical? For that matter, Can you even have a tradition without a liturgy of some kind?

At least, I thought, we know what *tradition* is. But not so! If scholarship were a disease, the spate of recent studies of tradition would qualify as an epidemic. Conservatives like T. S. Eliot have always been fascinated by tradition, of course. And not for nothing is the official journal of Orthodox Jewish thought, published by the Rabbinical Council of America, named *Tradition*. What is new is tradition's attraction to radicals on the left as well. In the Jewish world, for example, the distinctly unorthodox *chavurah* movement—that is to say, the countercultural revolutionaries of the sixties who reached adulthood in the seventies and adopted religion by the eighties—launched in 1985 its own counterjournal named *New Traditions*. Martin Marty likens the intellectual recovery of tradition to the recovery of ethnicity a generation ago and observes that "tradition occupies something of the space that 'the sacred' once did. The *mysterium tremendum et fascinosum* has become *tradition tremendum et fascinosum.*"[1] There is a reason why people flocked to hear Zero Mostel sing "Tradition, Tradition!" in *Fiddler on the Roof* and a reason, too, why of all the satirical Purim parodies at my very liberal seminary, the one I recall best is a student dressed up like Tevya and singing about Reform Judaism: "*No* tradition, *No* tradition!"

Not that unbounded traditionalism is such a good thing; the wholesale recovery of Grandma's favorite ethnic foods also turns out to be less wholesome than we anticipated. Particularly for minorities, cultural underclasses, and women, the call for a recovery of tradition ought to sound very suspect—like the promise of living again off a steady diet of eastern European heavy, fried, fatty foods. The wrong traditions, like the wrong foods, can kill. Still, one of the most remarkable features of the women's movement is that a significant segment insists on basing its revolution on traditional sources, recovering traditional ceremonies to celebrate its own identity, and the like. Edward Shils notes that "only traditions that have ceased to be possessions are viewed with indifference."[2] We might say, then, that although the victims of tradition wish to cease being possessed by their collective past, they clearly want instead to possess it; or, alternatively, to create or recreate or regenerate it anew; or to substitute a freshly remade countertradition—but in any case to *own* whatever it is they are willing to call *their* tradition.

Before worrying about how tradition becomes liturgical, then, we ought to say something about tradition in its own right and at least explain why we have come to the point where we can put together a series of books, not on the topic of two liturgical faiths or two liturgical histories, for example, but on two liturgical *traditions,* edited in part, mind you, by a Reform Jew, a member of the very movement whose ancestors once tried to move Shabbat to Sunday and whose descendants know that the student singing "*No* tradition" was on to something.

In what follows, I want to know: (1) Why do we yearn for tradition? (2) What is a tradition? (3) What makes a tradition liturgical? I shall conclude by saying that tradition is best likened to a work of art, while liturgy is the art form in which the work takes shape. Moreover, I shall argue that all traditions are, by definition, liturgical.

Why Do We Yearn for Tradition?

Why then do we yearn for tradition? Tradition's appeal lies, I believe, in our human search for immortality, since whatever tradition may be, it is, by definition, that which transcends any single human life. Tradition is to time what family is to space. We do not always like our families, either, but family (like tradition) is, at least ideally, our ticket to having a home.

It was those who saw their traditional home as repressive who first tried burning it down. Jaroslav Pelikan cites two culprits: the Protestant Reformation and the eighteenth-century Enlightenment, the latter personified by Thomas Jefferson, for whom "tradition was chiefly a hindrance."[3] People who grow up and revisit their childhood home may find that its old spiritual architecture has begun to look pretty run down. Just so, Jefferson glanced back at the European tradition whence he had broken free and found it shoddy and constraining. That critique of the past passed down methodically through one revolution after another: first in the United States, which turned its back on British tradition; then in France, where even the calendar was to be renumbered; and finally, throughout Europe, in revolutions both quiet and noisy. The quiet kind is best symbolized by Max Weber, who applauded modern Prussia's rationalized bureaucracy in contrast with what he called a "traditional" mode of authority. The noisy variety broke loose with Lenin and has not left us alone since.

But tradition has had its supporters too. I do not mean just the yahoo reactionaries who embrace the ancien régime, the good old days, and the old-time religion. I mean even the opponents of the old traditions, including the most thoughtful of the revolutionaries themselves, who began instituting new traditions where the old ones had failed. Can you even have *new* traditions? You certainly can. From a book unabashedly entitled *The Invention of Tradition,* we learn that only "between the late 1870s and 1914" did the British monarchic ritual, such as coronations and the changing of the palace guards, move from being "inept, private, and of limited appeal" to become "splendid, public and popular."[4] As late as Queen Victoria's coronation, the ceremony was considered of little enough import that the clergymen had not bothered to rehearse the rite and the trainbearers chattered away in obvious disinterest.[5] Jaroslav Pelikan dates the Catholic church's recovery of tradition to Cardinal Newman, who left the Church of England in 1845. And not only Catholics. Though high church symbolism among Anglicans was certainly not new in the 1880s, it was then that "vestments, surplices, incense and altar candles became increasingly common in cathedrals and city churches."[6] That too was the age that gave Germany its ceremonies of rampant nationalism, like planting oak leaves and reciting teutonic myths that claimed, at least, to be antique in origin. That same time too gave France its Bastille Day, which does not date to the revolution but only to 1880; and almost simultaneously, we Americans instituted the daily pledge of allegiance to our national flag.[7] What sociologists call *civil religion* thus had its roots in late nineteenth-century nationalism, which denied the centrality of religion but replaced it with its own traditional structures that were said to be older than they really were.

In general, then, we have seen a repetitive cycle that works like this:

First (1), a party of change challenges accepted traditions, either partially or completely. In so doing, its members justify their actions by reaching back further into the tradition than the traditionalists do. Do Abraham Geiger and Edward Schillebeeckx have anything in common? They both seek (or sought) roots in strata of their tradition that precede the established theory of traditionalism that they oppose.[8] Even the most thoroughgoing deniers of tradition, the Enlightenment rationalists, challenged the church precisely by citing a state of nature that, they said, existed even before there was a church.

In response (2), the traditionalists take refuge in a garrison mentality: recognizing that they cannot hold fast to everything, they erect defensive barriers around "sheltered species of tradition,"[9] the symbolic truths that cannot fall, come what may. What emerges is *Kulturkampf* with two warring sides doing battle over symbol systems.

No one escapes unscathed. When it is all over (3), the traditionalists emerge with their tradition changed. The Counterreformation is hardly a return to a prereformation church, after all, just as modern Jewish Orthodoxy is just that: not only Orthodox, but modern. And most surprising of all, (4) we find the antitraditionalists establishing their own brand of tradition.

This latter move amazes. Why do they bother? I think the flush of revolutionary zeal promises immortality in its own charismatic instant. The sacred community of reformers finds not only solace but salvation in each other's arms. Only thus are they led to the excesses called for by the moment: selfless devotion, violence, or even martyrdom. But in their ebullience, they hardly need the promise of eternity entailed in the link with generations past. So they willingly eschew tradition, until the next generation, when the initial charisma of the moment is thoroughly rationalized and people wonder what their mothers and fathers bothered dying for.

That is where we stand today, isn't it? Remember the radicals of the sixties? Now they practice *New Traditions* born of countercultural Judaism; their "Bible" is a best-seller called the *Jewish Catalogue,* a sort of whole earth catalogue of do-it-yourself Judaism, from building a Hebrew vocabulary to weaving amulets. Something happened to America in the aftermath of Pearl Harbor. It was the decline of a European center, and not just for Jews, who lost six million, but for American Christians too, who emerged from the European conflagration with the need to agonize over what they had witnessed and to wonder just what to do, now that America had no Europe to go home to. At first, we tried to ignore the change, as if we could just unenlist, check out of our battalions, turn back the clock, and go home again to business as usual: the Eisenhower years' call to generalized faith as Protestant, Catholic, or Jew (it did not really much matter, as long as it was faith in something);[10] women back in the kitchen, feeding the babies they could not have during the war; blacks back to the ghettos; and for the privileged, symbolized by Eisenhower himself, back to making money, with time out for golf. It did not work: the baby-boom children grew up to remind us that nothing could be the same as it was. That was their message of the sixties—an internal revolution against Eisenhower's old certainties. It was the Camelot years in Washington, then a peace corps and civil rights, and, eventually, kids thumbing their noses at established religion, or at least rewriting it. A new generation of active Jesuits moved their Woodstock seminary north to the action in Harvey Cox's "secular city," while Arthur Waskow composed a Haggadah for *Ramparts* magazine in which Huey Newton and Malcolm X star as the prophets of our time.[11]

That revolution, however, ran its course, and we now look again for proof that life is not a "tale of sound and fury told by an idiot." Ergo our return to tradition, not as it was, but as Karl Rahner conceives it, a "selective retrieval," in which, among other things, Protestants find roots in Catholicism, Catholics find roots in Judaism, and Jews claim integral connectedness with their branches called Christianity.

This retrieval of tradition is nowhere so evident as in the liturgical renewal that has gripped Christians and Jews equally, particularly in Canada and the United States. Out of nowhere, it seems, the 1970s gave us American-style liturgies: with modern English; democratic interaction; singable music, even folk-rock masses with guitar; and, for a philosophy of what we are about, if not power, at least empowerment, and certainly prayer, to the people.

I thus have an answer to my first question: Why has the renewal of interest in tradition taken root even among liberals, whose very liberalism ought to alienate them from the conservative force that tradition inherently represents? Answer: Tradition is the means to immortality for the second generation, the one that comes after the revolution and cannot live on the nostalgia generated by revolutionary memories alone. Since their newfound hankering after tradition is most clearly seen in liturgical forms, I turn now to the second issue, a definition of tradition that makes it inseparable from its liturgical expression.

What Is a Tradition?

To begin with,[12] the *Oxford English Dictionary* calls *tradition* "a saying handed down, an instruction or doctrine delivered, as in *traditio evangelica, catholico traditio* (Tertullian).'' English theological use goes back at least as far as Tyndale (1534), who spoke of the ''traditions of the elders,'' and even Wycliffe (c. 1380), who contrasts our own ''veyn tradiciouns'' with ''Goddis [com]maundements.''[13] The root, as we all know, is the Latin *tradere*, ''to hand over,'' paralleled, incidentally, by the Hebrew equivalent *masoret* (tradition) from *masar*, ''to hand over.'' In Roman law, *traditio* was a means of handing over, not doctrine, but private property, from one owner to another. For a while, early English, too, used *tradition* in the purely legal sense of handing over title or deed to property.[14]

Now what was *traditio* if not a ritualized action, a symbolic gesture denoting a particular agreed-upon public meaning? And what is liturgy if not the same thing? Ownership is a social, not a physical, fact and requires publicly recognizable markers. The first point of my definition, then, becomes this: *Liturgy* is the public act of *traditio*, the symbolic marker by which tradition is owned. Or, put another way: *Tradition* is a public property of the past, which we inherit by means of the equally public and symbolic proclamation of *traditio*, which is our liturgy.

Let us push the term *traditio* farther and see how it develops beyond mere laws of acquisition to become, not so much the passing *over* of an entity, as the passing *down* thereof. In a way, this must be a presumption from the beginning, since even in the acquisition of property, the seller must possess the object sold before the buyer does. However, there are degrees of sequential ownership, and as the legal *traditio* of property sale becomes the liturgical *traditio* of tradition transmission, the span of time between successive owners is increased. Hence the accent on a tradition's age; a tradition must be something that goes well back in time and has been handed down to us by an older generation. I mentioned above the curious fact that even new traditions claim rootedness in times more ancient than the old traditions that they replace. The very nature of tradition is to be clothed in garb that appears older than living memory. Claude Lévi-Strauss notes that primitive cultures, responding to the question of why something is done, attribute their otherwise inscrutable ritualizing to—"We've always done it," which is to say, with Tevya, "It's a tradition!" And Tevya is not alone; he could have gotten it (but did not) from the Talmud, which regularly attributes its acted-out, old-new ideas to those who are dead and cannot deny its allegations: *masoret hi*, "It is a tradition";[15] *masoret beyadenu*, "It is a tradition in our hands";[16] *masoret beyadi me'avi aba*, "It is a tradition handed down to me from my father's father";[17] and so on. When I told my teacher and colleague Harry M. Orlinsky the topic of this essay, he wrote me a short but not so cryptic note capturing the essence of tradition's traditional claim to being old, and, on that very account, good: "Tradition?" he wrote, "Why, tradition is just a lie going back at least a century." C. S. Lewis put it less succinctly, far more justly, but equally revealingly, in his *Letters to Malcolm: Chiefly on Prayer:* A man or woman is "a two-fold creature—not only . . . political, but also . . . spiritual. . . . You and I and Plato think it a fact; tens of thousands, perhaps millions, think it a fantasy. The neutral description of it is 'a traditional doctrine'."[18]

I said before that *tradition* is the public property of the past, which we inherit by means of the equally public and symbolic proclamation that is our liturgy. We can add that tradition is a *generational* legacy, a recollection that is passed down—as it were, endlessly—all the way from that single charismatic moment of initial insight in which our religious tradition had its origins. *Traditio* is the liturgical act by which each generation accepts its legacy as its own; *tradition* is the generational legacy itself, ceremoniously passed down as public property, through the liturgical act of *traditio*. Ownership is crucial here. If we, the recipients, do not take it as owned, it is not tradition any more.[19]

Ownership is also the essence of liturgy. Those who meet in sacred assembly accept the doctrines of the centuries as their own. In our ritualizing of prayer, we do more than go through the words. We necessarily make them our own in that ceremonial act called *worship,* which is itself the formal act of *traditio* that makes us willing heirs of what our forebears cared most about. We recite its creeds, rehearse its formulas, internalize its memories, and, in effect, paraphrase the promise Ruth made to Naomi (Ruth 1:16) as we say to generations past: "Where you have gone, we will go. Where you have lodged, we will lodge. Your people will be our people, and your God, our God."

It is not the case, however, that we go through the liturgical form of accepting the legacy of the past because we already believe it. We believe it because we have committed ourselves to making it ours. Pelikan illustrates what I mean when he notes that John Henry Cardinal Newman was baffled by apparent inconsistencies between Scripture and patristic literature. He therefore posited a precredal "traditionary system going back to Apostolic times" that mediated the now only apparent antitheses between the Bible and official church teaching. This novel theological fiction, if I can call it that for a moment, led Lewis Carroll to parody Newman's disciple W. G. Ward as someone who was careful to "believe as many as six impossible things before breakfast."[20] But Carroll did not understand Newman accurately. Newman's category of tradition did not include things believed because of their believability. Tradition's whole point was that it would transcend contradictions inherent in opposite pairs of dogmatic statements taken from the Bible, on the one hand, and church authority, on the other. Tradition could hardly be yet more dogma itself, that is, a third realm of belief intended to mediate between two others. So Newman posited tradition as something liturgical rather than propositional. It was a liturgical, not a theological, fiction. The act of believing impossible things may indeed be difficult, before or after breakfast. But the liturgical expression of continuity with a past is an exercise, not in believing the impossible, but in acting out the drama of the world that we have inherited in such a way that it thereby becomes irrefutable.

We understand then why the new traditions of the late nineteenth century were not doctrines but ceremonial actions, as if their authors had internalized Newman's message. Vestments, candles, oak leaves, and flags are all liturgical ritualizations, not statements of faith. A *liturgical tradition,* then, is not something in which one believes so much as it is something in which one participates, even when—perhaps especially when—the beliefs alone are beyond logical or empirical demonstration.

That is why there are scientific traditions, too, these being the very premises of the scientific undertaking that are passed down in the many rites that mark what Thomas Kuhn and others have called the process of "paradigm formation," the means by which discrete individuals come to see themselves as a "scientific community."[21] Scientific conferences do more than pass on knowledge; they pass down the scientific tradition (!), with banquets, honorees, and the rest of the panoply that we know (in our parallel context) as liturgical. Tradition for them is the same thing as tradition for us: it is a public good that one willingly takes as one's own; the framework within which we learn to recognize our world, and without which there could be no knowledge at all.

In sum, tradition is a set of nondemonstrable realia lacking a documented trail back to its putative source; it is passed down by the liturgical act of *traditio,* such that each succeeding generation willingly inherits it as its own and uses it now as a lens through which to see the world. Tradition is not the mere citing of a fact that we presume to be a demonstrably accurate photograph of the world it describes. For tradition does not so much describe as it attributes. Seen as mere belief, tradition is indeed a lie, or at least an impossible thing. Acted out in worship, it is as old as it says it is; for its liturgical perspective extends all the way back to the primal act of faith from which the community was once born, that moment of presumed theophany that liturgy recreates anew and without which we would never dare to imagine a world made better, if not now, then some day.

What Makes a Tradition Liturgical?

What then is a liturgical, rather than a nonliturgical, tradition? In the sense with which I use the word *tradition,* I venture to say: There are no nonliturgical traditions. Every tradition is by definition liturgical, in that its content is not as much reasoned, like so many Aristotelian syllogisms, as it is shaped by some form of practiced ritualizing in which one generation reenacts the taking possession of what past generations of forebears lived and died for. The ritual may be obvious, like high church ceremonial; or less than obvious—the Friends' meetinghouse ritual—or even, by analogy, the simple act of mutual greeting that does not proclaim the truth that we are friends so much as it ritualizes the possibility that we may become so.

Liturgical tradition is thus closer to being a painting than an argument; its content is denoted as present[22] rather than connoted as true. Pelikan calls it an *icon,* by which he means, not an " 'idol'—that purports to be the embodiment of that which it represents, but [really] directs us to itself rather than beyond itself; nor a 'token'—a purely arbitrary representation that does not embody what it represents"; but an icon in the religious sense of being a unique work of art that, while "not coextensive with the truth it teaches, does present itself as the way that we who are its heirs must follow, if we are to go beyond it—through it, but beyond it—to a universal truth that is available only in a particular embodiment, as life itself is available only in a particular set of parents."[23]

The key phrase here is "work of art." A much-cited tale is told of Picasso, who presented Alice B. Toklas with a portrait he had made of Gertrude Stein. "Gertrude doesn't look like that," Toklas is said to have commented. "She will," countered Picasso, "she will."

So critics say of our liturgies and their visions of a world where—going back to C. S. Lewis's example—men and women are characterized as being both political and spiritual. "They don't look spiritual," goes the objection—as if that were enough to render the traditional doctrine invalid, and were our religious doctrines mere scientific fact, it might suffice. But religionists reply, "They will; they will." And not only because human beings are changeable and so may become spiritual, whereas in fact, now they are not—that is not the point at all. They are no more and no less changeable than Gertrude Stein's face, which Picasso assures us will look different now that he has painted it other than the way we are used to seeing it. So too, the world looks different now that we enforce tradition as an icon—a work of art— upon it. Through the liturgical act of *traditio*, we see the world anew. Liturgy ritualizes our tradition's way of seeing.

Liturgy as Art Form, Tradition as Art Work

My final suggestion, then is to speak seriously of liturgy as an art form, and tradition as an art work. Speaking seriously about art, however, is no easy task. It runs counter to two thousand years of western thought, during the course of which art was imagined as being either trivial or troublesome. We can blame Plato for the whole misunderstanding, if we like, since on the one hand, he thought art to be but a pale reflection of life which is itself one step removed from the eternal world of the Ideas; so that art became one step yet further removed from truth—that is, trivial, when it comes to representing reality as it actually is.[24] But on the other hand, he knew that people were easily beguiled by artistic untruths, so he removed artists from power in his republic, thinking them dangerously false in what they say. Since Plato, we too have systematically expelled artists from our midst, shutting them up on society's fringes, the Greenwich Villages and Left Banks of our cities, and forcing them into Bohemian identities that fit our image of what artists should be like. With what love we rehearse the story of Van Gogh cutting off his ear! (It now turns out the poor man may only have been trying, rationally enough, to alleviate excruciating ear pain: he wasn't mad at all; he suffered from Meuniere's disease).[25] What satisfaction we receive from the play *Amadeus*, where we watch the *infant terrible*, Mozart, as opposed to his mainline opponent, Salieri, who cannot compose for his life but who at least looks respectable. Poor Beethoven, too, reappears on *New York Review of Books'*

David Levine T-shirts as a wild-eyed, bushy-haired maniac—
that is, as unmistakably an artist. Blame Plato again: artists,
he said, are inspired directly by the gods. They are not like
you and me.

Plato's etiology of art should remind us of ourselves, the
religionists of the world, who like to think it was not just
artists, but prophets too, who enjoyed direct access to divine
sources of wisdom.[26] Religious virtuosi have also been side-
lined onto society's margins, where they may choose from
among three roles. First, they are called "mystics," which
means they may dress funny and commune with God, as long
as they do not bother people. When their vision forces them
to confront society's leaders with an alternative to the way
things are, we call them "prophets," which means they bear
watching. If they are not careful, they make it to the final
role allotted to religious souls on fire, "martyrs," which is to
say, we set their bodies on fire too, for treason, which is just
another derivative of *tradeo*—the tradition as the opposition
sees it. Jeremiah and Ezekiel too seemed mad to the kings
and nobles of their day, who defined who belonged and who
did not. There is a reason why artists live in colonies and
religionists go on retreats. We, like artists, live at the boundaries of social structure, whence we serve up our critiques,
which are said to be of God. I do more than liken religion to
art, then. I maintain that religion *is* art, and we are its artists; our collective vision is our tradition, with its alternative
construction of the world we live in. Our liturgies are our
dramatic symbolizations by which we rehearse that alternative world to each other.

The essence of both religion and art, then, is our common
insistence on questioning how other people put the world together. We are all Picassos redrawing the world's portrait until people agree to see it our way. And insofar as scientists
join us in our pursuit of new world visions, they too are artists—we should not make the common error of mistaking the
dronelike laboratory technicians who follow out implications
of paradigms with the people who manufacture the paradigms from their own imagination, that is, from their own

artistic, and even religious, genius. Einstein too has a T-shirt bearing his portrait; the great social scientists, from Max Weber to George Simmel and even Karl Marx, as Robert Nisbet reminds us,[27] were all artists, who—no less than the poets and the visual artists—taught us to see cities and working classes, progress and the proletariat. There are religious and artistic drones also: the workshop painters who mass-produce motel art for Hiltons and Holiday Inns as if painting by number, and the apparatchiks who run religious institutions but have forgotten why, and who process people's lives "by number." They are no more artistic or religious than the unimaginative technician is a scientist. When Werner Heisenberg suggested desisting from a particular experiment because of its political consequences, Enrico Fermi objected, "But it is such a *beautiful* experiment!"[28] At the pinnacle of accomplishment, we are all the same, artists to our core. St. Augustine was a scientist who wrote treatises on time. The mathematician, Marston Morse proclaims himself an artist (choosing mathematical patterns for their "beauty's sake").[29] Leibnitz gave us calculus, and Einstein relativity; both spoke of God and eternity. Newton no less than Spinoza was convinced of God's reality made manifest in the sublime mysteries of equations.

In sum, the world is stocked full with profoundly religious visionaries who go by various names: artists, scientists, prophets, and sages. What they have in common is their own alternative way of seeing the world. Only very rarely, if at all, however, is their insight created *de novo* out of their own head. Instead, the normal course of things is to reject first the commonsense view of reality (which is the set of recipe knowledge with which ordinary people get through their day-to-day existence) and to adopt instead an alternative model of the world, a model learned from others, normally the others who have come before, which is to say from our traditions.[30] Thus, to cite a scientific example, Einstein could never have discovered relativity without Newton's laws of gravity, Clerk Maxwell's experiments in electromagnetism, Ernst Mach's insight into mechanics, and the rest of what we call the scientific tradition. What made him a genius is the fact that he did more than accept this tradition; he entered into dialogue with it, wrestled with it as Jacob wrestled with the angel, and proclaimed a new truth. Similarly, Picasso's cubism is inconceivable without the artistic tradition whence he sprang. Thornton Wilder's *Our Town* was composed in conscious reaction to the stage tradition that the playwright had inherited.[31] Harold Bloom tells us that every poet stands on the shoulders of prior poets, fighting an oedipal battle with those worthy predecessors. The prophets thus hark back to recollections of Abraham and Exodus and a covenant at Sinai, just as Jesus or the rabbis look back at the prophets. Tradition is first and foremost, therefore, an artistic phenomenon, what Nelson Goodman calls a *way of worldmaking*. "There is no perception without [prior] conception," he reminds us; and where do we get our alternative potential for perception, if not from our traditions?[32] In similar fashion, Nisbet looks at the naive view of scientists objectively droning away in a laboratory without prior visions that determine where they are to go. He calls it "the stork story of science."[33] "It is the theory that decides what can be observed," Einstein told Heisenberg.[34] In one way or another, we are all dependent on our traditions, "the theory that decides what we can observe," the handed-down way of seeing that we consult as our own critique on common sense. Even when we stand in open revolt against it, we are dependent on it, as Einstein was on Newton, Luther on Augustine, or the Abbot Suger on the anonymous Romanesque builders.

So I see tradition as the art work of the past. As with any art work, it is made of grand themes that provide continuity and of a series of conventional ways of expressing those themes.[35] Artists in every age gloss those conventional themes with their own newly discovered contemporary style, thus formulating the latest chapter in traditionary (or art) history.[36] As worshipers in the closing years of the twentieth century, we stand within our respective traditions, holding firmly to our inherited themes and conventions. At the same time, as members of our own age, we experiment with the styles that differentiate our generation from others. Style cuts across different lines of tradition, and that is why American Jews and Christians in this present moment can make comments about themselves that apply equally to each other as well.

If indeed tradition is a work of art growing through time as themes and conventions are met by a series of ever-novel styles, we have precisely what traditions have always said they are, that is, a continuously expanding commentary in which each new age considers the past as it has been handed down and then glosses it with its own stratum of comment. This is exactly what at least one modern philosopher, R. A. Sharpe, finds as the very essence of art too, namely, that a work of art is an object for interpretation. Sharpe dispenses with the usual explanations of art as mimetic representation, or the expression of our emotions, or even as necessary illusion. Art, he maintains, provides an alternative world whence we learn to see, hear, and feel the so-called real world differently from how we otherwise might. "I think of art," Sharpe concludes, "as the creation of objects which the public can interpret. . . . Art sustains multiple interpretations, no one of which is necessarily the only correct [one]. . . . The variability of interpretations depends mainly on the variety of possible readings of a complex object."[37]

That, I maintain, is exactly so: art is the establishment of themes that successive conventions comment upon.[38] And that, too, is what a tradition is—a handed-down thematic arrangement of reality; the grid through which we see freshly; the alternative world that we call Judaism or Christianity, by means of which we see things others do not.

Now at last, I can conclude with the liturgical part of the equation. I said before that by definition and following a suggestion by Cardinal Newman, we can understand all tradition as liturgical, in that liturgy is the acting out of a script for seeing the world.[39] Liturgy is our drama of the centuries providing us with the themes that persist through time, the assortment of conventions we have used to express those themes, and the experience of each new style as it emerges.

We leave the ritual arena having acted out our people's grand opera of time and space, postulating such impossibilities as creation and redemption, sin and punishment, incarnation and resurrection, covenant and commandment, or however else it is that we have been taught to see the world. These are our themes, the textual chapters of church and synagogue. We perceive a variety of conventions and commentaries passing through our liturgies as the grand story unfolds—its musical motives, its sacred spaces, its actors living and dead, its hopes and fears. And we go out into the world to live our liturgies by enforcing their vision on the two-dimensional cardboard world of common sense, where there is nothing grander than the need to fix the car muffler, cook a TV dinner, or get to work on time.

We care about our liturgical traditions, not solely because they are academically enticing, but because they are ours by virtue of our own reiterated liturgical act of *traditio*. Like the celebrated double helix of the DNA molecule, Christians and Jews have mapped a common path through time and space. As works of art, our traditions are like amassed sediments of interpretation on the raw text of life, layer after layer of the church or the Jewish people's way of worldmaking. Some of those constructions came about because of one another; others, despite one another; relatively few, in blissful disregard of one another.

We share also this happy time in which we meet—the new Reformation of our age, in which church and synagogue are being remade, not only before our eyes, but also in, with, and by our own hands. We are not only witnesses to history in the making; we are the history being made, or, better, we are the history-makers. This volume, the second in the series, considers how this is so. The Mishnah is fond of saying such things as "There are two kinds of going out [on the Sabbath] which are really four." Perhaps we should gloss that text with this: "There are two liturgical traditions which are really one," and we are they, bound like two atoms whose historical mass destines us to swirl endlessly through time as one larger molecular whole, and greater together, therefore, than we ever might hope to be as mere atomic isolates. For we, together, are committed by the very essence of the *traditio* that is our liturgies, to make the world over in the traditional vision we call God's.

NOTES

1. Martin E. Marty, "Tradition," *RAIL* 2/1 (Fall, 1984): 10, 13.

2. Edward Shils, *Tradition* (Chicago, 1981), p. 44.

3. Jaroslav Pelikan, *The Vindication of Tradition: The 1983 Jefferson Lecture in the Humanities* (New Haven and London, 1984), pp. 43–45.

4. David Cannadine, "The British Monarchy," in Eric Hobsbawm and Terence Ranger, eds., *The Invention of Tradition* (Cambridge, 1983), p. 120.

5. David Cannadine, *Splendor out of Court: Royal Spectacle and Pageantry in Modern Britain, c. 1820–1977,* cited in David Kertzer, *Ritual, Politics, and Power* (New Haven, 1988), p. 176.

6. Cannadine, "British Monarchy," p. 131.

7. Eric Hobsbawm, "Mass-Producing Traditions: Europe 1870–1914," in Eric Hobsbawm and Terence Ranger, eds., *The Invention of Tradition* (Cambridge, 1983), pp. 277, 271, 280.

8. See Marty, "Tradition," p. 14.

9. See Pelikan, *Vindication of Tradition,* pp. 46–47, for examples.

10. See Will Herberg's classic, *Protestant, Catholic, Jew: An Essay in American Religious Sociology* (New York, 1955).

11. Arthur Waskow, "A Radical Haggadah for Passover," in *Ramparts* 7/11 (April 1969): 25–33.

12. One gets an impression from the earliest of sources in Judaism, Christianity, and Islam, too, that *tradition,* properly speaking, is *oral* material handed down by tradents. From this it follows that an oral tradition is a redundancy, while, more to the point, a liturgical tradition, if *liturgical* is associated solely with written records like prayer books, would be an oxymoron. Whatever a liturgical tradition is, it will have to be something other than a set of texts that we catalogue like so many books on a library shelf.

13. Both cited in the *Oxford English Dictionary,* s.v. "Tradition."

14. See Reginald G. Marsden, ed., *Select Pleas in the Court of Admiralty,* 1540: "The byer . . . may entre and take possession of the said shype goods . . . withowte any furthere tradicion or delyvery" (cited in *Oxford English Dictionary,* s.v. "Tradition").

15. For example, B.R. 99b.

16. Meg. 31a.
17. P.T. San. 11:5.
18. C. S. Lewis, *Letters to Malcolm: Chiefly on Prayer* (New York and London, 1963 and 1964), p. 32.
19. Interestingly, the same Latin *tradere* gives us the English "treason" and "traitor," which, as we all know, is what characterizes *other* people who hand down doctrines without due regard for their accuracy. *We,* on the other hand, think always of ourselves as loyal traditionalists. Loyalty to what one has received can go too far, certainly. In *Richard III,* Buckingham accuses the cardinal of being "too ceremonious and traditional"; and Milton accuses his entire age of being perverse because, while "eager in the reformation of Names and Ceremonies," the people of that era are "as traditional and as ignorant as their forefathers." But in general, we prefer the label "zealous traditionalist" to that of "misguided traitor," even though it is not always easy to know which is which.
20. The discussion, including Carroll's parody, can be found in Jaroslav Pelikan, *Vindication of Tradition,* pp. 26–29. Newman's notion of tradition, however, is more complex than that. It changed over time. He seems originally to have gotten the idea from Edward Hawkins at Oxford, who emphasized "the Church's mode of teaching [which] hands on its message orally from generation to generation" (see Guenter Blemer, *Newman on Tradition* [1967], English ed., trans. Kevin Smith, [London, 1961], p. 45). Hence, Newman argued that the "safeguard against its [tradition's] corruption was the unanimity of its witnesses. The Canon of Scripture was another. Also . . . the Creed, that is, by a fixed form of words" (p.45). But he was unhappy with this thesis alone, so by 1836, in his *Brothers Controversy,* he posited two countervailing sources of tradition: first, the Apostles' Creed and matters passed on orally from bishop to bishop in the form of dogmatic statements of faith; and second, "primarily in the *liturgies,* in the literature of controversy, in sermons and the like . . . [that is,] the prophetic tradition" (p. 47; emphasis mine). After his conversion (1845), he referred to the former as *verbum dei objectivum* and to the latter as *verbum dei subjectivum* (pp. 57–58). Recent Newman studies thus do not, it seems to me, bear out the notion that Newman's understanding of liturgy as discussed by Pelikan was central to him, though there is no denying that Newman did proclaim the doctrine as at least part of his larger message. Cf. Thomas J. Norris, *Newman and His Theological Method* (Leiden, 1977); and Jovett Lynn

Powell, *Three Uses of Christian Discourse in John Henry Newman* (Missoula, Mont., 1975), which barely refer to liturgy throughout their discussions.

21. Cf. Thomas S. Kuhn, *The Structure of Scientific Revolutions* (Chicago, 1962); Alan E. Musgrave, "Kuhn's Second Thoughts," in Gary Gutting, ed., *Paradigms and Revolutions: Applications and Appraisals of Kuhn's Philosophy of Science* (Notre Dame and London, 1980); and references to Kuhn's later work in Musgrave's bibliography, p. 52.

22. See Susanne Langer's classic characterization of art as "presentational" symbolism (*Philosophy in a New Key* [Cambridge, Mass., 1942]); similarly, I hold that liturgy, through which tradition is passed down, is its own unique art form and thus is "presentational," denotative as a painting.

23. Pelikan, *Vindication of Tradition*, pp. 55–57.

24. There were, on the other hand, nineteenth-century art critics, like G. Albert Aurier, who applied Plato positively to art and argued that the Platonic "Ideas are mystical essences . . . manifested as symbols in this world, and brought to life [only] through art." See Patricia Mathews, "Aurier and Van Gogh," in Kathleen J. Regier, ed., *The Spiritual Quest in Modern Art* (Wheaton, Ill., 1987), p. 16.

25. *New York Times,* July 25, 1990, p. C11.

26. See the discussion by David Tracy, *The Analogical Imagination: Christian Theology and the Culture of Pluralism* (New York, 1981), pp. 12–13. His claim, especially, is that artists are "antennae to new visions of human possibility" (p. 12), that religious thinkers too "disclose permanent possibilities for human existence," much as a classic in general does. Thus religious thought produces "some classical expression of the human spirit on a particular journey in a particular tradition." Classics, moreover, are "always public, never private" (p.14). But society marginalizes just such visionaries, so that "where art is marginalized, religion is privatized." Cf. references provided by Tracy in his discussion.

27. Robert Nisbet, *Sociology as an Art Form* (New York, 1976).

28. Werner Heisenberg, *Tradition in Science* (New York, 1983), p. 7.

29. "Discovery in mathematics is not a matter of logic. It is rather the result of mysterious powers which no one understands, and in which the unconscious recognition of beauty plays an important part. Out of an infinity of designs, the mathematician chooses

one pattern for beauty's sake." Cited in Nisbet, *Sociology as Art Form*, p. 5.

30. Cf. Jacques Barzun, *Darwin, Marx, Wagner: Critique of a Heritage* (Chicago and London, 1941). All three scientific or artistic geniuses, though claiming independence and absolute novelty, actually depended on their traditions, Darwin's ideas going back as far as Diderot, for example, who recognized the idea of the survival of the fittest as early as 1754 (p.42).

31. See Thornton Wilder, introduction to *Three Plays* (New York, 1957).

32. Nelson Goodman, *Ways of Worldmaking* (Indianapolis and Cambridge, 1978), p. 6.

33. Robert A. Nisbet, *The Sociological Tradition* (New York, 1966), p. 18.

34. Heisenberg, *Tradition in Science*, p. 10.

35. For greater detail, see Lawrence A. Hoffman, *The Art of Public Prayer* (Washington, D.C., 1988).

36. See Jacob Neusner's work (for example, his *First Principles of Systemic Analysis: The Case of Judaism within the History of Religion*, Studies in Judaism [Lanham, Md., 1987]) emphasizing the notion that Jewish tradition is really not tradition, in that tradition builds on its predecessors as a diachronic unfolding, while the classics of Jewish literature, though pretending to be just that, are actually their own statement on the world in which they are composed. Thus the Mishnah, though apparently built out of scripture, actually ignores much that the Bible says and states its own systemic and synchronic account of reality. The Babylonian Talmud, especially, addresses this dissonance between scripture and Mishnah, taking up the task to link Mishnah with biblical prototype. His opponent in the debate seems to be Gershom Scholem, whose view was republished in Neusner, *Understanding Jewish Theology* (New York, 1973).

37. R. A. Sharpe, *Contemporary Aesthetics: A Philosophical Analysis* (New York, 1983), pp. 183–85.

38. See Hoffman, *Art of Public Prayer*, for a detailed understanding of terms used here, namely, *theme, convention,* and *style*.

39. For Newman, the liturgical act of *traditio* overcame successive, but conflicting, interpretations of truth. We can adopt my artistic analogy and my literary-anthropological discussion of text to Newman's insight, seeing his alternative truths as successive conventions of the same theme, or, alternatively, as commentary and

supracommentary on the church's cultural text. In either case, there is no reason to expect automatic total consistency between successive conventions or commentaries—not if Sharpe is right in seeing art as unfolding essentially the possibility of multiple interpretations. It happens that theologians worry about harmonizing these necessarily incongruous layers of tradition—either through scholastic interpretation, as in the high Middle Ages, or in historical development theory, as the nineteenth century preferred. But those who live the tradition need not posit consistency as a necessary attribute of artistic truth. Their liturgical drama engages them in different strata as if they are consistent, and that suffices.

PART 1

Liturgical Traditions and Theologies of ''the Other''

Introduction

Liturgical traditions specify the identity and beliefs of the faith community that rehearses them. But identity can be inclusive or exclusive: the way our group is like everyone else, or the way it is not. From the very moment that Christianity emerged as an independent faith no longer identical to some variety of Judaism, it necessarily emphasized its exclusivity vis-à-vis its Jewish origin; and Judaism too took pains to clarify what made Christianity different in essence from what Jews could accept as authentically Jewish. Throughout most of the Middle Ages this exclusive definition of each other, colored further by theological polemic on both sides, became codified in liturgical expression, with the result that Christians and Jews learned about each other as much from what their prayers said as from their actual experience with each other on the street or in the marketplace.

The Christian theological perception of Jews is better known than the Jewish theological perception of Christians, primarily because the reality of Christian power and Jewish powerlessness resulted in anti-Jewish legislation and popular, or even governmental, violence against Jews. But if Christians in the Middle Ages were not positively disposed toward Judaism, Jews were equally not enamored of Christianity. Both groups thus developed an exclusive view of self and a negative theology of "the other," both of which were preached in powerful ways in their liturgies.

By contrast, a significant characteristic of our own time is the gradual development of an inclusive definition of our two religious communities. Phrases like "the Judeo-Christian heritage" or the act of worship in common on American

29

Thanksgiving, for instance, betray the desire of most modern Christians and Jews to see each other as positively related in some familial sort of way. Reflecting this new perception of ourselves, both church and synagogue have scrutinized their liturgies in an effort to purge them of an old and dangerous negative theology of "the other."

Samuel E. Karff is rabbi of Congregation Beth Israel in Houston and past president of the Central Conference of American Rabbis. He teaches also as Adjunct Professor at Rice University's Department of Religious Studies. John Gurrieri, a Roman Catholic priest, is an archdiocesan consultant for liturgy in the Archdiocese of Los Angeles and has served as the executive director of the Bishops' Committee on the Liturgy of the National Conference of Catholic Bishops. He lectures also at Mount St. Mary's College in Los Angeles and is Adjunct Professor of Liturgy at St. John's Seminary, Camarillo. In this part, Karff and Gurrieri explore their liturgies past and present, explicating their respective theologies of "the other."

The Perception of Christians
in Jewish Liturgy: Then and Now

SAMUEL E. KARFF

In moments of worship a religious community defines itself.[1] Through its liturgy a people asks, as do Jews near the end of the Yom Kippur service, in this traditional translation of an equally traditional prayer:

> What are we? What is our life? What is our goodness? What is our virtue . . . What can we say to Thee, Lord our God and God of our ancestors. . . . Yet from the first Thou didst single out mortals and consider them worthy to stand in Thy presence. . . . Thou, Lord our God, didst graciously grant us this day of atonement ending in the complete forgiveness of all our iniquities.[2]

Through the inspired flow of a liturgist's pen the members of a community proclaim a double paradox: I, a finite creature, have been granted the dignity of a covenant with the infinite God; the infinite God of all creation is uniquely bonded to the people of Israel. Through that bond I, a Jew, find my primary path to forgiveness and renewal of life even in the midst of my brokenness.

Although the early rabbis focused primarily on God's relationship to Israel, they viewed the Jewish covenant within the matrix of God's relation to all humanity. The covenant with Adam and Noah preceded the covenant with Abraham. Nor does the covenant with Abraham invalidate those earlier covenants.

Rabbinic literature reflects an abiding awareness of God's relation to every human creature through the use of such

31

terms as *adam* or *enosh* (human being) or *beriyot* (human-kind). Thus we read: "If one sees the sages of the peoples of the world one should say: 'Praised be thou who has given of his glory to humanity' (literally: 'his creatures,' *beriyotav*)."[3]

To be sure, the acknowledgment of the universal is almost always enmeshed in an affirmation of the particular. Thus, in the prayer cited earlier, the infinite God's relation to *enosh*, all finite creatures, is followed by the assertion that Yom Kippur's reconciling power is God's special gift to his people Israel. Note, there is nothing here to suggest that other people have no access to divine forgiveness; only that this particular medium for reconciliation reflects the special bond between God and Israel.

When one lays claim to a special covenant with the Eternal, one may at times speak as a child who, in the intimacy of parental embrace (and in the physical absence of siblings), acts as if his or her bond with father or mother is not only different from, but more precious than, the others. Let us press the metaphor. If the relation between siblings is sorely strained, that moment of intimacy with a parent may also be a time for hostility against the others and an appeal to the parent for deliverance from them; perhaps even a time to challenge their claim to equal consideration by the parent.

Given the painful, bruising quality of much of the Jewish-Christian encounter in history, we should expect some liturgical traces of antisibling, i.e., anti-Christian, sentiment. Let us briefly examine the record.

The Liturgy of Premodernity

We begin with the more subtle polemics. The Mishnah informs us of a time when the daily recitation of the *Shema* ("Hear O Israel, the Lord our God, the Lord is One") was preceded by the recitation of the Decalogue. Why was the Decalogue subsequently omitted from the service? The Talmud explains: "So that the *minim* [sectarians] might not charge that these commandments alone were given to Moses at Sinai."[4] According to some scholars this reference to *minim* could well refer to Christians who no longer felt the binding character of the biblical ritual commandments or the oral Torah of the rabbis.[5] The rabbis therefore replaced the Decalogue with a prayer that declares that God so loved Israel, God gave Israel the Torah. "Incline our hearts to perceive, learn, and teach, to observe, do, and fulfill gladly, *all the teachings of your Torah*."[6]

Liturgical polemics were frequently much more confrontational and invidious. Consider, for example, the poetic insertions (*piyyutim*) that probably originated in Palestine during the fifth and sixth centuries. During that period of Byzantine hegemony Christianity flourished. Even as Justinian (reigned from 527 to 565) built great churches in the Holy Land, he severely constricted the Jewish community. Some Jews were forcibly converted. Synagogues were transformed into churches. The study of the oral Torah was banned. In this grim environment the polemical *piyyut* was born. In measured cadences these liturgical poems expressed immeasurable pain and hostility. Yannai (fl. sixth century), one of the most prolific of the early poets, wrote *piyyutim* that directly challenged the faith claims of the church. In one poem Yannai denies that God gave birth to a son and asserts that Christians revered a dead man rather than the living God.[7]

The most anti-Christian *piyyut* came to be incorporated in the Yom Kippur liturgy. It was entitled "Who Does Not Fear You Who Are the King of the *Goyim* [the non-Jews]?" In this poem Jesus is described as the son of a wanton woman. Even when included in the liturgy, however, such expressions were printed ambiguously with letters or words omitted, and in any event, all such *piyyutim* have long since disappeared from the Jewish prayer book; but they offer historical traces of Jewish anguish and anger seeking a liturgical catharsis. They bear witness to the grimmest periods in the encounter of synagogue and church.[8]

The twelfth benediction of the *Tefillah*, part of the very core of the daily liturgy, has also been shaped by the Jewish-

Christian encounter. In its present form this benediction reads: "May the slanderers have no hope; may all wickedness perish instantly; may all Thy enemies be soon cut down. Do Thou speedily uproot and crush the arrogant. . . . Blessed art Thou, O Lord, who breakest the enemies and humblest the arrogant."[9]

Known as *Birkat minim* (the benediction concerning sectarians), this prayer dates back in one form or another at least to the end of the first century. Scholars theorize that the word *malshinim* (slanderers) may well have been directed at Jews who converted to Christianity and who then proceeded to malign the texts and teachings of their abandoned heritage. In place of *malshinim* (slanderers), an earlier version of the prayer contained the word *meshumadim* (apostates)—that is, those who were baptized. Several texts of this benediction taken from the Cairo Genizah go further still, identifying the subject of hostility not only as *minim* (sectarians) but as *notzrim* (literally, Nazarenes, or Christians).[10] Whether, as some claim, the prayer was originally directed against Jewish sectarians or, as others insist, against Judeo-Christians,[11] there is no reason to doubt that over the centuries this prayer was directed against enemies of the people of Israel, among whom Christians were often to be reckoned.

The *Alenu* prayer too has a polemical dimension. Rooted in antiquity, this prayer has been used since the fourteenth century to conclude the worship service. The *Alenu* begins by praising God for having singled out the people Israel for a special covenant and witness ("Who has not made us like the nations of the world") and concludes with the hope that some day "the world shall be perfected under the reign of the Almighty" and all will "accept the yoke of Thy dominion."[12]

Originally the prayer included an invidious distinction between Israel and those who "prostrate themselves to vanity and emptiness and pray to a God who cannot save them" (based on Isaiah 30:7 and Isaiah 45:20). Jewish apologists over the centuries have claimed that this paragraph was directed against pagan idol worshipers of antiquity alone, but there is some evidence that in post-Crusades Europe this paragraph expressed both anti-Christian and anti-Moslem animus. A commentary from the period notes:

> I have heard that one should say "vanity and emptiness" because the arithmetic sum represented by the Hebrew letters that constitute these words is the same as the sum of the Hebrew letters that make up "Jesus and Mohammed." Therefore, all who believe in the two of them "prostrate themselves to vanity and emptiness."[13]

Either in self-protection or in response to the demands of government censors, this paragraph of the *Alenu* was dropped from the liturgy of Ashkenazic Jews. Yet we can actually find it restored in several contemporary Orthodox prayer books.[14]

For the final entry in this cursory survey of anti-Christian polemics, we turn to the Passover home prayer book (the Haggadah). At one moment in the seder ritual, the door is opened so that Elijah, the harbinger of the messiah, may be welcomed into our homes. As the doors open, participants recite:

> Pour out Your wrath on the nations who know You not and upon the kingdoms that call not upon Your name (Psalm 79:6–7).
> For they have devoured Jacob and laid waste to his habitation. Pour out Your indignation and let the fierceness of Your anger overtake them (Psalm 69:25).
> You will pursue them in anger and destroy them from under the heavens of the Eternal (Lamentations 3:66).[15]

This declaration on seder night probably dates from *Machzor Vitry* (c. eleventh-twelfth century) and may well have been fully integrated into the Passover liturgy after the depredations of the Crusaders.[16] Those biblical verses, originally directed at Israel's enemies in antiquity, seemed painfully resonant to medieval Jewry. The underlying sentiment may be paraphrased: "Why, O Lord, do You seemingly direct your wrath at us who bear the price of serving You in this unredeemed world? Pour Your wrath upon those who by their actions express contempt for Your purposes."

Nineteenth- and Twentieth-Century Liturgical Reform

Such liturgical hostility toward "the other" remained unchallenged as long as it mirrored the world of the Jewish worshiper. It became problematic only when new social and political developments spurred some western-European Jews to view the world through different eyes. Particularly, as the liturgy was translated, its editors felt the need to respond to the afterglow of the Jewish Emancipation from the ghetto, the promise of citizenship, and the aura of Enlightenment—with its declaration of a human sphere that transcended all religious particularism. Some Jews now felt the need for a new prayer book, with Israel no longer imaged as "a people who dwell apart" and the world no longer perceived as enemy camp.

In particular, Reform Jews of nineteenth-century Germany perceived themselves, and wished to be perceived by others, as a religious fellowship (not a nation) proclaiming the universal message of ethical monotheism in a spirit of reconciliation with the enlightened sectors of the non-Jewish world. The liturgical implications of this new self-image were obvious to rabbis like Abraham Geiger (1810–1874), a leading advocate of reform, and rabbi in Breslau, Frankfort, and Berlin, who declared: "The separation between Israel and the other peoples which existed at one time has no right to be expressed in prayer. Rather ought there to be an expression of joy that such barriers are increasingly falling."[17] If indeed the prayers of the synagogue were to be recited increasingly in the language of the land—the language we and our neighbors understood—and if under the new climate our neighbors would more likely venture into our synagogues from time to time, it was all the more essential that our liturgy not even appear to alienate us from them.

The new liturgical spirit came to be embodied most eloquently in the prayer books of the American Reform movement. Indeed, with one exception, the remainder of this essay will focus on American Reform liturgy, which has been at the cutting edge in articulating a post-Emancipation theology of "the other."

The classical liturgical statement of American Reform Judaism is to be found in its *Union Prayer Book* (*UPB*) of 1894–1895. Though revised twice since then (in 1924 and again in 1940), it remained in essence Reform Judaism's book of worship here until the 1970s, when the *Gates* series supplanted it. Conspicuously missing from all editions of the *Union Prayer Book* are the poems that lament our degradation at the hands of others. Gone completely is the twelfth benediction of the *Tefillah* which invokes God's wrath against the slanderers of our people. Deleted from the *Union Haggadah: Home Service for Passover* (1923) are the words, "Pour out Thy wrath upon the nations who know Thee not." Added however, is a prayer for "grace to fulfill [our] mission with zeal tempered by wisdom and guided by regard for other men's [and women's] faith."[18]

Gone also is the phrase in the *Alenu* prayer that praises God for having not "made us like the nations of the lands." Featured instead is the part of the prayer that proclaims that the God we worship is the creator of all. Elsewhere, in place of the phrase, "Grant peace to us and all Israel your people," the Hebrew is changed to read: "Grant peace . . . to us and all who revere your name."[19]

The Reform liturgical consensus that prevailed during the first half of the twentieth century accentuated and made explicit the universalism implicit in classic Judaism. This liturgical model was reappraised and found wanting after World War II, when the Reform prayer book's balmy spirit of meliorism and its tilt toward universalism seemed strikingly incongruous to a Jewish community that had emerged from the Holocaust. Real enemies remained in our world. A Jew who prayed history could not liturgically ignore the Holocaust or the traumatic rebirth of a Jewish state called Israel. The Messianic Age was not virtually within human grasp, as Reform liturgy had suggested.

And yes, the accent on universalism had rendered Reform too porous a vessel for a millennial heritage. Was not Judaism's staying power a function of its sinewy particularism? If our covenant was too bland, too undifferentiated, how could it engage and nourish us? A rebalancing was necessary to mirror a post-Holocaust world and to respond to American society's new respect for pluralism and diversity. Our liturgists were now challenged to be at once unapologetically particularistic and patently respectful of "the other." So the *UPB* gave way to *Gates of Prayer* and *Gates of Repentance*.[20]

These new Reform prayer books restored to the *Alenu* the words claiming that God has indeed "set us apart from the other families of the earth, giving us a destiny unique among the nations," even as they retain the universal hope for the time when "all will acclaim You as their God and, forsaking evil, turn to You alone."[21] After considerable debate the new Reform Haggadah continued to omit the words, "Pour out Your wrath upon the nations who know You not," even though the artist, Leonard Baskin, commissioned to provide art for the work, had included a full-page illustration to accompany the phrase in question. (Baskin's rendering was omitted as well.) By way of illustrative contrast, we note that the Conservative movement's new Haggadah retained the formula but only with this clarifying meditation:

> Why does the impassioned invocation of divine wrath belong in our celebration of freedom? Because by opting conveniently for chronic amnesia, the world compels us to remember freedom's foes. So we remember the Hadrianic persecutions, the Crusades, the ritual murder accusations, the inquisition, the pogroms, the Holocaust. . . . And we remember God-fearing men and women of all nations who risked their lives for us in so many valleys of the shadow of death.[22]

One can virtually hear the studied effort to balance a remembrance of Israel's particular pain with an embrace of those who risked all for the sake of a shared vision of the sacred. Here, too, is an open particularism.

Conclusions: Particularism, Not Ethnocentrism

Surely the last liturgical word has not been written, nor the final edition of our liturgy been published. In every generation, implicitly or explicitly the liturgy proclaims a theology of "the other." What guidelines emerge from the tradition and from the efforts of contemporary liturgical poets?

1. Liturgy is intrinsically particularistic. The worship service is a time for the community to evoke its inner history—its own singular experience of the living God. So, for example, after duly celebrating God's creation of the world, classic Jewish liturgy praises God for redeeming our ancestors from Egypt and giving us the Torah. The Yom Kippur liturgy proclaims the paradox of an infinite God's relation to all human creatures, but then the service acknowledges the special gift of Yom Kippur to the people Israel. The moment of worship is Israel's private time with the divine parent. It is the hour to confirm our special bond with the One who has become known to our ancestors and to us. That evocation of Israel's covenant with Adonai gives Jews a sense of the particular claims that the covenant makes upon us and upon God. Thus in the midst of confessing our sins and seeking forgiveness on Yom Kippur we hear the cantor and choir recite the medieval poem:

> We are your people; You are our king.
> We are your children; You are our parent.
> We are your possession; You are our portion . . .
> We are your beloved; You are our friend.[23]

2. The liturgical moment is also a time for a mission statement—a time to affirm the transcendent significance of Israel's particular witness to God in the world, a time to confirm that God's world needs Israel's testimony. So we say, "It is our duty to give thanks to thee, to praise and glorify thee, to bless and hallow thy name. How good is our destiny, how pleasant our lot, how beautiful our heritage."[24] As part of its mission statement the liturgy also confirms that the meaning of my life derives from being faithful to Israel's covenant and sharing Israel's task.

3. But responsible liturgy does not permit a moment of intimacy to become a moment of theological ethnocentrism. Our prayers must allow that the One we call Adonai is in some sense known by those outside our covenant and is involved redemptively in their lives too. After all, the biblical heritage proclaims that the One who redeemed Israel from Egypt also freed the Philistines from Caphtor (Amos 9:7). And the One who became known to Moses was also heard by the non-Israelite prophet Balaam (Numbers 22:9–12, 23:26, 24:1–2).

Thus, after duly affirming God's redemption of Israel from Egyptian bondage, *Gates of Prayer* translates the Hebrew phrase, "who answers his people," as "who is the answer to all who cry out to him." And elsewhere: "We give thanks for our sages and teachers of all peoples and faith who have brought many to deeper understanding of you and your will."[25]

Be it granted that on occasion our classic literature and liturgy did proclaim an exclusive paternal-filial bond of love between God and Israel. Today's liturgist should help us preserve the mystery of Israel's election without implying a greater divine love for Israel than for others and without even appearing to denigrate the integrity of God's other covenants. There is a subtle, but real, difference in tone between praising God "for not having made me a non-Jew," as does the traditional liturgy, and praising God for "having made me a member of the household of Israel"—as does our new Reform liturgy.

Is it really necessary during my people's private time with God to explicitly affirm Adonai's relation to those outside my covenant? Given the many centuries of liturgical ethnocentrism, it is time for some "affirmative action." If there are others who still make me pay a price for being Jewish in

an unredeemed world, I have even more reason to acknowledge that some of God's noblest servants are also others.

4. *These preliminary guidelines for contemporary liturgy
do not encompass a special dimension of the Jewish-
Christian encounter today.* Christians visiting a synagogue
may be inclined to join in, in the English responses. Such
visitors report feeling at home with the general spirit, if not
with all the specific claims, of the Jewish liturgy. After all,
was not Jesus a son of the synagogue? In opening themselves
to the experience of Jewish worship, are not Christians re-
claiming their Judaic roots?

This phenomenon is asymmetrical. Christians feel more
comfortable in a synagogue (especially where there is substantial English in the liturgy) than do Jews in a church. For
Christians the Jewish liturgical experience is a pilgrimage to
their roots. For Jews, the Christ-centered liturgy of the
church marks the gospel we cannot profess.[26]

The Christian's empathetic response to Jewish worship
creates no theological problems for Judaism. Non-Jews were
welcome to pray—even to bring offerings to God—in the ancient temple. Christian responsiveness to Jewish worship may
be considered an intimation of messianic times.

However, the Christian's role in Jewish worship does become more problematic when one moves from reading or
hearing prayers in a pew to a visible role on the *bimah* (pulpit). Consider the case of a mixed marriage. Suppose the
children are being raised as Jews and the time has come for
the child's bar- or bat-mitzvah ceremony. Both parents will
be on the *bimah*. In many Reform synagogues the mother of
the child recites the blessings over the kindling of the Sabbath lights. There may also be a symbolic transmission of the
Torah scroll from grandparents to parents to child—signaling
the child's acceptance of the privileges and obligations of his
or her heritage.

If the child's mother is Christian, shall she be invited to
kindle the lights and lead the congregation in the blessings?
The Responsa Committee of the Central Conference of

American Rabbis concludes: "It would be appropriate to have that parent participate in some way in that service, but not in the same way as the Jewish parent."[27] The traditional blessing praises God "who has sanctified us by his commandments and commanded us to kindle the lights of the Sabbath." The Christian does not feel accountable for such ritual commandments. For that reason Jews traditionally regard Christians as members of the Noahide covenant: they feel bound by the moral laws applicable to all God's creatures and have rejected idolatry. Hence, strictly speaking, the Christian mother of the child does not live under the commandment to kindle those Sabbath lights. The non-Jewish mother may be asked to recite another text or that part of the kindling liturgy that does not declare the unique covenantal obligations of a Jew.

Our synagogue's Torah transmission ceremony makes the same distinction. The non-Jewish parent helps dress and undress the Torah scroll and stands with the child when he or she reads from it, but the Jewish parent alone affirms some variant of the words, "This is *our* Torah which I now hand to you."

Such attention to boundaries is ultimately more respectful of each tradition. Christians who profess a love for their Jewish neighbor or spouse or child and who feel a bond to the synagogue are, from a Jewish perspective, the equivalent of *Yirei Adonai*, God-fearing gentiles. While they may feel part of Israel, and the church regards itself as the "new Israel," they cannot be so regarded by the synagogue. The new spirit of mutual respect that is so precious a part of our interreligious scene and the realities of mixed marriage summon us to love each other without denying our otherness.

5. Nor does civility and openness compromise the Jewish liturgical claim to transcendent truth. Our liturgy proclaims that we are charter witnesses to a truth not yet acknowledged or fully lived by us or the world. By being Jews we acknowledge that truth. When we live our covenant, we do the most we can to further the coming of God's dominion. The new

Reform prayer includes: "You have chosen us and set us apart from all the peoples, and in love and favor have given us the Sabbath day as a sacred inheritance."[28]

Our liturgy (including the *Alenu* prayer) presumes that Israel's vision of God is in some sense fuller and truer than alternative visions and that others will, in time, acknowledge ours. I expect a corresponding claim from my Christian neighbor. We leave it to God to bring ultimate clarity to our separate visions and to arbitrate our conflicting claims. In the interim our task is to be faithful to the truth entrusted to us and to respond with respect to those whose noble vision differs from our own.

Buber wisely observed:

> The mystery of another lies deeply within him [or her] and it cannot be observed from without. No man [or woman] outside of Israel knows the mystery of Israel and no man [or woman] outside Christianity knows Christianity. But in their ignorance they can acknowledge each other in the mystery.[29]

To be sure, this capacity to "acknowledge each other in the mystery," to be stirringly particular without violating the integrity of the other, is ultimately a function of the social climate in which the liturgy and the liturgical people live. In periods of enforced isolation and persecution, ethnocentrism rears its head. Our current liturgical spirit is a tribute to the openness and freedom of America. May its benign ambience continue to inspire the liturgies of tomorrow.

NOTES

1. I am grateful to Lawrence A. Hoffman for directing me to some of the relevant sources consulted in the first part of this paper.

2. Phillip Birnbaum, ed. and trans., *Machzor Hashalem Lerosh Hashanah Veyom Kippur: High Holiday Prayer Book* (New York, 1951), pp. 1004–6.

3. Ber. 58a.

4. Ber. 12a, P.T. Ber. 3c.

5. See G. F. Moore, *Judaism in the First Centuries of the Christian Era* (Cambridge, 1927), vol. 3, pp. 95–96, n. 64.

6. See Philip Birnbaum, ed. and trans., *Hasiddur Hashalem: The Daily Prayer Book* (New York, 1949), p. 76.

7. See Tzvi Rabinowitz, *Machzor Piyyutei Rabbi Yannai Latorah Velano'adim* (Jerusalem, 1985), pp. 45–60.

8. See E. D. Goldschmidt, *Machzor Layamim Nora'im* (Jerusalem, 1970), pp. 186–87. Cf. the discussion by Goldschmidt in his "Hashlamah Lamachzor Leyom Hakippurim," *Kiryat Sefer* 31 (1964): 146–51; and the brief listing by Israel Davidson, *Otsar Hashirah Vehapiyyut,* reprint ed. (New York, 1970), vol. 2, p. 181.

9. Birnbaum, *Hasiddur,* p. 88.

10. Cf. Jacob Mann, "Genizah Fragments of the Palestinian Order of Service," reprinted in Jakob J. Petuchowski, ed., *Contributions to the Scientific Study of Jewish Liturgy* (New York, 1970), p. 416.

11. See Reuven Kimelman, "*Birkat Haminim* and the Lack of Evidence for an Anti-Christian Jewish Prayer in Late Antiquity," in E. P. Sanders, ed., *Jewish and Christian Self-Definition,* vol 2: *Aspects of Judaism in the Greco-Roman Period* (Philadelphia, 1981), pp. 226–44, notes on pp. 391–403; and Lawrence H. Schiffman, *Who Was a Jew?* (Hoboken, N.J., 1985), pp. 53–61, notes on pp. 94–97.

12. Birnbaum, *Hasiddur,* p. 138.

13. See E. A. Urbach, ed., *Arugat Habosem* (Jerusalem, 1939), vol. 3, pp. 468–69.

14. Cf. the standard Israeli prayer book, *Siddur Rinat Yisrael,* p. 193; and in America, *ArtScroll Siddur* (New York, 1969), p. 84. Even E. D. Goldschmidt restores the line to his scientifically "accurate" text of the daily service, both for the standard Ashkenazic rite of northern Europe, and for Hasidic congregations who altered that rite in accordance with what they believed to have been the practice of Isaac Luria (sixteenth century). Cf. E. D. Goldschmidt, *Siddur Tefillat Yisra'el lefi Nusach Ha'ashkenazim Ba'arets Uvachuts La'arets* (Israel, 1969), p. 71; and *Siddur Tefillat Yisra'el lefi Minhag Hachasidim Lerabot Chasidei Chabad* (Israel, n.d. [1969?]), p. 88. Both works are compiled "along with additions that were deleted by censors" (see title pages).

15. Cf. Menachem M. Kasher, ed., *The Passover Haggadah* (New York, 1962), p. 197; Philip Birnbaum, ed., *The Birnbaum Haggadah* (New York, 1976), pp. 114–15.

16. See discussion in E. D. Goldschmidt, *Haggadah Shel Pesach Vetoldoteha* (Jerusalem, 1970), pp. 62–64.

17. Quoted in Jakob J. Petuchowski, *Prayerbook Reform in Europe* (New York, 1968), p. 299.

18. *Union Prayer Book* (1940 ed.), p. 34 (hereafter *UPB*).

19. Ibid., p. 141. For earlier attempts by Reform editors to expunge *Alenu's* particularistic message, see Petuchowski, *Prayerbook Reform*, pp. 298–306. For Reform Judaism's attempt to recapture its particularistic message, without, however, blunting its universalism, particularly in its *Gates* liturgy in use today—and for a survey of the tension between universalism and particularism in American Reform liturgies preceding the *UPB*—see Lawrence A. Hoffman, "The Language of Survival in American Reform Liturgy," *CCAR Journal* 24/3 (1977): 87–106.

20. For details, see Hoffman, "Language of Survival."

21. *Gates of Prayer* (New York, 1975), p. 615 (hereafter *GOP*).

22. Rachel Anne Rabinowicz, ed., *Passover Haggadah: The Feast of Freedom* (New York, 1982), p. 101.

23. Cf. traditional text in Birnbaum, ed., *Machzor*, pp. 545–48; and Reform version in *Gates of Repentance* (New York, 1978), p. 279.

24. Birnbaum, *Hasiddur*, p. 26.

25. *GOP*, pp. 304, 322.

26. On the phenomenon of a liturgical gathering containing both Jewish and Christian worshipers, cf. Lawrence A. Hoffman, "Worship in Common," *Cross-Currents: Religion and Intellectual Life* 40/1 (Spring 1990): 5–17; and the responses that follow, pp. 18–46.

27. Walter Jacob, ed., *American Reform Responsa* (New York, 1983), p. 23. Cf. Lawrence A. Hoffman, "Non-Jews and Jewish Life Cycle Liturgy," *Journal of Reform Judaism* 37/3 (Summer 1990): 1–16; and the response thereto by Gunther Plaut, pp. 17–20.

28. *GOP*, p. 719.

29. Martin Buber, quoted in *The Jewish-Christian Argument* (Die Stunde und die Erkenntnis, p. 155) (New York, 1963), p. 167.

The Perception of Jews
in Christian Liturgy: Then and Now

JOHN GURRIERI

A quarter of a century has passed since the promulgation in 1965 of *Nostra aetate*, the Declaration on the Relationship of the Church to Non-Christian Religions.[1] After centuries of suspicion, persecution, pogroms, and the greatest tragedy of this century, the Holocaust, Catholic-Jewish relations have been transformed, particularly in the United States, where, as Pope John Paul II put it:

> The same basic religious principles of freedom and justice, of equality and moral solidarity, affirmed in the Torah as well as in the Gospel, were in fact reflected. . . . Jews and Catholics have contributed to the success of the American experiment in religious freedom and, in this unique context, have given to the world a vigorous form of interreligious dialogue between two ancient traditions.[2]

The key words today are *reconciliation* and *transformation*. As John Paul II stated in Miami, "Differences in faith should not cause enmity but open up the way of 'reconciliation,' so that in the end 'God may be all in all' (1 Cor 15:28)."[3]

The experience of persecution did not result solely or even principally from socioeconomic reasons, or even because ethnic or racial differences grew as the church became increasingly gentile. The experience was predicated on the theology that Christians formulated over centuries, a theology rooted in a Christian misinterpretation, sometimes willful, of the events narrated in the four Gospels concerning the death of

Jesus, whom we call "the Christ." That misinterpretation of the death of Jesus is already found in the Christian canonical Scriptures,[4] and because it is present in the writings that Christians hold and cherish as the Word of God, the liturgy itself was tainted by it.

In other words, with regard to Jews and Israel, Christians had constructed a theology of "the other" in which "the other"—that is, Jews—were the subject of persecution and even near-obliteration. That theological view did not allow Jews to define themselves in the light of their own experience of God's revelation. Rather, Christians defined Jewish experience and identity and did so negatively, holding that

1. God's covenant with Israel was historically abrogated by a new covenant established in Jesus Christ;
2. the Jews were once and for all responsible for the crucifixion and death of Jesus, the Son of God;
3. responsibility inhered in the people of the time and in their descendants as an eternal curse;
4. and therefore only Christians constituted God's people of the new covenant who possessed, through baptism, the only authentic and meaningful share in the kingdom of God and its eternal promise.

This theology of "the other" informed and often shaped elements of Christian worship, catechesis, music, art, and even the Christian appropriation of Hebrew scriptures. It understood the Old Testament to be old precisely in the sense of fulfilled, abrogated, and, in Christian practice, practically discarded. We did not mean Old Testament in the sense of the ancient testament or covenant between God and Israel; we did not mean Old Testament in the sense that our New Testament was born of the continuing and valid covenant established between God and Abraham and his descendants.[5]

But in the latter half of the twentieth century, perhaps because of the Holocaust and perhaps because of new biblical studies among Christians, a genuinely new theology of "the other" has emerged that affirms Christians and Jews as mutually covenanted peoples, with each group enjoying individual validity. *Nostra aetate* invites us, *letaken olam bemalkhut Shaddai*, "to mend the world under the sovereignty of God," as Rabbi Waxman stated in Miami.[6] We should be led to ask ourselves: Who are the Jews? What are Christians? How do we speak about each other, not to one another but within our own circles?

If we Christians attempt to answer these questions in the sociopolitical realm, we will turn toward the same dark alleys of the past. We will suspect; persecute; persist in our mistrust. If instead we look to our worship of God, the language we use in our liturgy and how we use the biblical Word, then we may be surprised to find not only cause for sorrow but also reason for joy and hope.

Finding the Jews and Israel in Christian Liturgy

I write as a liturgist who worked for the National Conference of Catholic Bishops. My intention is to probe the present Roman Catholic liturgy to see: (1) how Jews and Judaism are presented there, and (2) what opportunities Christian preachers have to present Jews and Judaism properly. I will stress particularly a project on which the Bishops' Committee on the Liturgy has worked for nearly three years, the document, *God's Mercy Endures Forever: Guidelines on the Presentation of Jews and Judaism in Catholic Preaching.*[7]

God's Mercy instructs preachers in the liturgical context how to interpret biblical texts that speak of Jews and Judaism. The guidelines are predicated on basic assumptions of Christian life: in the events of the Torah we Christians see ourselves alongside the people of Israel; in the Exodus we see our salvation; in the crossing of the Jordan we see our own promised land with the Jews; in the Prophets we see ourselves taken to task and chastised by God; in the Psalms we sing our praise, our thanksgiving, our penitence, our supplication, and even our despair together with Jews. We Christians see what John Paul II called our "spiritual fraternity" with the people to whom God first revealed the Name and to whom was given the Law. In other words, our love for the scriptures means we have cast our lot with the Jews. This basic fact of salvation history must be presented in all Christian preaching and theology.

Jews are present in Christian liturgy not by happenstance but, as Christians believe, by divine plan. Christianity issued from Israel and from Judaism. *God's Mercy* attempts to signal that presence and interpret it correctly, that is, without the historical or contemporary prejudices that cloud the vision of Christian eyes.

The Document's Background

God's Mercy draws heavily from the Vatican's 1985 document, *Notes on the Correct Way to Present Jews and Judaism in Preaching and Catechesis of the Roman Catholic Church,*[8] one of several postconciliar initiatives to implement *Nostra aetate*. Among the other projects of the Bishops' Committee on the Liturgy, such as dealing with the Good Friday *Improperia,* or "Reproaches,"[9] the participation of Catholics at seders,[10] joint prayer services to remember the Holocaust,[11] and the Good Friday bidding prayer for the Jews, *God's Mercy* seeks to correct the Christian view of the Jew as "other" in the liturgy while at the same time enriching Catholic understanding of the relationship between Christian liturgy and Judaism.

Jewish Roots of the Liturgy

The document begins by affirming the findings of liturgical scholarship with regard to the relationship of Jewish and Christian liturgy, citing John Paul II on the relationship of Christian liturgy to Judaism:

> Our common spiritual heritage [with Judaism] is considerable. To assess it carefully in itself and with due awareness of the faith and religious life of the Jewish people as they are professed and practiced still today, can greatly help us to understand better certain aspects of the life of the Church. Such is the case with

the liturgy, whose Jewish roots remain still to be examined more deeply, and in any case should be better known and appreciated by the faithful. (*God's Mercy*, no. 1)

The document thus holds, "Nowhere is the deep spiritual bond between Judaism and Christianity more apparent than in the liturgy" (*God's Mercy*, no. 2). The Catholic liturgical tradition owes "the very concepts of a liturgical cycle of feasts and the *lectio continua* principle of the lectionary" to Jewish liturgical practice. "Easter and Pentecost have historical roots in the Jewish feasts of Passover and Shavuot," although their Christian meaning is quite distinct (*God's Mercy*, no.2). In the central act of Christian worship, the eucharist, Christianity is linked historically and inextricably with Jewish ritual (*God's Mercy*, no. 3).

> The term for Church, *ecclesia*, like the original sense of the word synagogue, is an equivalent for the Hebrew *keneset* or *kenesiyah* (assembly). The Christian understanding of *ecclesia* is based on the biblical understanding of *kahal* as the formal "gathering" of the people of God. The Christian *ordo* (order of worship) is an exact rendering of the earliest rabbinic idea of prayer called a *seder*, that is, an "order" of service. Moreover, the Christian *ordo* takes its form and structure from the Jewish *seder:* the Liturgy of the Word, with its alternating biblical readings, doxologies, and blessings; and the liturgical form of the Eucharist, rooted in Jewish meal liturgy, with its blessings over bread and wine. Theologically, the Christian concept of *anamnesis* coincides with the Jewish understanding of *zikaron* (memorial reenactment). Applied to the Passover celebration, *zikaron* refers to the fact that God's saving deed is not only recalled but actually relived through the ritual meal. The synoptic gospels present Jesus as instituting the Eucharist during a Passover *seder* celebrated with his followers, giving to it new and distinctly Christian memory. (*God's Mercy*, no. 3)[12]

Similarly, the document affirms the relationship of the Our Father, the liturgy of the hours, and other prayer forms with rabbinic Judaism and contemporary synagogue prayers

(*God's Mercy*, no. 4). Without a doubt *God's Mercy* presumes and affirms what liturgical scholarship now takes for
granted: Christian liturgy is the "new branch from the common root."

Historical Perspectives and Contemporary Proclamation

"The strongly Jewish character of Jesus' teaching and that
of the primitive Church was culturally adapted by the growing Gentile majority and later blurred by controversies alienating Christianity from emerging rabbinic Judaism at the end
of the first century" (*God's Mercy*, no. 5). Begun in the
third century, the process of de-Judaizing the church has existed, in some or another shape or form, throughout the history of Christianity. *God's Mercy* cites the extreme position
of the heretic Marcion, who taught the "complete opposition
of the Hebrew and Christian Scriptures" and that "different
Gods had inspired the two Testaments." "Despite the
Church's condemnation of Marcion's teachings, some Christians over the centuries continued to dichotomize the Bible
into two mutually contradictory parts. They argued, for example, that the New Covenant 'abrogated' or 'superceded'
the Old, and that the Sinai Covenant was discarded by God
and replaced with another" (*God's Mercy*, no. 6).[13]

Together with the pernicious notion of the "collective
guilt of the Jews" in the arrest, trial, and death of Jesus, the
opposition of the Christian scriptures, with their implied or
explicit abrogation of the Sinai covenant, was responsible for
most Christian oppression of Jews throughout the centuries.
Both ideas found their way into the Christian liturgy, especially in homilies and other forms of preaching. It is still possible to hear from Catholic (and other Christian) pulpits and
ambos, especially in Holy Week and the Easter triduum,
preaching that blames the death of Jesus on the Jews, preaching that belittles God's covenant with Israel. *God's Mercy*,
therefore, establishes guidelines for preachers to present Jews
and Judaism correctly and justly.

These guidelines arise from contemporary church teaching, but they are supported by scholarship that demonstrates the extent to which even problematic biblical texts do not warrant the misinterpretations that have buttressed abrogationism, supersessionism, and the theory of collective guilt. It must be understood that "the Christian proclamation of the saving deeds of the One God through Jesus was formed in the context of Second Temple Judaism" (*God's Mercy*, no. 8). Particularly, one cannot understand Christianity and early rabbinic Judaism without taking into account the destruction of the Temple in 70 C.E. For just as the Temple's destruction had an enormous impact on the development of rabbinic Judaism, so too for Jewish Christians and the gentiles among whom the disciples preached, the razing of the Temple meant a radical break with the past. Rabbinic Judaism itself influenced the growth of its "sibling,"[14] Christianity, as it strove to make some sense of a world where sacrificial worship according to the precepts of the Torah was impossible and where at the same time a new phenomenon called Christianity now existed.

God's Mercy holds that the Christian attitude toward Jews and Judaism, positive or negative, has consequences for the church itself, in that "false or demeaning portraits of a repudiated Israel" after the destruction of the Temple "may undermine Christianity as well. How can one confidently affirm the Covenant with all humanity and creation in Christ (see Romans 8:21) without at the same time affirming God's faithfulness to the Covenant with Israel that also lies at the heart of the biblical testimony?" (*God's Mercy*, no. 8).

Homilists must, therefore, "confront misinterpretations of the meaning of the lectionary readings, which have been too familiar in the past. Specifically, homilists can guide people away from a triumphalism that would equate a pilgrim Church with the Reign of God." They "can confront the unconscious transmission of anti-Judaism through clichés that derive from an unhistorical overgeneralization of the self-critical aspects of the story of Israel as told in the scriptures (e.g., 'hardheartedness' of the Jews, 'blindness,' 'legalism,' 'materialism,' 'rejection of Jesus,' etc.)'' (*God's Mercy*, no. 8).

Specific Guidelines for the Liturgical Seasons

One of the great innovations of current Catholic liturgical reform has been the inclusion of readings from the Hebrew scriptures into nearly every eucharistic liturgy. Some may debate the usage of this or that reading, questioning perhaps the typological linkage of Old and New Testament readings according to ancient patristic principles (e.g., the prefiguring of Christ in the Old Testament books); nevertheless, for the first time in a millennium, Catholics are hearing the Word of God proclaimed from the Hebrew scriptures. It might be argued that the previous near total absence of the Old Testament (except for the Psalms) in the pre–Vatican II lectionary indicated a certain disdain, even distaste, for the ancient scriptures and the relationship of God and Israel contained therein, now "superseded" by the new covenant. The genius of the new Roman lectionary and other cycles of readings derived from it rests in the nearly complete inclusion of the Hebrew scriptures into Catholic liturgy. However, the use of the Hebrew scriptures varies according to season, so that *God's Mercy* clearly states how the readings are used and how best they might be approached by the homilist or preacher.

In the section *Advent: Relationship between the Scriptures,* the document is at pains to clarify the relationship between the Hebrew scriptures and the New Testament, so that preachers may avoid the pitfall of abrogationism. While Christians see in the prophecies of the Hebrew scriptures their fulfillment in the coming of Jesus, it is not beyond Christian doctrine to understand that Jews, who still await the messiah, may interpret these same texts in other senses.

> Christians believe that Jesus is the promised Messiah who has come (see Lk 4:22), but also know that his messianic kingdom is

not yet fully realized. The ancient messianic prophecies are not merely temporal predictions but profound expressions of eschatological hope. . . . This hope includes trust in what is promised but not yet seen. While the biblical prophecies of an age of universal *shalom* are "fulfilled" (i.e., irreversibly inaugurated) in Christ's coming, that fulfillment is not yet completely worked out in each person's life or perfected in the world at large (1974 *Guidelines*, no. 2). It is the mission of the Church, as also of the Jewish people, to proclaim and to work to prepare the world for the full flowering of God's reign, which is, but is "not yet" (cf. 1974 *Guidelines*, II). Both the Christian "Our Father" and the Jewish *Kaddish* exemplify this message. Thus, both Christianity and Judaism seal their worship with a common hope: "Thy kingdom come!" (*God's Mercy*, no. 11)

Christians and Jews, then, have a common task: to proclaim the kingdom and to work for its coming.

The liturgical season of Advent, which prepares for the Christian celebration of Jesus' birth, by tradition and by its very nature links the ancient prophecies of Isaiah and Jeremiah with the Christian belief that Jesus is the messiah, the Christ of God. The season cannot do otherwise. But in so doing it must not, and cannot, undo God's special covenant with Israel whose expression is also found in these same prophets. The people of God, Jewish and Christian, can arrive at a richer understanding that both tend "toward a like end in the future: The coming or return of the Messiah—even if they start from different points of view" (cf. 1985 *Notes*, nos. 18–19, in *God's Mercy*, no. 12).

The document confronts potentially problematic readings directly. An uncritical reading and hearing of Isaiah on the second Sunday of Advent (cycle A) and Baruch in cycle C by a Christian homilist and assembly "can leave the impression that pre-Jesus Israel was wholly guilt-ridden and in mourning and Judaism virtually moribund." Such an impression is often reinforced by Christian Advent hymns and customs and our woeful ignorance of rabbinic literature, an ignorance with

precedent in the writings of the church fathers. "In fact, in
their original historical settings, such passages" found in the
Advent liturgy "reveal Judaism's remarkable capacity for
self-criticism" and *teshuvah*, or turning back to God in faithful repentance and conversion, a theme endemic to the Christian season of Lent in which the church does penance to be
converted anew. "Judaism was and is incredibly complex and
vital, with a wide variety of creative spiritual movements vy-
ing for the people's adherence" (*God's Mercy*, no. 13).

Of particular concern for the season of Lent is the issue of
typology, a hermeneutic based on the symbolism of resemblances, by which Christians see anticipation of the New Testament in the "Old Testament" and thus appropriate the
Hebrew scriptures as their own biblical literature. In 1 Corinthians 10:1–13, for example, Paul draws a parallel between
the experiences of Israel in the desert and that of the Christian Corinthians. In the situation of the former, according to
St. Paul, the Corinthian community can see types or resemblances of their own experiences.[15] By the second century,
Christian literature went beyond types as resemblances to a
spiritual exegesis based on allegory, seeing in the parallel experiences of Israel and the church the very presence of
Christ. Clement of Alexandria and Origen were the most notable for developing a typological hermeneutic. "Clement
based his exegesis" of the scriptures "on the existence of a
Christian gnosis, i.e., the secret knowledge of the profound-
est truths of the Christian faith, to which the elite were initiated. The key to the gnosis was an allegorical interpretation
of the Bible."[16]

The patristic use of typology and allegory influences
Christian biblical hermeneutics to the present day. Nowhere
is this more evident than in Advent and in the lectionary
readings of Ordinary Time. Texts are often paired on the basis of the *sensus plenior* (fuller meaning) that Christian interpretation gives to the person or event (e.g., Moses, the
Exodus) described in a lectionary text. At other times, the
principle of typology links an Old Testament reading with a

New Testament text, "in which biblical figures and events are seen as 'types' prefiguring Jesus" or the church (*God's Mercy*, no. 14).

To be sure, hermeneutic principles such as *sensus plenior* and typology represent an ancient tradition for Christians. However, they are not the only interpretative guides on which Christian preachers have relied. In fact, literal exegesis is just as old a technique as the others. Likewise, the pairing of Old and New Testament texts in the lectionary often relies on "New Testament precedent and interpretation of the messianic psalms and prophetic passages. Matthew 1:23, for example, quotes the Septuagint, which translates the Hebrew *almah* (young woman) as the Greek for *virgin* in its rendering of Isaiah 7:14. The same biblical text, therefore, can have more than one valid hermeneutical interpretation, ranging from its original historical context to traditional Christological applications" (*God's Mercy*, no. 15).

Typological interpretation of the Hebrew scriptures has always made Jews uneasy, to say the least, a fact with which all Christians must come to grips. While breaking no new ground in the area, *God's Mercy* at least alerts the Catholic preacher to the inherent difficulty of relying on typology. In this regard, the document cites the important statement found in the Vatican's 1985 *Notes*: Typological hermeneutics "should not lead us to forget that" the Hebrew Bible "retains its own value as Revelation that the New Testament often does no more than resume (1985 *Notes*, no. 15; cf. *Dei Verbum*, 14–18)" (*God's Mercy*, no. 15).

Lent: Controversies and Challenges

Nowhere is the problem of lectionary selections more evident than in the season of Lent. This section of *God's Mercy* is an important step in Catholic reflection on the use of the Hebrew scriptures and how Christians comprehend the role of the Jews in the life and death of Jesus. All of Lent, but particularly Holy Week and the Easter triduum, have been times of anguish for Jews throughout the common era on account of Christian mobs—stirred into fury by homiletic harangues on "Jewish responsibility" for the death of Jesus—mobs who launched pogroms during this season which was meant to be the holiest for Christians.[17] Christians hearing of "hypocrites in the synagogue" (Ash Wednesday), John's depiction of an angry Jesus in the Temple (third Sunday of Lent, cycle B), and Jesus' conflicts with the Pharisees (fourth Sunday of Lent, cycle C) "can give the impression that the Judaism of Jesus' day was devoid of spiritual depth and essentially at odds with Jesus' teaching. References to earlier divine punishments of the Jews . . . can further intensify a false image of Jews as a people rejected by God" (*God's Mercy*, no. 17).

Do these readings reflect either history or the biblical authors' intentions? *God's Mercy* offers the following reflection:

> In fact, however, as the 1985 *Notes* are at pains to clarify (sec. III and IV), Jesus was observant of the Torah. . . . , he extolled respect for it. . . . , and he invited obedience to it (see Mt 8:4). Jesus taught in the synagogues (see Mt 4:23 and 9:35; Lk 4:15–18; Jn 18:20) and in the Temple, which he frequented, as did the disciples even after the Resurrection (see Acts 2:46; 3:1ff). While Jesus showed uniqueness and authority in his interpretation of God's word in the Torah—in a manner that scandalized some Jews and impressed others—he did not oppose it, nor did he wish to abrogate it. (*God's Mercy*, no. 18)

The homilist is urged, therefore, to communicate the Jewishness of Jesus, not only in his birth, but especially in his observance of the Torah.

Jesus' affinity with the religious vision of the Pharisees of his time, which may have been "a reason for many of his apparent controversies with them," is a case in point. "Jesus shared with the Pharisees a number of distinctive doctrines: The resurrection of the body; forms of piety such as almsgiving, daily prayer, and fasting; the liturgical practice of addressing God as Father; and the priority of the love commandment. . . . Many scholars are of the view that Jesus was not so much arguing against 'the Pharisees' as a group, as he was condemning the excesses of some Pharisees, excesses of a sort that can be found among some Christians as well'' (*God's Mercy*, no. 19). Such controversies were more likely the result of Jesus' participation in various internal debates among the Pharisees than of his opposition to the Pharisees as a religious party, e.g., divorce or the *lex talionis*. "Jesus' interpretation of biblical law is similar to that found in some of the prophets and ultimately adopted by rabbinic tradition as can be seen in the *Talmud*" (*God's Mercy*, no. 19).

The problem that Christian homilists face today concerning the controversies recorded in the Gospels has more to do with the historical distancing of the church from Judaism. Thus, certain controversies that may actually have taken place between church leaders and rabbis toward the end of the first century were read back into the life of Jesus:

> Some [New Testament] references hostile or less than favorable to Jews have their historical context in conflicts between the nascent Church and the Jewish community. Certain controversies reflect Christian-Jewish relations long after the time of Jesus. To establish this is of capital importance if we wish to bring out the meaning of certain gospel texts for the Christians of today. All this should be taken into account when preparing catechesis and homilies for the weeks of Lent and Holy Week (1985 *Notes*, no. 29; see no. 26 below). (*God's Mercy*, no. 20)

The greatest challenge is to be found in the ancient and tragic charge of Christ-killer made against Jews by many Christians. Nowhere is this more salient than in how Christians appropriate or comprehend the mysteries celebrated in Holy Week and in the proclamation of the Passion narratives during the Holy Week and triduum liturgies. In March 1988, the Bishops' Committee for Ecumenical and Interreligious Affairs disseminated principles to guide dramatic presentations of the Passion.[18] Concerned with the reading or proclamation of the Passion narratives in the liturgy, *God's Mercy*, on the other hand, holds:

1. The purpose of proclaiming the Passion narratives "is to enable the assembly to see vividly the love of Christ for each person, despite their sins, a love that even death could not vanquish" (no. 22).

2. "To the extent that Christians over the centuries made Jews the scapegoat for Christ's death, they drew themselves away from the paschal mystery" of Christ's death and resurrection (no. 22).

3. The Passion narratives "do not offer eyewitness accounts or a modern transcript of historical events. Rather, the events have had their meaning focused, as it were, through the four theological 'lenses' of the gospels" (no. 23).

4. All four accounts share certain common historical elements essential to the narrative: "A growing hostility against Jesus on the part of some Jewish religious leaders" (note that the Pharisees are not mentioned by the synoptic Gospels, which refer only to the "chief priests, scribes, and elders"); Jesus' Last Supper with the disciples; the betrayal by Judas; the arrest of Jesus outside the city ("an action conducted covertly by the Roman and Temple authorities because of Jesus' popularity with his fellow Jews"); the interrogation before the high priest, and not necessarily a Sanhedrin trial; formal condemnation by Pontius Pilate, who bears sole responsibility for it, according to the Apostles' and Nicene Creeds, even though some Jews were involved in Jesus' death; crucifixion by Roman soldiers; affixing the title "King of the Jews" on the cross; the crucifixion, death, and burial; and the resurrection (no. 24).

5. Other elements are unique to the individual Gospels; e.g., the use of the phrase "the Jews" by John, the crowd shouting "his blood be upon us and on our children" in Matthew. These and similar elements must be understood in the context of the particular evangelist and the community for which he was writing.

Reflecting contemporary biblical scholarship,[19] *God's Mercy* further concludes: "Often, these unique elements reflect perceived needs and emphases of the [gospel] author's particular community at the end of the first century, *after* the split between Jews and Christians was well underway."

The homilist is also cautioned about readings assigned to the Easter season in general, especially those from the Acts of the Apostles that if read out of context might give the mistaken impression of collective Jewish responsibility for Jesus' death. The liturgical assembly is, therefore, to be told of the growing rift between the Christian and Jewish communities, particularly in Jerusalem. Likewise, the homilist is to refer to current church teaching on this matter as stated in *Nostra aetate* and recent papal statements. For Christians it is important to hear these readings because they reflect the enthusiasm of the post-Easter church in proclaiming Jesus as the risen Christ. "But in so doing, statements about Jewish responsibility have to be kept in context. This is part of the reconciliation between Jews and Christians to which we are all called" (*God's Mercy*, no. 26).

Pastoral Activity during Holy Week and the Easter Season

God's Mercy (nos. 27–29) offers advice concerning other pastoral activity in which Christians often participate during the Easter season, such as Passover seders, joint liturgies of reconciliation on Passion (Palm) Sunday, and the remembrance of the Holocaust.

Concerning participation in Passover seders, the Bishops' Committee on the Liturgy had already offered the following advice in 1980:

> When Christians celebrate this sacred feast [Passover] among themselves, the rites of the *haggadah* for the seder should be respected in all their integrity. The seder . . . should be celebrated in a dignified manner and with sensitivity to those to whom the seder truly belongs. The primary reason why Christians may celebrate the festival of Passover should be to ac-

knowledge common roots in salvation history. Any sense of "restaging" the Last Supper of the Lord Jesus should be avoided. (*God's Mercy*, no. 28, citing the Bishops' Committee on the Liturgy *Newsletter*, March 1980, p. 12)

In other words, there should be no attempt to "baptize" or "Christianize" the Passover, especially by ending the seder with New Testament readings, "or worse," by turning it "into a prologue to the Eucharist. Such mergings distort both traditions. . . . Seders arranged at or in cooperation with local synagogues are encouraged" (*God's Mercy*, no. 28).

The increasing awareness among Christians of the importance of remembering the victims of the Shoah is reflected in *God's Mercy*. The document urges Catholics to pray in the celebration of the eucharist (especially in the general intercessions, or prayer of the faithful) on the Sunday closest to Yom Hashoah for the victims of the Holocaust and their survivors. Likewise, it encourages joint services or liturgies of remembrance commemorating the victims of the Shoah, again without attempting to deny the essential Jewish significance of the event. Christians must come to believe with all their hearts that "God's mercy endures forever" for the Jewish people in spite of Christian antisemitism through the centuries. The Holocaust is an event that Christians ignore at their own peril (*God's Mercy*, Introduction).

Preaching throughout the Year: General Principles

God's Mercy concludes with nine general principles that are intended as guides to Catholic preaching throughout the liturgical year, for the "challenges that peak in the seasons of Advent, Lent, and Easter are present throughout the year in the juxtaposition of the lectionary readings." Since "all Scripture, including the New Testament, deals with Jews and Jewish themes," there is hardly an occasion in the calendar of feasts and seasons when "a reference to Jews or Judaism in a homily based upon a text from the Scriptures" can be

avoided. After all, Jews and Judaism are, in the end, part of
the Christian reality (*God's Mercy*, no. 30).

Those general principles, found in the penultimate paragraph (no. 31) of the document, are of a practical nature and
serve as ample conclusion to this summary of the church's
newly evolving theology of "the other":

1. Consistently affirm the value of the whole Bible.
   While among all the scriptures, even those of the New
   Testament, the Gospels have special preeminence (*Dei
   Verbum*, 18), the Hebrew Scriptures are the Word of
   God and have validity and dignity in and of themselves (ibid., 19).
2. Place the typology inherent in the lectionary in a
   proper context, neither overemphasizing it nor avoiding
   it. Show that the meaning of the Hebrew scriptures for
   their original audience is not limited to, nor diminished
   by, New Testament applications (1985 *Notes*, II).
3. Communicate a reverence for the Hebrew Scriptures
   and avoid approaches that reduce them to a propaedeu-
   tic or background for the New Testament. It is God
   who speaks, communicating Godself through divine
   revelation (*Dei Verbum*, 6).
4. Show the connectedness between the two sets of scriptures. The Hebrew Bible and the Jewish tradition
   founded on it must not be set against the New Testament in such a way that the former seems to constitute
   a religion of only retributive justice, fear, and legalism,
   with no appeal to love of God and neighbor (cf. Dt 6:5;
   Lv 19:18, 32; Hos 11:1–9; Mt 22:34–40).
5. Enliven the eschatological hope, the "not yet" aspect
   of the *kerygma* (proclamation). The biblical promises
   are realized in Christ. But the church awaits their perfect fulfillment in Christ's glorious return when all creation is made free (1974 *Guidelines*, II).
6. Emphasize the Jewishness of Jesus and his teachings
   and highlight the similarities of the teachings of the
   Pharisees with those of Christ (1985 *Notes* III and IV).

7. Respect the continuing validity of God's covenant with the Jewish people and their responsive faithfulness, despite centuries of suffering, to the divine call that is theirs (1985 *Notes*, VI).

8. Frame homilies to show that Christians and Jews together are the "trustees and witnesses of an ethic marked by the Ten Commandments, in the observance of which humanity finds its truth and freedom" (John Paul II, Rome Synagogue, 13 April 1986).

9. Be free to draw on Jewish sources (rabbinic, medieval, and modern) in expounding the meaning of the Hebrew scriptures and the apostolic writings. The 1974 *Guidelines* observe that "the history of Judaism did not end with the destruction of Jerusalem, but went on to develop a religious tradition . . . rich in religious values." The 1985 *Notes* (no. 14) thus speak of Christians "profiting discerningly from the traditions of Jewish readings" of the sacred texts.

God's Mercy concludes by citing the following words of the 1985 *Notes*:

> Attentive to the same God who has spoken, hanging on the same word, we have to witness to one same memory and one common hope in him who is master of history. We must also accept our responsibility to prepare the world for the coming of the Messiah by working together for social justice, respect for the rights of persons and nations, and for social and international reconciliation. To this we are driven, Jews and Christians, by the command to love our neighbor, by a common hope for the kingdom of God, and by the great heritage of the prophets. (1985 *Notes*, no. 19; see also Lv 19:18, 32)

NOTES

1. See Walter M. Abbott, ed., *The Documents of Vatican II* (New York, 1966), pp. 663–68. For a list of Catholic statements and documents, Vatican and American, on Judaism, see John T.

Pawlikowski and James A. Wilde, *When Catholics Speak about Jews: Notes for Homilists and Catechists* (Chicago, 1987), pp. 68–70.

2. *Origins* 17/15 (24 September 1987): 241.

3. Ibid., p. 242.

4. See Raymond E. Brown, S.S., and Sandra M. Schneiders, I.H.M., "Hermeneutics," in *New Jerome Biblical Commentary* (Englewood Cliffs, N.J., 1990), pp. 1157–58.

5. See *Nostra aetate*, no. 4.

6. *Origins* 17/15 (24 September 1987): 240.

7. Washington, 1988.

8. Holy See, Commission on Religious Relations with the Jews, *Notes on the Correct Way to Present the Jews and Judaism in Preaching and Catechesis of the Roman Catholic Church* (Washington, 1985).

9. "Good Friday Reproaches (*Improperia*)," in *Bishop's Committee on the Liturgy Newsletter*, March 1980.

10. "Celebrating the Passover Seder," in *Bishops' Committee on the Liturgy Newsletter*, March 1980. See also Leon Klenicki, *The Passover Celebration* (Chicago, 1980).

11. "Days of Remembrance of the Victims of the Holocaust," in *Bishops' Committee on the Liturgy Newsletter*, March 1988. For examples of such services of remembrance, see Elie Wiesel and Albert H. Friedlander, *The Six Days of Destruction: Meditations toward Hope* (New York and Mahwah, 1988); and Irving Greenberg and David Roskies, *A Holocaust Commemoration for Days of Remembrance* (Washington, 1981).

12. On *zikaron* and Paul's use of the term *anamnesis*, see Kenneth Stevenson, *Eucharist and Offering* (New York, 1986), p. 10.

13. See Brown and Schneiders, "Hermeneutics"; See also Jaroslav Pelikan, *The Christian Tradition: A History of the Development of Doctrine*, vol. 1: *The Emergence of the Catholic Tradition (100–600)* (Chicago, 1971), pp. 71–81.

14. See Hayim Goren Perelmutter, *Siblings: Rabbinic Judaism and Early Christianity at Their Beginnings* (New York and Mahwah, 1989), pp. 16f.

15. See Jerome Murphy-O'Connor, "The First Letter to the Corinthians," in *New Jerome Biblical Commentary*, p. 807.

16. See Brown and Schneiders, "Hermeneutics," p. 1154.

17. See Paul Johnson, *A History of the Jews* (New York, 1987), pp. 164–65. Even among those who did not hold that modern Jews

were responsible for Jesus' death, anti-Judaism (and persecution) became the natural outgrowth of the view that Jews had obstinately refused to accept Christ, in spite of witnessing his miracles (see Johnson, *History*, pp. 206ff).

18. *Criteria for the Evaluation of Dramatizations of the Passion* (Washington, 1988).

19. Cf. Raymond Brown, *The Community of the Beloved Disciple* (New York, 1979); idem, *The Churches the Apostles Left Behind* (New York, 1984).

PART 2

American Reform or Second Reformation?

Introduction

On 21 June 1988 a historic dialogue occurred. On a single stage, together for the first time, those with some responsibility in one way or another for the current liturgies of six church and synagogue bodies explained to each other and to an assembled audience of several hundred Christians and Jews what they and their committees had accomplished as their own contribution to what we have called this second Reformation through which we are living. Their remarks demonstrated clearly how Catholics, Protestants, and Jews—regardless of denomination—are all affected by considerations emerging from the culture and time that they share in common. This part consists of an expanded version of the panel's remarks.

Speaking for Roman Catholicism is Kathleen Hughes, Professor of Liturgy at the Catholic Theological Union in Chicago. She served on the advisory committee of the International Commission on English in the Liturgy (ICEL), which was charged with the task of translating the revised rites into English. Hughes is former chair of ICEL's subcommittee charged with developing original English supplementary prayer texts.

Eugene L. Brand is Director of the Division of Studies of the Lutheran World Federation. He played a major part in the production of the *Lutheran Book of Worship (LBW)* of 1978.

Charles P. Price, the William Meade Professor (Emeritus) of Systematic Theology at the Protestant Episcopal Theological Seminary in Virginia, has taught liturgics as well as theology. He was a member of his church's standing liturgical commission from 1967 to 1985.

Hoyt L. Hickman directs worship resource development for the General Board of Discipleship of the United Methodist Church. He has edited or written much of the worship literature of his church and had major staff responsibilities in the development of the *United Methodist Hymnal*. His editorial responsibility also extends to the book of worship to be submitted to the 1992 General Conference.

Jules Harlow, a Conservative rabbi, has worked on the Rabbinical Assembly's publications committees since his ordination in 1959. As the director of publications, he is the editor and translator of the Conservative movement's High Holy Day *machzor* (1972) and its daily and Shabbat *siddur* (1985).

A. Stanley Dreyfus, a Reform rabbi, has taught liturgy courses at the Hebrew Union College–Jewish Institute of Religion in New York and chaired the liturgy committee of the Central Conference of American Rabbis during most of the period when the Reform movement's current worship books were conceived and composed.

The Changing Face of Roman Catholic Worship

Kathleen Hughes

The celebration of the eucharist is the central act of Roman Catholic worship. Catholics gather to hear the word of the Scriptures, both Hebrew and Christian, and to celebrate the Supper of the Lord at eucharist, an event that we believe makes Jesus' supreme act of sacrificial love sacramentally present. The eucharist is a meal of thanksgiving mandated by Jesus on the night before he died; a memorial of Jesus' death for the life of the world; and a sacrament of Jesus' abiding presence in the community of his disciples. The earliest description of the Sunday eucharist, that of Justin Martyr (c. 150 C.E.), remains remarkably apposite today:

> On the day which is called the day of the Sun we have a common assembly of all who live in the cities or in the country, and the memoirs of the apostles or the writings of the prophets are read, as much as there is time for. Then, when the reader has finished, the one presiding provides, in a discourse, admonition and exhortation to imitate these excellent things. Then we all stand up together and say prayers, and, as we said before, after we finish the prayer, bread and wine are presented. He who presides likewise offers up prayers and thanksgiving, to the best of his ability, and the people express their assent by saying *Amen*, and there is the distribution and participation by each one in those things over which thanksgiving has been said, and these are sent, through the deacons, to those not present. The wealthy, if they wish, contribute whatever they desire, and the collection is placed in the custody of the president, and he helps the

orphans and widows, those who are needy because of sickness
or any other reason, and the captives and the strangers in our
midst; in short, he takes care of all those in need. The day of the
Sun, indeed, is the day on which we all hold our common assembly, because it is the first day. On it God, transforming dark-
ness and matter, created the world; and our Savior Jesus Christ
arose from the dead on the same day.[1]

While the essence and the basic ritual pattern of the eucharist have not changed over time, the external forms of celebration have undergone extraordinary mutations. In the
course of centuries, particularly as the community expanded
into different regions and cultures, shifts have occurred: from
improvised prayers to fixed texts; from charismatic leadership to ordained male presidency; from the participation of
the whole assembly to liturgy as the preserve of the clergy;
from reclining at table to kneeling before a distant and often
elevated altar; from the simplicity of word and table fellowship to the celebration of mysterious rites with the celebrant's back to the community; from the language of the
people to a tongue no longer understood; from participatory
psalms and hymns to intricate choral pieces; from house-
church to ornate basilicas.

Gradually the understanding of eucharist as meal was lost.
The laity knelt to receive a wafer of bread; the chalice was no
longer offered to them; the reception of communion, once an
integral part of the celebration, became infrequent. Over
time, central symbols were obscured by secondary accre-
tions; prayers multiplied; popular—and sometimes question-
able—extraliturgical devotions flourished. By the turn of this
century, when the modern liturgical movement was in its in-
fancy, the community was largely estranged from its rites.[2]

The watershed that irrevocably shaped patterns of contemporary Roman Catholic worship was the Second Vatican
Council (1962–1965) and the liturgical reforms that the council mandated. The principles of reform and the concrete proposals for change that were elaborated at the council were
part of a vision of renewed worship that the liturgical movement in Europe and North America had enthusiastically pro-

moted for decades.[3] Liturgical reformers had envisioned a liturgy in which people would (1) experience themselves once again as participants rather than spectators; (2) experience full, conscious, and active participation in the rites through the use of vernacular languages in place of Latin; and (3) recognize the intimate connection between worship and the demands of justice and charity that authentic eucharistic participation placed on their daily lives.

The goal of the early liturgical movement that was later carried forward officially in postconciliar policies might best be captured in its oft-repeated aspiration that the community once more learn to "pray the Mass" rather than simply "pray at Mass." To this end, the movement promoted the use of hand missals, abbreviated copies of the Roman missal, the book used by the priest at the altar. Forbidden for use by the laity until the reforms of Leo XIII (pope from 1878 to 1903), these prayer books, with Latin and the vernacular on facing pages, made it possible to follow and to understand the words and actions of the priest. The unfolding of the feasts and seasons of the liturgical year and, more importantly, the scriptures and the prayers of the eucharistic celebration were now available to the assembly, inviting Roman Catholic laity to a new liturgical spirituality. One such prayer book, affectionately called the "Stedman you-can't-get-lost missal,"[4] sold over fifteen million copies in the thirties and forties, an eloquent index of the growing desire among the laity for full participation in the church's worship.

The Reforms of Vatican II

The first document to issue from Vatican II, promulgated on 4 December 1963, at the end of the council's second session, was The Constitution on the Sacred Liturgy. Its introduction sums up conciliar goals that would be mirrored in the sweeping liturgical renewal that followed:

This sacred Council has several aims in view: it desires to impart an ever increasing vigor to the Christian life of the faithful;

to adapt more suitably to the needs of our own times those institutions that are subject to change; to foster whatever can promote union among all who believe in Christ; to strengthen whatever can help to call the whole of humanity into the household of the Church. The Council therefore sees particularly cogent reasons for undertaking the reform and promotion of the liturgy.[5]

The council's bishops envisioned liturgical reform as a two-stage process,[6] the first of which was a complete revision of the rites of the church based on thorough theological, historical, and pastoral studies. Not only the eucharist, contained in the missal, but all of the church's sacraments—initiation, reconciliation, pastoral care of the sick, marriage, and ordination—were to be revised. The latter were contained chiefly in the Roman ritual but were scattered also in other books, including the liturgy of the hours, the book of blessings, the pontifical, the rites of religious profession, the dedication of a church and an altar, and the order of Christian funerals.[7] The first stage of reform was itself a mammoth task. No less so was the second stage of liturgical renewal mandated by Vatican II: the adaptation of the liturgy to various cultures and peoples once a new library of service books was created.[8]

The Constitution on the Sacred Liturgy had spelled out broad principles of liturgical reform and empowered a postconciliar commission to be responsible for the research that would inform each of the revised rites. Various subcommittees of this commission drafted the individual reformed rites, using a variety of methods: excision, addition, restoration, accommodation, and development.[9]

Excision or suppression involved omitting unnecessary duplications and suppressing devotional additions that tended to obscure the central prayers and rites, for example, prayers that had been added to the core of the celebration but whose purpose had been forgotten or superseded.[10] Excision also had the effect of streamlining the church's liturgical calendar, in which the multiplication of saints' feasts had almost obliterated the central focus of the liturgical year: the mysteries of the life of Christ.

The second mode of reform, addition or accretion, was the obverse of the first in that it added elements where variety was clearly desirable. For instance, a three-year cycle of readings replaced a single cycle of scripture for the Sunday eucharist, thus inviting the community to a deeper appreciation of the Word of God. Perhaps more surprising, nearly all of the rites whose prayers were invariable now have an ample selection of optional texts. A notable example of the addition of texts is the ancient Roman canon, the only eucharistic prayer in use in the Roman rite from roughly the sixth century until the council, which has now been supplemented with a variety of other texts; a total of nine eucharistic prayers is presently authorized for use in the United States.

Thorough historical investigations dictated a third mode of reform, namely, reform by revival or restoration. Examples abound: the ancient pattern of preparation for baptism has been revived for the initiation of adults into the community of faith; rites that recognize the communal nature of reconciliation have been recovered; pastoral care of the sick, relinquished when the focus of sacramental pastoral care shifted to the dying—and, therefore, colloquially referred to as "the last rites"—has now been restored.

Because of a renewed appreciation for the variety of cultures in the universal church, a fourth mode of reform was employed, namely, reform by accommodation, the adjusting of the church's ritual patterns in light of the needs of different times and places. Most obviously affected by this method are rites that mark significant moments of passage, for example, funerals, marriages, and initiation. Such rites of passage have now become more hospitable to local customs and cultures. In addition, music, dance, architecture, and other aesthetic considerations are all the subject of reform by accommodation.

A final operative method of reform was development, a method dictating that any new forms or rites grow organically from forms already existing. The ongoing development of original texts exemplifies this mode of reform. Original texts now in preparation are new prayers written to meet new situations or particular needs, but they are crafted according to the structures of traditional liturgical genres.

Each of these five different approaches to liturgical re-form—excision, addition, revival, accommodation, and de-velopment—was employed in the reform of the texts and rites of the Roman Catholic church in general, so that each of them is operative to one degree or another in the reform of the eucharist in particular. Noteworthy aspects in the renewal of the eucharistic celebration are the following: (1) the basic structure of Word and Table has been recovered together with much-simplified introductory and concluding rites; (2) pri-vate devotional prayers and repetitive prayers have been ex-cised; (3) intercessory prayer and the exchange of peace have been restored; (4) the homily is now strongly encouraged, particularly on Sundays and feasts; (5) reception of commu-nion is again normative. Justin Martyr would recognize once more the Sunday assembly and its worship.

The Work of the International Commission on English in the Liturgy

The use of the vernacular had surfaced early as a question for conciliar debate. At first, a rather modest concession to vernacular translations for readings, exhortations, and some of the hymns and prayers was envisioned,[11] but a further de-cision remanded the question of extensive use of the vernac-ular to regional groups of bishops.[12] By the time the new service books were prepared, the vernacular had been autho-rized across the world for virtually all of the rites.

During the closing days of the council, the probability that extensive authorization of the vernacular would be sanc-tioned led to the establishment of other kinds of committees. Called "mixed commissions," these translation bodies were to be international in character and to be of service to coun-tries that used the same language. Thus was born the International Commission on English in the Liturgy (ICEL), a mixed commission serving eleven major English-speaking conferences of bishops, including the National Conference of Catholic Bishops of the United States and a number of associate member conferences.

ICEL was faced with a Herculean task. Within ten years of the close of Vatican II, every major rite of the church was revised and promulgated in what is called the *editio typica*, the Latin text that would serve as the original in the work of translation. The texts of the Roman missal alone—the book containing everything necessary for the celebration of the eucharist—numbered more than eighteen hundred texts, and that book, while central to the reform, was only one of many projects to be completed by a small ICEL staff.

The work was further complicated both by the lack of models of good, contemporary, English prayer texts and by a paucity of research into the question of how liturgical language functions to produce meaning. In its early days, therefore, ICEL had to make decisions about language register, international English, literal vs. faithful translation, the role of poetic expression, the meaning and function of each text, and the performative character of liturgical prayer.

Of all of these decisions, perhaps the most vexing was that of language register. Is there, or should there be, a special hieratic language? The Elizabethan English of the Reformers no longer seemed appropriate for use in late-twentieth-century translations—though some outside of ICEL vigorously promoted its use. On this topic there was wide, often heated, debate, as suggested by one commentator:

> There are those who would prefer a liturgical translation that is not really English, wishing to preserve the sacral remoteness of the Latin liturgy by retaining an archaic form of language in which to express it. What is at issue here is not language at all but an approach to liturgy that would wish to keep it at arm's length and undefiled by the world. Good language there must be, but should one look for a "religious" form of language, and

if so, which is it? A pastiche, not to say imitation, of earlier styles is not expressive of good liturgy or of good language.[13]

Those opposed to the development of a new sacral language believed that it would lead in time to a new estrangement and, in fact, would be from the outset a stumbling block for many. Josef Jungmann, doyen of the liturgical movement, was asked his opinion on the topic. His response: "Every language that possesses a literature is suitable for divine worship if used in the right way. It is the elevated speech used on formal occasions. It need not be remote from the world; it is simply the language of religious dignity."[14]

ICEL thus selected the language of formal discourse as its register. It transcended idiomatic and colloquial differences existing on opposite sides of the Atlantic. Furthermore, the choice of contemporary, formal discourse demanded that translators employ faithful, but nonliteral, translations. In its turn, this decision necessitated abandoning the elegant and terse periodic construction typical of Latin rhetoric but impossible to replicate in good contemporary English.

The ICEL episcopal board and advisory committee were well served by experts in classics, languages, liturgy, scripture, and other disciplines. By 1974 nearly all of the rites had been released at least in draft form. Meanwhile, another realization was dawning, well captured in an instruction issuing from Rome involving questions of translation:

> Texts translated from another language are clearly not sufficient for the celebration of a fully renewed liturgy. The creation of new texts will be necessary. But translation of texts transmitted through the tradition of the Church is the best school and discipline for the creation of new texts so "that any new forms adopted should in some way grow organically from forms already in existence."[15]

Composition of Original Texts

Renewal of the community's prayer demands new texts to supplement prayers translated from the Latin, for how else will the community's new experiences find their way into the language of its prayer? In light of this need, ICEL established a subcommittee for the preparation of original texts.

Feminism is one such experience that has had a profound effect on the ways that we name one another in the community of faith and in our understanding of appropriate metaphors for God. These questions have sometimes been lumped together under the rubric *inclusive language,* and have been distinguished from each other as "horizontal" and "vertical" language. These distinctions are not helpful. For one thing, the distinction suggests that God is in some up-down spatial relationship to the community; for another, God-language is not of the same order as language referring to the community and, while God-language has employed a preponderance of masculine images (Father, King, Lord), the appropriate solution is not so simple as to augment these titles with feminine metaphors. God is neither masculine nor feminine, neither father nor mother—like both, perhaps, in some limited sense, but in fact escaping all such human categories. Feminism urges a language of prayer that recognizes and names the personhood of all believers; it has, at the same time, made us question our predominantly male categories for our God who will never be adequately named or known— and perhaps suggests that we ought continually to search for an ever-broader range of metaphors in order to break open our categories and perhaps break down our idols.

In 1975, after a long and thorough debate, the advisory committee of ICEL resolved to avoid words that ignore the place of women in the Christian community or that seem to relegate women to a secondary role. The debate about discriminatory language raised broader concerns. ICEL further determined to study and implement policies regarding other forms of discrimination in language, including racism, clericalism, antisemitism, and language that discriminates against the disabled. These are among the concerns brought to bear in the translation and revision of liturgical texts.[16]

Evolving theological understandings will always have an impact on the language of prayer. For example, a contempo-

rary evolutionary appreciation of creation has been captured
in the following original preface to a eucharistic prayer:

> Blessed are you, strong and faithful God.
> All your works, the height and the depth,
> echo the silent music of your praise.
>
> In the beginning your Word summoned light:
> night withdrew, and creation dawned.
> As ages passed unseen,
> waters gathered on the face of the earth
> and life appeared.
>
> When the times at last had ripened
> and the earth grown full in abundance,
> you created in your image man and woman,
> the crown of all creation.
>
> You gave us breath and speech,
> that all the living
> might find a voice to sing your praise.
> So now, with all the powers of heaven and earth,
> we chant the ageless hymn of your glory:
>
> Holy, holy, holy Lord, ...[17]

A contemporary appreciation of the participation of humankind in establishing the justice and the reign of God has
further prompted prayers that do not ask God to do thus and
such but ask that God empower the community to be agents
of justice and reconciliation. A comparison of the following
texts—the first, antedating the council; the second, a product
of the revisions—will suggest a shift in the role of the praying community from passive recipient to active participant in
establishing the reign of God:

> *For Peace*
>
> O God,
> source of all holy desires,

right counsels and just works,
grant your servants
that peace which the world cannot give
so that we may be obedient to your commands
and under your protection
enjoy peace in our days
and freedom from fear of our enemies.[18]

For Peace and Justice

God our Father,
you reveal that those who work for peace
will be called your sons [and daughters].
Help us to work without ceasing
for that justice
which brings true and lasting peace.
We ask this. . . . [19]

World concerns will naturally inspire a new corpus of texts. Recent writing has questioned the loss of lament in our prayer, especially in light of the perilous nature of our world and the horrendous sufferings we have caused and continue to inflict on one another. One section of the missal contains a collection of texts for "diverse circumstances" which provides for some of these concerns. To supplement the present collection are drafts of prayers for social justice; for human rights; for the progress of peoples; in time of war or conflict; for a reverent use of creation; for the poor and neglected; for the unemployed.

Furthermore, our new desire for ecumenical and interfaith collaboration causes us to examine carefully the language of prayers to be used in common to ensure that they are both hospitable, in recognition of the faith that binds us together, and thoroughly honest about what continues to separate us.

Finally, new texts have been prepared for certain rites issued by Rome that did not anticipate all of the quite particular pastoral situations when the rite would be used. The revised order of Christian funerals is an apt example of a ritual in need of supplementary new texts to express the very particular grief occasioned by suicide, violent or sudden death, the death of an infant or young child, stillbirth, and other tragic circumstances.

In the course of preparing original texts and attempting to commission authors for this work, the original text subcommittee discovered that there was no blueprint for the crafting of new prayers. It is much easier to say what prayer is not than what it is, much easier to spot what we do not like in a composition submitted to us and much more difficult to instruct authors about what results we had hoped for. The committee gradually developed some guidelines that continue to be refined as its work progresses. These guidelines fall into three general areas: the structure and function of prayer; its content and style; and specific trinitarian concerns.

Issues of structure and function include the exercise of care both for the function of a particular prayer, for example, petition, as well as the prayer's place and function in the rite; knowledge of the purpose of a particular rite; the proclamatory nature of liturgical prayer, including its oral and aural effects; and care for logical coherence and unity.

Issues of content and style include guidelines that texts be doctrinally sound but not self-consciously so, respecting the distinction between first and second theology.[20] Authors are encouraged to find their inspiration in the scriptures, the liturgical seasons, and the theology of the particular rite; to incorporate enough substance to draw the community into the prayer; to use themes that are sufficiently universal to meet the needs of an international community; to employ a consistency of images and a wide-ranging vocabulary with attention to rhythm, cadence, and sense lines for easy proclamation. In addition, authors are invited to use language that is "clear, forceful, interesting, consistent, and imaginative"—no small order!

Trinitarian concerns are chiefly about the ways that prayer is addressed and concluded. Christian prayer has traditionally been addressed to the first person of the Trinity, the creator; through the mediation of Jesus Christ, the redeemer; in the power of the Spirit, the sanctifier. Authors are instructed to show care for this trinitarian economy of grace.

The ICEL Revisions Program

From the beginning of its work, ICEL recognized that revision would be necessary after the testing of its work in communities of prayer across the English-speaking world. Shortly after completing the last of the major rites, a careful and thorough program of revision was developed. Over a period of approximately fifteen years all of ICEL's texts will undergo a process of revision based on study and wide consultation.

The rite of funerals was selected as a revisions pilot project both because it represented one of ICEL's first translation efforts and because it was a reasonably brief and self-contained rite. Procedures that evolved in the course of this revision would then be refined for the rest of the revisions work. A consultation book for the project was developed and sent to bishops and consultants throughout the English-speaking world. Respondents were invited to comment on the present liturgical texts of the funeral rite and to answer questions regarding original texts needed for the rite, ways the rite might be better presented for pastoral use, particular pastoral situations not taken into consideration in the present rite, the translation of the introduction and the rubrics, and about the whole of the revisions program as it might be conducted over the next decade or so.

In light of the responses, the liturgical texts of the funeral rite were completely revised, original texts were prepared, and pastoral introductions and directions were added. The new order of Christian funerals is a stunning tribute to the professional and pastoral work of the International Commission on English in the Liturgy in serving the worship needs of the English-speaking Roman Catholic church. The revision of the Roman missal is the major project presently underway and due for publication in the 1990s. Other rites will follow.

Critique

In a sense, the revisions program of ICEL is its own evaluation and critique. Some of the first translations were done in haste. Some of the Latin texts upon which ICEL based its work were less than inspired. Only slowly was ICEL able to assemble experts in various fields as translators, composers, and critics. Only gradually was ICEL able to refine its plan "for the translation of liturgical texts and the provision of original texts where required, in language which would be correct, dignified, intelligible, and suitable for public recitation and singing."[21] The work is in process; guidelines continue to be refined; English-speaking communities have been and continue to be well served by this body.

Two points are remarkable in the story of the changing face of Roman Catholic worship. The first is the high degree of satisfaction that the revised liturgy has engendered in worshiping communities. The Catholic church has achieved a renewal of its liturgical prayer, unprecedented in both scope and speed. By and large this renewal has been the impetus for a deeper and more vibrant life of liturgical prayer and faith. The second point worthy of note, and illustrated by this very volume, is the amazing collaboration that has been occasioned by a simultaneous renewal of liturgical forms throughout mainline Christian churches. Denominations that looked to Roman books for some of their texts will be happy to discover that their own books were sources of inspiration to ICEL in the revision process. Such liturgical collaboration among Christians cannot help but have profound ecumenical impact in years to come. Christian and Jewish dialogue on the nature and function of liturgical language as well as the quite specific concerns faced by each liturgical tradition have proven equally fruitful for mutual respect and collaboration in this awesome work of ours.[22]

NOTES

1. *The First Apology*, no. 67, in Daniel Sheerin, trans., *The Eucharist*, Message of the Fathers of the Church (Wilmington, Del., 1986), p. 35.

2. See *Roman Missal* (New York, 1966) for the texts and rubrics of the eucharistic rite, essentially unchanged since 1570. Publications of the missal after 1965 but before 1969 contain an interim English translation of the Latin texts that antedate the conciliar reforms. See n. 4 below, for a lay prayer book containing similar material. Excellent secondary sources include: *The New Catholic Encyclopedia* (New York, 1966): see, particularly, "Mass," "Liturgical Movement," "Liturgical Participation," "Liturgical Reform," "Liturgical Year," and "Liturgiology." More extensive treatment of preconciliar worship may be found in Gerald Ellard, *Christian Life and Worship* (New York, 1933). For a popular treatment of the pre- and postconciliar eucharistic celebration, see M. Basil Pennington, *The Eucharist Yesterday and Today* (New York, 1984).

3. The liturgical movement's early emphasis on rubrics rapidly yielded to the more fruitful historical study of the liturgy, which in turn opened up questions of genuine adaptation of liturgy to various cultures in light of history and scripture. See L. G. M. Alting von Geusau et al., *Liturgy in Development* (Westminster, Md., 1966), pp. 1–7, and passim. On the liturgical movement in general, see "Liturgical Movement," in *The New Catholic Encyclopedia*. A delightful first-person account of the liturgical movement is Bernard Botte, *From Silence to Participation*, trans. John Sullivan (Washington, 1988).

4. Joseph F. Stedman, *My Sunday Missal* (New York, 1938).

5. Constitution on the Sacred Liturgy (hereafter CSL), no. 1, trans. in International Commission on English in the Liturgy, *Documents on the Liturgy 1963–1979* (hereafter *DOL*), 1, no. 1. *DOL* is the standard reference for all conciliar, papal, and curial liturgical documentation for the fifteen years following the council. For an excellent commentary on the Constitution on the Sacred Liturgy, see Frederick R. McManus, "The Constitution on the Liturgy: Commentary," *Worship* 38 (1964): 314–74; 450–96; 515–65.

6. CSL, in *DOL* 1, nos. 23 and 37–40.

7. For an explanation of various ritual books, see "Liturgical

Books of the Roman Rite," in the supplement of *The New Catholic Encyclopedia*, vol. 17.

8. For an introduction to cultural adaptation, see Anscar J. Chupungco, *Cultural Adaptation of the Liturgy* (New York, 1982).

9. These five methods are spelled out generally in John W. O'Malley, "Reform, Historical Consciousness, and Vatican II's Aggiornamento," *TS* 32 (1971): 573–601. I am responsible for applying O'Malley's general principles specifically to liturgical reform.

10. An interesting case in point is a collection of prayers appended to the celebration of the Mass during the nineteenth century and prescribed for use in the Papal States. Leo XIII extended the prescription to include the whole church in 1886 and added the invocation to the archangel Michael. Under Pius X, a threefold invocation of the Sacred Heart of Jesus was added. Pius XII made the special intention of these prayers "the conversion of Russia." The original reason for the addition of the prayers disappeared over time, but the prayers themselves disappeared only with the reforms of Vatican II.

11. CSL, in *DOL* 1, no. 36:1–2.

12. CSL, in *DOL* 1, no. 36:3–4.

13. John Ainslie, *Making the Most of the Missal* (London, 1976), p. 17.

14. Anon., "The Language of the Liturgy," *Herder Correspondence* 3 (1966), p. 171.

15. "On the Translation of Liturgical Texts," *DOL* 123, no. 43.

16. The most significant actions taken with regard to the portrayal of Jews in Roman Catholic liturgy are the following: In March 1959, Pope John XXIII ordered the deletion of negative references to Jews in the solemn prayers of Good Friday; in 1978, ICEL developed a position paper on antisemitic language referring again to the Good Friday orations and highlighting the textual difficulties of the Gospel of John; in 1988 the National Conference of Catholic Bishops of the United States issued *God's Mercy Endures Forever: Guidelines on the Presentation of Jews and Judaism in Catholic Preaching*. See above, John Gurrieri's essay, "The Perception of Jews in Christian Liturgy: Then and Now."

17. ICEL, Eucharistic Prayer A (Washington, 1986). This text has not yet been approved for liturgical use.

18. *Roman Missal* (New York, 1966).

19. *Sacramentary* (New York, 1985).

20. First and second theology is an ancient distinction marking the community's most immediate expression of its faith in worship (first theology) and its more systematic articulation of its belief (second theology).

21. From the mandate entrusted to ICEL by its episcopal committee in 1964, cited in Frederick R. McManus, *ICEL: The First Years, an ICEL Occasional Paper* (Washington, 1981), p. 13, an excellent source of information about ICEL, its mandate, organization, and early history.

22. Cf. readings suggested in note 2 (above); and Edward J. Kilmartin, "Theology of the Sacraments: Toward a New Understanding of the Chief Rites of the Church of Jesus Christ," in R. Duffy, ed., *Alternative Futures for Worship*, vol. 1: *General Introduction* (Collegeville, 1987), pp. 123–75.

New Lutheran Liturgy for the United States and Canada

Eugene L. Brand

BACKGROUND OF LITURGICAL REFORM

Lutheran history in the United States and Canada has been punctuated by the merging of scores of ethnic Lutheran churches into increasingly unified American/Canadian churches. Except for the Lutheran Church–Missouri Synod and other small, ultraconservative Lutheran groups who have held themselves aloof from the process, the goal of Lutheran church unity has been all but achieved in the formation of the Evangelical Lutheran Church in Canada (ELCC) in 1986 and the Evangelical Lutheran Church in America (ELCA) in 1988. Because the ethnic churches have been culturally diverse—they were founded by successive waves of immigrants from Germany, Scandinavia, Finland, and central Europe—their coming together was not only a matter of finding their place in an alien Anglo-American milieu but also equally a matter of combining their own ethnic heritages. Thus American Lutheran history has strong cultural and sociological parallels with American Roman Catholic history.

Chief among the problems of inculturation was language. Real progress toward unity tended to parallel the abandoning of the former languages and the adoption of English as the medium of worship and instruction.

Lutheran mergers have been accompanied—and to some extent accomplished—by new books of worship. The *Common Service Book*, 1918, became the book of the newly formed United Lutheran Church in America. The eight churches that published the *Service Book and Hymnal* (*SBH*) in 1958 had become two churches by 1962. *The Lutheran Book of Worship* (*LBW*), 1978, preceded the formation of the ELCC by eight years and the ELCA by ten. There can be little doubt that the common use of English made possible the liturgical unification of Lutheranism in North America, and that the liturgical process both influenced and was influenced by the structural process of merger. But that is only part of the story.

American Lutherans were in the vanguard of world Lutheranism's nineteenth-century rediscovery of its Reformation liturgical heritage. The eucharist of the *Church Book*, 1868, and especially that of the *Common Service*, 1888, mark the recovery of the fullness of the liturgy of the Reformation *Kirchenordnungen* (church orders), particularly the western Mass, which the early Lutheran reformers had consciously retained, albeit reformed of medieval "errors." Thus Lutheran liturgical history has significant parallels with that of the Anglican Communion: both traditions have striven to remain in the liturgical tradition of western catholicism.

The inclusion of the 1888 *Common Service*—the full evangelical-catholic tradition in English—in the 1918 *Common Service Book* united American Lutherans liturgically in the first half of this century. The *Service Book and Hymnal* was the apotheosis of Lutheranism's restoration phase, as well as the signal that a new phase had already begun.[1]

MOTIVATIONS TOWARD LITURGICAL REFORM

What motivated the American Lutheran Church (ALC) and the Lutheran Church in American (LCA) to join the Lutheran Church–Missouri Synod (LC-MS) in work on what was to become the *Lutheran Book of Worship* (*LBW*) less than a decade after publication of their *Service Book and Hymnal*? Chiefly the force of the long-held dream of all American Lutherans using one book, sharing one form for worship. In the mid-1960s it looked as though the LC-MS was poised to join the majority of North American Lutherans in using a common liturgical and hymnological resource.

But the work of the newly established Inter-Lutheran Commission on Worship (ILCW) had scarcely begun in 1966 when conservatives gained leadership in the Missouri Synod. Though they continued to participate in the commission until the manuscript of the *Lutheran Book of Worship* was finished, they saw to it that the *LBW* was not approved for publication. Their own *Lutheran Worship*, 1982, however, contains large portions of the *LBW*, often slightly revised. One cannot avoid the judgment that the leaders of the Missouri Synod rejected the *LBW* because, from their more conservative posture, they could not risk putting a powerful symbol of Lutheran unity in the hands of parishioners.

Another reason for the development of the *Lutheran Book of Worship* was that in terms of its diction the *Service Book and Hymnal* was out of date already by the day it was published. Its framers could not have foreseen the challenge of the Revised Standard Version of the Bible to the Jacobean style of the Authorized Version and of the *Book of Common Prayer*. In the 1960s the clergy especially were restive with the ''thee-thou'' style and its archaic verb endings.

Finally, the growing impact of the broader liturgical movement gained in appeal through the revision of the Roman Catholic liturgical books both before and after the Constitution on the Sacred Liturgy of the Second Vatican Council, 1963. What is sometimes called the pastoral phase of the liturgical movement had special resonance among Lutherans and suggested that they pursue further the ecumenical path that had already been opened in the *Service Book and Hymnal*. Though the *Lutheran Book of Worship* is a hymnal as well as a service book, and though its hymnological accomplishments must not be ignored, the *kairos*—the opportune time for grace—was clearly liturgical and only to a lesser degree musical. Among Lutherans themselves, two organizations became the focus and impetus for discussion leading up to work on the *LBW:* the Lutheran Society for Worship, Music, and the Arts, founded in 1958, and the Valparaiso University Institute of Liturgical Studies, founded in 1949.

The manuscript of the *Lutheran Book of Worship* was prepared by four committees—Liturgical Texts, Liturgical Music, Hymn Texts, Hymn Music—of the Inter-Lutheran Commission on Worship (ILCW), which was itself officially appointed by, and responsible to, the cooperating Lutheran churches. Some of the work of the liturgical texts committee was done by subcommittees or task forces, e.g., lectionary, Holy Week, eucharistic prayers. At first, the worship executives of the churches shared staffing responsibilities. But in 1975 a full-time project director was appointed with chief responsibility for coordination. The project director was also responsible for assembling the manuscript, seeing it through the official review processes, and, together with editors functioning on behalf of the publishers, to see it through the process of publication.

The *Lutheran Book of Worship* was published jointly in 1978 by the American Lutheran Church's Augsburg Publishing House and the Lutheran Church in America's Board of Publication. It is actually a small library of books: (1) the standard pew edition, which contains the chief liturgical material and hymns; (2) the minister's edition, or altar book, which contains all the liturgical material and complete notes on the services; (3) the minister's desk edition of the altar book, and (4) the accompaniment edition for the liturgy. Companion volumes are *Manual on the Liturgy*, 1979, *Hymnal Companion*, 1981, and, most recently, *Commentary on the LBW*, 1990.

The Inter-Lutheran Commission on Worship quickly abandoned the idea that it could first lay a theoretical, or even theological, foundation for its work and, having done so, then address itself to the tasks of structure, texts, and music. Instead it opted for a more synthetic approach that, in the end, would let the liturgies speak for themselves. The basic issues discussed below should therefore not be seen as an a priori agenda to which the liturgy was made to comply.

Rather, they emerged as the work progressed, or they are judgments made on the finished body of work.

ISSUES AND JUDGMENTS IN LITURGICAL REFORM

Ecumenical Convergence

By its inclusion of a litanylike Kyrie along Eastern Orthodox lines and of a eucharistic prayer, the eucharist of the *Service Book and Hymnal* had already in 1958 ventured beyond the "common consent of the pure Lutheran liturgies of the sixteenth century." That step gave liturgical expression to a growing appreciation among Lutherans of their catholic heritage. Inspired by the revelations of the biblical and liturgical movements and by the far-reaching reforms of the Roman rite according to the principles of Vatican II, the Commission on Worship was determined not to carry on its work in a confessional vacuum. Convinced that to be truly Lutheran is to be truly catholic, the commission wished to do as much of its work as possible together with other communions having similar liturgical convictions. It therefore remained in touch with the Roman Catholic International Committee on English in the Liturgy (ICEL) and especially with the Standing Liturgical Commission of the Episcopal Church in the United States of America.

These ecumenical contacts were fostered by the American Consultation on Common Texts and later by the International Consultation on English Texts (ICET). The commission thus took an approach to its Lutheran mandate and heritage that differed from previous liturgical commissions, an approach suggested by the new direction of the liturgical movement. In the earlier recovery phase, the goal had been to restore the fullness of the classic confessional heritage. In the new pastoral phase, the goal was to act on the conviction that Lutheranism is a legitimate bearer of the western catholic tradition and thus should be a partner in the current shaping of that tradition.[2]

The use of ICET texts gives evidence of this growing partnership. From the beginning, the commission participated in the ICET task and was committed to the results.[3] At a later stage when the issue of inclusive language was having its influence, the commission stood firm on retaining the ICET texts even if they did not always meet its standards for inclusive language. The commonality of the texts was judged the more important factor.

The use of a modified version of the Roman Catholic eucharistic lectionary is a second example of ecumenical convergence. In this case, it was not just a matter of harmony with Roman usage but of being part of a far-reaching American consensus. Continental Lutheranism was determined to maintain the traditional one-year cycle of pericopes in a somewhat revised form, and the Lutheran World Federation acted as coordinator in a project aimed at making a pericope system for use among Lutherans worldwide. The project collapsed because the American Lutherans judged it more important to read the same pericopes as their American sister churches than to be in harmony with Lutherans overseas. This was a difficult, but wise, choice.

The choice of the Psalter prepared by the Episcopalians for their own prayer book is a third example. The *Service Book and Hymnal* had used the Authorized Version Psalms, but the ILCW judged its successor, the Revised Standard Version Psalter, unsuitable for singing and infelicitous for unison reading. The Episcopal version was selected after considering other alternatives because it was made for liturgical use, but also because it would forge a common bond between the two communions.

The inclusion of a eucharistic prayer in the Great Thanksgiving is a final example. With a few notable exceptions, Lutheran liturgies had followed the 1523 and 1526 models of Luther himself, which excised most of the Roman canon for theological reasons but put nothing in its place. Lutheran liturgies thereby gave the words of institution a prominence unprecedented in Christian history, lending to them, in the opinion of an increasing number of liturgiologists, an almost mechanistic force as a formula of consecration. That development was, of course, the opposite of Luther's intention. He wished to disencumber the *Verba* from a context that muted their proclamatory potential as gospel in microcosm. The opinion is still held by many, even after the rediscovery of the genre of thanksgiving, that because the *Verba* are a proclamation (addressed to the assembly), they cannot be placed in the context of a prayer, which by definition is addressed to God.

The duration of Lutheran practice and the theological interpretation it has produced made it necessary to offer two alternatives to the eucharistic prayer: (1) the *Verba* alone, (2) a brief prayer of thanksgiving, followed by the *Verba*. But the ILCW argued its case strongly and doggedly, both on theological and ecumenical grounds, with the result that a eucharistic prayer is the preferred usage in the *Lutheran Book of Worship* and that three alternative eucharistic prayers appear in the minister's edition.[4]

Ecumenical convergence and the common use of ICET texts have produced striking parallels, especially in the Masses of the English version of the missal of Paul VI, the 1979 *Book of Common Prayer* (ECUSA) and the *Lutheran Book of Worship*.

Baptismal Focus

Baptism functions as the foundation of the theology of the modern ecumenical movement. It played a crucial role in the theology of Martin Luther also, but, until recently, Lutherans had not drawn the liturgical consequences from that fact. Not only did Lutheran baptismal liturgies suffer in form and amplitude from the scholastic debate about the essence of a sacrament, but the rites themselves were commonly buried in clerical manuals, since baptism had come to be thought of as an occasional service.

The *Service Book and Hymnal* took an initial step forward by including several of the occasional services at which congregations are normally present. But it remained for the

Lutheran Book of Worship to place the baptismal liturgy in the chief liturgical section of the book and to restore to it its own thanksgiving and the elements of confirmation.[5] No longer a brief interruption in the normal course of a Sunday service, baptism is now a full sacramental celebration with appropriate dignity and ritual action.

The baptismal focus is not limited to holy baptism itself: it penetrates the entire liturgical corpus. The various orders for the confession of sin are cast as clear baptismal *anamnesis*. The inclusion of the Easter vigil places baptism at the center of the celebration of Jesus' passover from death to life. The order for burial begins with a baptismal remembrance and contains other allusions to that rite. Thus, more than any of its predecessors, the *LBW* gives clearer liturgical expression both to the nature of the Christian community and to the Christian person.

Presidency and Lay Leadership

Prior to the nineteenth-century liturgical review, Lutheran liturgy had often degenerated into a pastor's monologue framing the sermon. The congregation was present merely as an audience. But even with the recovery of the dialogic character of the liturgy, dialogue tended to be limited to the pastor and the congregation. The pastor had absorbed all of the traditional ministries of liturgical leadership, with the possible exception of cantor (precentor). Descriptors such as *celebrant* and *liturgist* and *officiant* betray what the former mindset really was. Though the *LBW*'s predecessors had simply used *minister* to label all leadership functions, and though somewhere in the rubrics that term was so interpreted as to include certain lay functions, in practice the pastor did everything labeled *minister.*

Only gradually is that mindset being overcome with the emerging understanding of the pastor's role as the presidency over an action in which there are multiple leadership roles, some of which belong by right to laypersons. The *LBW* assists in the process by using varied leadership designations:

(P) for presiding minister; (A) for assisting minister, who should be an ordained person only if lay leadership is unavailable; (C) for congregation as a whole; and (L) for leader of daily prayer offices and other nonsacramental services. Since American Lutherans lack a clearly defined diaconate, the role of deacon does not appear. And though the churches have bishops, no role is designated clearly for them liturgically apart from ordination.

Ten years into the era of the *Lutheran Book of Worship*, lay lectors have become common and laypersons assist at the communion more and more frequently. Laypersons also lead the intercessions in some places. But old habits are tenacious, and change is often resisted by the laypeople themselves. In parishes with two or more pastors, the sharing of leadership is often illogical and all too often precludes lay leadership.

A concept of ministry that embraces all members of the church is the goal that the *LBW* attempts to foster. Lay leadership should give liturgical expression to and the assembly should recognize the dignity of every Christian ministry. Moreover, the ministry of all in their several vocations should come to expression in the offering both of money and of bread and wine.

There is a danger that the offertory can assume too dominant a role, and Lutherans, with their gift theology of the eucharist, are especially anxious about that. But if the risk is not taken, the liturgical expression of Christian vocation in general is thwarted, and thus an important moment in the complex relationships of the eucharist remains unexpressed. In the offertory rubrics, the offertory song, and the offertory prayer, the *LBW* gives evidence of a clear theology of offering, connecting it to the oblation of Christ that is, of course, the supreme moment in the eucharistic complex.

A final and most significant point. If the ILCW intended to present a declericalized liturgy for the whole church, it needed to reach that goal with the participation of the whole church. Thus the trial use of liturgical reforms must be regarded as more than a popular ploy. The series of ten *Contemporary Worship* booklets provided the possibility for congregations to be involved in the process.[6] Reactions, both critical and positive, were taken seriously. They resulted either in changes in the final form of the liturgy or revealed areas where education was especially needed. This more informal process was intensified where the eucharist was concerned, with a more scientific test of the semifinal draft.

Not only did the process produce a better liturgical book—at least in the sense of pastoral realism—but it insured more ready acceptance of the *LBW*. The book did not seem to come down from on high. People and pastors, to say nothing of musicians, were already familiar with at least some of the contents.

Inclusive Language

Sensitivity to the active involvement of the whole worshiping community also calls for sensitivity where inclusive language is concerned. In 1966, when the ILCW held its organizational meeting, few were already conscious of the issue. But its advocates increased, and their voices began to register. A few examples illustrate the change. In the trial use liturgy for Holy Communion, 1970, the rubrics about actions of the ministers used the pronoun *he*: "He includes prayers for . . . " One of the offertories contained the line, "Gather the hopes and dreams of men." In the *LBW* the corresponding texts read: "Prayers are included for . . . ," and "Gather the hopes and dreams of all."

With the exception of the ICET texts (see above), all the language referring to persons is inclusive. The God-language remains masculine, however, for at least two reasons: (1) it was not yet a major issue when the manuscript was made final, and (2) good and generally acceptable alternatives had not yet been developed. In the mid-1970s church review committees were not yet ready for *Godself* and similar innovations.

The body of collects was, however, reviewed, and the forms of invocation revised to fit the main theme. Such biblical images as "God of compassion," "Almighty God, our redeemer,'' and "God our creator" replaced "Father" or "Lord" in several places.

The concern to make language inclusive does not stop at avoiding sexism. Problems of racial exclusivity were also noted, as was the picture presented, especially in the Holy Week services, of the Jewish people. In the bidding prayer of the Good Friday liturgy, the traditional prayer for the conversion of the Jews was transformed:

> Let us pray for the Jewish people, the first to hear the Word of God, that they may receive the fulfillment of the covenant's promises. *Silent Prayer*.

> Almighty and Eternal God, long ago you gave your promise to Abraham and his posterity. Hear the prayers of your Church that the people you first made your own may arrive with us at the fullness of redemption.[7]

After an abortive attempt to expand the *Improperia* to make clear its application to Christians, it was omitted altogether.

In retrospect it is clear that the *LBW* marks only a beginning in the struggle for a properly inclusive language that is also theologically sound. Another generation will find better and more widely acceptable solutions.

Liturgical Music

The 1960s, when the ILCW began its work, was a decade of upheaval in church music. Most of the pop and folk masses of the period have been forgotten, but the desire for variety that they represented—when they were not merely anarchistic—remains. It is impossible in one book designed for use by an entire denomination to include settings of the liturgy that fit all situations. Yet the effort had to be made because of the strong emphasis that Lutherans have traditionally placed on the congregational singing of the liturgy. Choral Mass settings are not unknown, but they are highly unusual in ordinary Lutheran worship.

The *LBW* presents three full musical settings of the Holy Communion: (1) a through-composed, vigorously rhythmic setting for unison voices with an organ accompaniment that is modestly dissonant, (2) a through-composed setting for unison voices somewhat reminiscent of modern English hymnody, (3) a unison chant setting adapted from the *Swedish Mass Book* of 1942 whose music goes back through the Reformation period to Gregorian originals. All three settings include intonations for the ministers. Morning and evening prayer have musical settings similar to the first setting for the Holy Communion. The Psalms are pointed for singing, and ten simple psalm-tones are provided.

CRITIQUE

From its official introductory date, Advent I, 1978, the *LBW* was rapidly and readily adopted by the congregations—much more so than its predecessor, *SBH*. The positive effect of the trial use procedure has already been mentioned. More important was the continentwide program of introduction mounted by the churches.

During September and November 1978, 722 congregational "cluster events" were held in the United States, Canada, and the Caribbean, giving every congregation the possibility of participation. Key to the program was an introductory kit that was designed for congregational use. Twelve thousand out of a possible eighteen thousand congregations participated in these events. This process demonstrated that the production of a book is only the beginning. It must be made accessible to congregations in a positive and helpful spirit. Various surveys made in 1988 after a decade of use show that whatever its shortcomings, the *LBW* is still functioning well in most places.

Most criticism has centered on the hymnal: its selection of hymns, its efforts at updating language and, mostly, its harmonizations. The liturgical portion has generally been well received, though some persistent questions are still debated. Chief among them is whether eucharistic prayers are possible for Lutherans (see above, Ecumenical Convergence). Another is whether the traditional eucharist meets the needs of an increasingly culturally diverse American Lutheranism. Is it still too northern European in form and ethos? Still another question is about retention of "traditional" God-language. Just as some pastors in the 1960s and early 1970s tried to modernize the Jacobean diction of the liturgy on the spot, so some pastors today try various solutions to avoid masculine pronouns for God.[8]

NOTES

1. I have described this process in greater detail in "The Lutheran 'Common Service': Heritage and Challenge," *Studia Liturgica* 19 (1989): 78–95. See also Luther Reed, *The Lutheran Liturgy* (Philadelphia, 1959).

2. In such an essay as this it seemed inappropriate to document from ILCW minutes the decisions mentioned below. The papers of the ILCW are deposited in the Archives of Cooperative Lutheranism, now in Chicago.

3. One modification of the ICET texts used in the *LBW* is the substitution of the traditional, "He descended into hell," for ICET's, "He descended to the dead," (Apostles' Creed). The ICET text is printed as alternative use.

4. For the debate, cf. essays in the *Lutheran Quarterly* 26 (1974): 110–224; and *The Great Thanksgiving* (ILCW, Contemporary Worship 8, 1975), pp. 1–7.

5. The logical implications of reuniting two of the initiation rites could not be realized, however. A separate liturgy for use in confirmation still exists. Note a similar inconsistency in the American *Book of Common Prayer*.

6. The series began in 1966 with a collection of hymns and was published by the participating churches under the auspices of the ILCW. It ended in 1976 with "Burial of the Dead," the tenth volume. In between were "The Holy Communion" (1970), "The Marriage Service" (1972), "Hymns for Baptism and Communion" (1972), "Services of the Word" (1972), "The Church Year: Calendar and Lectionary" (1973), "Holy Baptism" (1974), "Affirmation of the Baptismal Covenant" (1975), and "Daily Prayer of the Church" (1976).

7. *LBW*, ministers' edition, p. 140.

8. The following selective list of review articles will yield an accurate picture of the response:

Senn, Frank C. "Lutheran Book of Worship." *Dialog* 18 (1979): 301–5. Cf. further reactions in *Dialog* 19 (1980): 128–30; 295–97.

Routley, E. "The Lutheran Book of Worship." *The Hymn Society Bulletin* 9/5 (1979): 73–79.

Lathrop, Gordon W. "Pastoral Liturgical Theology and the LBW: A Reconnaissance." *Dialog* 18 (1979): 108–13.

Hoekema, David. "Worship for Today." *The Reformed Journal* 29/6 (1979): 18–22.

Boehme, Armand J. "Sing a New Song: The Doctrine of Justification and the LBW Sacramental Liturgies." *Concordia Theological Quarterly* 43/2 (1979): 96, 118.

Echols, James K. "A Theological Approach to the LBW from a Black Perspective." *LCA Partners* (December 1981).

Ramshaw-Schmidt, Gail. "Toward Lutheran Eucharistic Prayers." In *New Eucharistic Prayers*, Frank C. Senn, ed., pp. 74–79. New York, 1987.

Brand, Eugene L. "The LBW: A Shaper of Lutheran Piety in North America." *Word and World* 9/1 (1989): 37–45.

The *Book of Common Prayer:*
Revising the Liturgy of the American
Episcopal Church

CHARLES P. PRICE

The 1979 revision of the American *Book of Common Prayer* (henceforth *BCP* '79) constituted the most sweeping change of Anglican liturgical provisions since the first prayer book appeared in England in 1549 during the reign of Edward VI. Every congregation, from cathedral to university chapel to country parish church, had been required by law to conform to that first book; and to this day in all provinces of the Anglican Communion worship is expected to be in accordance with an authorized prayer book that in every instance bears a strong family resemblance to the English model. The book has gone through a number of subsequent revisions in England, Scotland, the United States, Canada, South Africa, and indeed in all parts of the Anglican Communion. Each revision has preserved the shape and general contents of the 1549 *Book of Common Prayer.* Each has introduced the changes that a changing church in a changing society requires.

Sixteenth-, seventeenth-, and eighteenth-century revisions were slight, for, despite political upheavals, society was relatively stable. Nineteenth- and twentieth-century revisions, however, are a different story. Social upheavals created by the industrial revolution have been major. Patient historical research has brought new understanding of liturgical development. These factors created both the pressure and the possibility for much more radical change. Enrichment by recovered liturgical treasure and new composition as well as flexibility to adapt to a wide variety of circumstances became the watchwords of liturgical advance.

Even so, revisions of the American book in 1892 and again in 1928 were cautious and left many issues unresolved. In 1928 the General Convention of the church authorized its revision but recognized that further change was inevitable and established a standing liturgical commission to study the needs of the church and to propose new forms of worship. By 1950 the commission began to publish the results of its work. In 1967, trial use of new proposals was authorized for the first time. For the next twelve years, congregations large and small throughout the church engaged in the evaluation of these proposals. Such a practice was a new departure for Episcopalians, and it bore much fruit in the form of criticism and suggestion. In more senses than one, *BCP* '79 is a book of *common* prayer.[1]

Once *BCP* '79 was approved, work began on a new hymnal. In the American Episcopal Church the texts of hymns as well as the *Book of Common Prayer* are authorized by the General Convention. This process went more smoothly and quickly than the revision of the prayer book. By 1982 a new set of texts had been approved, and a few years later, complete with music, *Hymnal 1982* was in the pews. Many of the same factors were at work in both processes.[2]

Seven features of the revision of the prayer book and hymnal bear closer examination: (1) modernization of language; (2) inclusivity of language; (3) comprehensiveness of church parties; (4) ecumenical convergences; (5) concern for social justice and ecology; (6) a changing attitude toward the Jews; (7) provisions to increase congregational participation.

Modernization of Language

Many branches of the Anglican Communion have published revisions of their liturgies during the past ten years or so. Down to this round of revision, prayer books had retained sixteenth-century language, which is deeply imprinted on Anglican consciousness, almost a sacred language, like Hebrew for Jews or Latin for Roman Catholics. Its splendid and majestic prose was formative of English style in past eras, when virtually all English-speaking persons were reared on it. To lure Episcopalians to address God in any other way proved difficult, and the 1979 revisers did not want to eliminate the old rhetoric completely. Consequently *BCP* '79 retains traditional language for one form (rite one) of the daily office—daily morning and evening prayer—for the eucharist, and for the burial of the dead; but all the material in the book in an alternative rite (rite two), including the daily services, the eucharist, and the burial of the dead, appears in a contemporary idiom. The commission made a determined effort to forge a new liturgical style that is adequate to express the worship of the people of God. A beginning has been made. In a religion centered in the Word made flesh, liturgical language should be the language of the people.

The change that symbolized the shift from sixteenth- to twentieth-century speech was the substitution of *you* for *thou* in addressing the deity. No change was harder to swallow, even for those willing to make the shift. In the sixteenth century, *thou* was an address of intimacy, whether one spoke to God or to another person. The use of *thou* paralleled the present-day French use of *tu* or the German *du*; these languages employ the familiar form of the second-person pronoun in love and religion. In English, however, the nonreligious use of *thou* has almost disappeared. Even in love poetry, it begins to sound quaint rather than to denote intimacy.

Consequently, *thou* in its religious setting has acquired a sense of distance and awe that it did not originally have and was not intended to have. The relationship to God that was then expressed by *thou* can be communicated today only by *you*. And that single change, of course, requires a complete reworking of liturgical diction. Our church has taken two decades to begin to worship in this new style.[3]

Inclusivity of Language

Like most other western churches, the Episcopal church has sought to achieve a more inclusive language for worship. All segments of God's people should be able to respond to prayer book language with ease and joy.

The term *inclusive language* has come to suggest primarily gender inclusivity. Yet language can also offend and exclude racial minorities and the handicapped. Associations between evil and blackness or goodness and whiteness and references to the mute as "dumb" are cases in point. Thus the phrase in a familiar eucharistic hymn which originally ran, "From tainting mischief, keep them white and clear," has been altered to read, "From tainting mischief keep them pure and clear."[4] Charles Wesley's line, "Hear him ye deaf; his praise, ye dumb," has become "Hear him ye deaf; ye voiceless ones."[5]

The feminist critique of the language of worship was not as fully developed during the years when *BCP* '79 texts were taking shape as during the formation of *Hymnal 1982*. *Hymnal 1982* shows more sensitivity of these concerns. The prayer book preserves masculine references to deity. The hymnal makes a few cautious attempt to be more inclusive in Godward reference as well as in human relations. One doxology runs,

> All praise, O unbegotten God,
> all praise to you, eternal Word,
> all praise, life-giving Spirit, praise,
> all glory to our God Triune.[6]

The hymnal revisers came to think that in the course of time parity between masculine and feminine images for God should obtain, and that it would be a grave mistake to eliminate gender-specific references altogether, since to do so would eliminate personhood altogether. It will plainly take a long time to reach parity.

Comprehensiveness of Church Parties

The third concern, comprehensiveness of church parties, represents intracommunal, but nonetheless very real, interests. It needs to be said that *BCP* '79 was designed so that it could be used by Episcopal congregations with quite different liturgical inclinations.

For one hundred years, from the mid-nineteenth to the mid-twentieth centuries, the Episcopal church was marked and often hampered by controversies among various ecclesiastical parties. High church congregations often imported unauthorized missals. Low church clergy often made up their own prayers. *BCP* '79 has amplified and enriched both the eucharistic services and the collection of occasional prayers. It introduced some formerly controversial material on an optional basis. Although it would be misleading to imply that no internal liturgical controversy remains, *BCP* '79 has in fact proved to be remarkably unifying and healing.

One feature of *BCP* '79 has contributed to this result in an unexpected way. For the first time, the eucharist is described as "the principal act of Christian worship on the Lord's day."[7] This provision pleased Anglo-catholics, for whom frequent celebrations of the eucharist had been customary for a long time. It also proved helpful in encouraging a renewed Evangelical emphasis on the eucharist as the communion meal that our Lord commanded. Wesley, Cranmer, and Calvin, it has been remembered, desired weekly celebrations. Many Protestant churches are also appropriating this insight and practice, and it may change the liturgical face of western Christendom.

Ecumenical Convergences

Ecumenical convergences appear in a number of texts.

One of the four eucharistic prayers in *BCP* '79, prayer D, is a slightly altered form of the earliest known version of the Liturgy of St. Basil.[8] In one form or another, this prayer is now shared not only by Eastern Orthodox churches, but also by Roman Catholics (prayer 4 in the missal) and several Protestant denominations. Although some textual variants in these denominational versions point to still-unresolved theological disagreements,[9] it is fair to say that for the first time since the Reformation, and perhaps since the Great Schism, progress is being made toward framing a eucharistic prayer that can be used throughout Christendom.

The three-year Sunday lectionary, which *BCP* '79 shares, with slight modifications, with Methodists, Lutherans, Roman Catholics, the United Church of Christ, and the liturgy of the Churches of Christ Uniting (COCU), is another ecumenical feature of contemporary Episcopal worship. This lectionary provides a lesson from the Hebrew Scriptures, a New Testament reading (usually, though by no means always, an Epistle), and a Gospel pericope for each Sunday and Holy Day. It can be used, of course, at either eucharistic or non-eucharistic services; but it allows the Old Testament to sound again at eucharistic celebrations in all the churches that used the ancient eucharistic lectionary (Roman Catholic, Lutheran, Anglican).[10] For the most part, the traditional lectionary provided only an Epistle and Gospel.

BCP '79 also uses texts of the Lord's Prayer, Apostles' Creed, Nicene Creed, and a number of canticles, which were published by the International Consultation on English texts (ICET), an ecumenical group convened to provide new common translations for widely used liturgical texts during the period of revision.[11]

Social Justice and Ecology

A glance at the section of *BCP* '79 that contains prayers for special occasions will reveal the scope of its concern for both social and ecological issues:[12] In Time of Conflict (No. 28), For the Unemployed (No. 30), For the Aged (No. 49), For the Human Family (No. 3). It is the first Anglican book with a specific prayer For Our Enemies (No. 6).

On the ecological side, there is a whole section of prayers for the natural order, including a prayer For the Knowledge of God's Creation (No. 40), For the Conservation of Natural Resources (No. 41), and For the Future of the Human Race (No. 44). Similar concerns come to expression in other places in the book. There is a new emphasis on God's creative activity, although, to be sure, such language was not absent in earlier books. God's work in creation is celebrated in all the new eucharistic prayers.[13] It had been mentioned in ancient thanksgivings, as in the Jewish *berakhah* on which they probably depend. It disappeared inexplicably from the canon of the Mass and was not restored in sixteenth-century Protestant reworkings of the text. Its reappearance now is welcome.

Changing Attitude toward Jews

Inspection of a succession of Anglican prayer books reveals a changing attitude toward Jews. *BCP* '79 intends to acknowledge the status of the Jewish people in their covenant with God, a covenant on which Christians depend. It is "irrevocable," to use St. Paul's word.[14] In the strength of this conviction, *BCP* '79 corrects earlier offensive language.

From 1549 through 1892, one of the solemn Good Friday collects contained the phrase, "Have mercy upon all Jews, Turks, infidels, and heretics; and take away from them all ignorance, hardness of heart, and contempt of thy Word." This language was mitigated in 1928 to read, "Have mercy on all who know thee not as thou art revealed in the Gospel of thy Son,"[15] and further in *BCP* '79:

Let us pray for all who have not received the Gospel of Christ;
For those who have never heard the word of salvation
For those who have lost their faith
For those hardened by sin or indifference
For the contemptuous and the scornful
For those who are enemies of the cross of Christ and persecutors of his disciples
For those who in the name of Christ have persecuted others.[16]

Jews are not mentioned, and the thrust of the prayer has been redirected toward the Christian community itself.

The revisers of *BCP* '79 included the Reproaches within the Good Friday liturgy in its penultimate form, as presented to the General Convention for approval. They had not appeared in earlier English or American books, but they had been widely used. They were conceived to describe the sins and failures of Christians and to express Christ's anguish in being crucified anew by his own people. Some Jewish friends, however, reminded the commission that the Reproaches, originally medieval devotions, had been taken in the past, and still could be taken, to blame the Jews for Jesus' death. Medieval and later congregations sometimes burst forth after hearing the Reproaches at Good Friday services and instigated unspeakable pogroms. Consequently, the Reproaches were simply omitted from the final text of *BCP* '79 as the surest way of removing this cause of friction and misunderstanding.

Increasing Congregational Participation

It would be difficult to describe all the measures taken to increase congregational participation. Worship in accordance with Anglican prayer books used to be virtually a solo performance by the priest except for the singing of hymns. Now a concerted effort is made to share leadership, both in the liturgy and beyond it. The role of the deacon has been expanded, particularly in the eucharist. Laypersons are encouraged to read lessons and some of the prayers. There are many litanies requiring congregational response; all the prayers of the people are cast in this form. Worship conducted by *BCP* '79 is envisioned as a choir with many voices united in a paean of praise to God.

Critique

What should have been done differently?

In retrospect it has become clear that much more attention should have been given to inclusive language, particularly in rite-one services. At the time, the liturgical commission desired to preserve the texts as nearly intact as possible, for the

sake of continuity and conciliation. The result has rendered
them in fact less useful to a generation more sensitive to this
issue and still desirous of the option of traditional language.
Pressure for further revision comes almost entirely from this
quarter. Experimental inclusive language liturgies were authorized by the General Convention in 1988. As in the case
of the hymns, new ways to speak of God must be sought to
supplement (though not to eliminate) masculine images for
God. The personal character of God and the continuity of the
theological tradition have to be conserved in this process.
These newer liturgies wrestle with that set of problems,
though they are still unsettled.

Unquestionably a number of things could have been improved. Some language is not felicitous; there was never
enough time to perfect it. Also, there should almost certainly
be an indication of the action that a bishop should perform
not only at confirmation but also at the reception of new
members and the reaffirmation of baptismal vows.[17] The ambiguity was originally creative. It is now confusing.

In general, perhaps greater ecumenical consultation during
the process of revision might have yielded even greater liturgical convergence than *BCP* '79 now displays.

NOTES

1. *The Book of Common Prayer and Administration of the Sac-
raments and Other Rites and Ceremonies of the Church According
to the Use of the Episcopal Church* (New York, 1979). See also
Marion J. Hatchett, *Commentary on the American Prayer Book*
(New York, 1980); and Charles P. Price and Louis Weil, *Liturgy for
Living* (New York, 1979.)

2. *The Hymnal 1982 According to the Use of the Episcopal
Church* (New York, 1982).

3. To choose only an example or two of this modernization of
language would be arbitrary; the whole book is a monument to it.
One of the more controversial changes is the alteration of the first
line of the *Te Deum*, which (in the traditional language) runs, ''We
praise Thee, O God,'' to, ''You are God, we praise you.'' The

sound of *you* is not as strong as the sound of *Thee*. Hence the radical change is necessary to preserve emphasis.

4. *Hymnal 1982*, hymn no. 337.

5. *Hymnal 1982*, hymn no. 493.

6. *Hymnal 1982*, hymn no. 55.

7. *BCP* '79, p. 13.

8. *BCP* '79, pp. 372–75.

9. Where the eucharistic prayer D in *BCP* '79 reads, "offering to you from the gifts you have given us, this bread and this cup," prayer IV in the Roman Catholic liturgy runs, "we offer you his body and blood, the acceptable sacrifice which brings salvation to the whole world."

10. *BCP* '79, pp. 887–931.

11. *Prayers We Have in Common: Agreed Liturgical Texts Prepared by the International Consultation on English Texts*, 2d rev. ed. (Philadelphia, 1975).

12. *BCP* '79, pp. 809–41.

13. For example, "All glory be to thee, O Lord our God, for that thou didst create heaven and earth, and didst make us in thine own image; and of thine tender mercy" (eucharist prayer II, *BCP* '79, p. 341). Cf. eucharist prayer I, "All glory be to thee, Almighty God, our heavenly Father, for that thou of thy tender mercy" (*BCP* '79, p. 334).

14. Romans 11:29.

15. *BCP* 1928, p. 157.

16. *BCP* '79, p. 279.

17. *BCP* '79, pp. 418–19.

Worship Revision in the United Methodist Church

HOYT L. HICKMAN

Historical Background

The United Methodist Church was formed in 1968 by the union of the Methodist church and the Evangelical United Brethren church, the latter having been formed in 1946 by the union of the Evangelical church and the United Brethren in Christ. The Methodist church arose from a movement within the Church of England led by a priest, John Wesley (1703–1791); the Evangelical church, from a movement in America led by a Lutheran lay preacher, Jacob Albright (1759–1808); and the United Brethren in Christ, from a movement in America led by a Reformed pastor, William Philip Otterbein (1726–1813), and a Mennonite preacher, Martin Boehm (1725–1812). It is significant that the traditions represented by the United Methodist church today (1) arose as reformations within Protestantism in the eighteenth century rather than as part of the sixteenth-century Protestant Reformation and (2) give United Methodists roots in all four major branches of the sixteenth-century Protestant Reformation: Anglican, Lutheran, Reformed, and Anabaptist (Mennonite).[1]

From its beginnings, Methodist worship has combined the use of printed texts with the freedom to use extemporaneous and even spontaneous acts of worship. As a priest of the Church of England, John Wesley was devoted to the 1662 *Book of Common Prayer;* and when the American Methodists organized as a church in 1784 he abridged and adapted that book for them in what he called the *Sunday Service of the Methodists in North America.*[2] On the other hand, Wesley frequently led informal services characterized by hymn singing and extemporaneous prayer and testimonies; and in the letter he sent with his *Sunday Service,* he wrote that the American Methodists "are now at full liberty, simply to follow the scriptures and the primitive church. And we judge it best that they should stand fast in that liberty, wherewith God has so strangely made them free."[3] The American Methodists found the *Sunday Service* largely unsuited to their needs and in 1792 abandoned much of it in favor of simple directions for the conduct of informal worship; they retained the printed texts from the *Sunday Service* only for the Lord's Supper, baptism, matrimony, the burial of the dead, and ordinations.

The subsequent history of the printed texts, which collectively became known as the Ritual, was recorded in Nolan H. Harmon's *The Rites and Rituals of Episcopal Methodism.*[4] William Nash Wade's *A History of Public Worship in the Methodist Episcopal Church and Methodist Episcopal Church, South, from 1784 to 1905*[5] goes beyond these texts, which were of secondary importance for Methodists, to examine the evidence of what was actually happening in American Methodist Episcopal worship and how it was evolving during the period. In the early nineteenth century the American Methodists divided into several denominations, of which the two covered by Wade's history are the chief. Those two, plus the Methodist Protestant church, reunited in 1939; but other Methodist denominations remain to this day.

Much of the history of American Methodist worship remains unresearched, but faculty and graduate students in the doctoral programs in liturgy at Drew University and the University of Notre Dame are doing work in this area. Primary source materials are in the archives of the United Methodist church at Drew University in Madison, New Jersey. The history of worship in the Evangelical United Brethren traditions and in American Methodist traditions other than Methodist

Episcopal has received very little attention. Research is now under way on the history of Methodist worship in the twentieth century.[6]

In practice, however, rather than any particular collection of prayer texts per se, including even Wesley's *Sunday Service,* it has been the hymnals of the United Methodists and their predecessors that have been the people's books of worship; in the twentieth century the hymnals have contained not only hymns but the texts of other acts and services of worship that needed to be in the people's hands. These hymnals have been increasingly supplemented at each service by a locally designed and duplicated bulletin specific to that service. The resulting freedom to design each service to meet local needs has led to great diversity in forms and styles of worship. Official reforms are not necessarily followed in local congregations, which may or may not adopt the latest official hymnal and which have almost complete freedom to design their worship as they please.

The Process of Revision

When The United Methodist church was formed in 1968, the Ritual of the Church was defined by its first General Conference (supreme legislative body) as "that contained in *The Book of Ritual* of the Evangelical United Brethren Church, 1959, and *The Book of Worship for Church and Home* of the Methodist Church [1965]."[7] Since few besides the clergy saw these books, however, the most important liturgical books were *The Methodist Hymnal* (1966; renamed *The Book of Hymns* in 1970) and *The Hymnal* (Evangelical United Brethren, 1957).

The 1968 General Conference also set up a commission on worship "to prepare forms of worship and to revise existing orders of worship for recommendation to the General Conference."[8] The members of this commission, which after 1972 became the section on worship of the newly formed General Board of Discipleship, were elected by an involved process that secured representation of each region of the United States, clergy and laity, women and men, and the principal ethnic minorities. Over a period of sixteen years, the commission (section) developed a complete new liturgy by an elaborate process of research and development that is described in detail in the *Companion to the Book of Services* ([Nashville, 1988], pages 9–26). At every stage of development, expert consultants and staff were utilized, as were a variety of survey and testing procedures. The liturgies that were developed in this way were submitted to the 1984 General Conference, were adopted as official alternatives to the older liturgies, and were published by the United Methodist Publishing House in 1985 as *The Book of Services.*

The 1984 General Conference also set up a hymnal revision committee, which represented all of the types of persons mentioned above, plus persons with handicaps, and this committee prepared a proposed hymnal that contained the new liturgies together with some of the old liturgies. This committee operated by a process described in detail in chapter 2 of *The Worship Resources of The United Methodist Hymnal,* by Hoyt L. Hickman (Nashville, 1989). The new official denominational hymn and worship book that resulted was adopted by the 1988 General Conference and published by the United Methodist Publishing House in 1989 as *The United Methodist Hymnal: Book of United Methodist Worship.* Work is well advanced on a further collection of liturgies which are to be presented for adoption in 1992. Together these constitute the most sweeping liturgical reform in our denomination's history.

From Premodern to Modern to Postmodern

The motivations behind this reform are complex—a variety of needs felt by very diverse factions of the United Methodist membership. Most of the specific debates centered on issues of inclusiveness, such as feminist or ethnic concerns, and legitimizing and accommodating diverse theologies and styles of worship. Underlying these specific issues, however, was a basic change of perspective from a modern to a postmodern world of experience and thought. And while there was relatively little debate about Jewish-Christian relations, perhaps because a changed attitude toward Judaism was already so pervasive, the implications of the new liturgies for Jewish-Christian relations are profound.

The history of the development of American Methodist worship in the nineteenth and early twentieth centuries is in many ways the story of the journey from a premodern to a modern world of experience and thought under the increasing influence of Enlightenment rationalism, which by mid-twentieth century had deeply affected Methodist liturgies. Scandalous particularities of the Christian story were suppressed in an attempt to affirm only what, it was hoped, everyone, especially our cultured despisers, might be persuaded to believe on the basis of universal human experience and reason. Immensely helpful as this shift was in moving Methodists and other Christians from intolerance to tolerance, there was an underlying goal of assimilation and antiparticularism that is ultimately both anti-Christian and anti-Jewish.

This movement toward rationalistic modernity perhaps reached its peak in *The Methodist Hymnal* of 1935. A second trend was evident in the 1966 hymnal—a trend that greatly accelerated after the union of 1968 under such diverse influences as recent philosophies and theologies, forces of feminist and ethnic empowerment, and recent liturgical movements, all of which saw that Enlightenment rationalism is far less universal, far more provincial, than had been imagined. In the latter half of the twentieth century we have become less literal minded and more appreciative of the mysterious and distinctive ways in which the language of our Christian story and teaching functions—more like an art than a science.

As a result, United Methodists are now using our distinctive Christian language more fully and boldly. This reassertion of our particular Christian heritage and peoplehood, far from being a move back to a premodern age, is profoundly postmodern. As such, it gives us as Christians an improved theological and liturgical basis for acknowledging the full validity of Judaism and for relating to Judaism and the Jewish community as equals.

The Reinterpretation of Universalistic Claims

Christian thought and liturgy have been permeated with universalistic claims such as the affirmation of Jesus' saving role for the world, and in the past these claims have been given an imperialistic interpretation. Our goal was for everyone to become a Christian. In modern times this imperialism often led, ironically, to a rationalistic theology of the least common denominator that, it was hoped, every reasonable person could accept.

These universalistic claims are increasingly being understood in new ways, which our liturgies have been designed to be open to and to encourage. One new understanding that has influenced our new liturgies sees these universalistic claims as an affirmation that by its righteousness, the Christian community can become a blessing to the whole world. To become so, the community is challenged to accept its status as one community among others and to develop what is best in its own particularity.

Such a claim requires an accompanying recognition that the Christian community can be, and has been, by its sin, a catastrophe for others. Our new liturgies reflect the beginnings of a struggle to confront what Christians and Christian teachings have done to Jews over the centuries and in our own lifetimes, and to begin, liturgically as well as otherwise, the radical and ongoing process of repentance. As Christians who live after the Holocaust, it is surely fitting that we take part in Days of Remembrance. In addition, we have felt led to incorporate this remembrance into the very heart of our Christian liturgy in the same liturgical act that has had the worst history of fostering anti-Judaism. We have rewritten the Reproaches in our Good Friday liturgy so that they are unambiguously directed against Christians rather than against Jews, as the following stanza indicates:

I grafted you into the tree of my chosen Israel,
    and you turned on them with persecution and mass murder.
I made you joint heirs with them of my covenants,
    but you made them scapegoats for your own guilt.[9]

Our new liturgies also reflect the early stages of an attempt, especially in our Holy Week liturgies where the dangers are greatest, to correct among United Methodists the false teaching that the Jews killed Jesus. Some of our problems in doing this lie in the scriptural Passion narratives themselves, and our Holy Week liturgies reflect our struggle to present the Passion story in ways that will accomplish good rather than harm.[10]

This new understanding of our universalistic claim is further indicated by the fact that our new liturgies reflect a plural covenant theology—in two senses of that term. First, we intend to say nothing that would deny the covenantal claims of Judaism or that would imply that Jews need any covenant other than the one they already have, while at the same time we affirm that the Christian community has been given its birth, its deliverance from slavery to sin and death, its baptismal covenant, and its peoplehood through Jesus, whom we call the Christ. The stanza from the revised Reproaches quoted above reflects this theology.

Second, we see the Christian community itself as relating to more than one covenant. Our new liturgies call for an enormous increase in readings from the Hebrew scriptures and in the use of the Psalms and other scriptural songs as corporate prayer and praise.[11] We are reminded in our liturgies of our participation in God's covenant with every living creature as declared in Genesis chapter 9.[12] Part of our comprehending that Jews and Christians alike are joint heirs of ancient Israel is the understanding that the Sinaitic covenant has in some sense been opened to Christians through the Christ event and functions for Christians as our old covenant—i.e., Old Testament. This theology is seen, for instance, in the self-identification as people of the Exodus that is so central to African-American Christianity and American Puritanism and that has become more prominent for all United Methodists in our increasingly multiethnic liturgies. It is also seen in our acknowledgment of the authority for Christians of such teachings as the Ten Commandments and in the fact that when we pray the Psalms we call ourselves Israel.

Our renewed sense of plural covenant relationships poses questions that may need to be discussed in further Jewish-Christian dialogue, but it is already bringing us important practical benefits. Praying the Psalms helps us recover the notes of lament, grief, anger, and other feelings that we had regarded as inappropriate in prayer and worship. Our identification with the people of the Exodus as well as with the Christ event strengthens the note of divine-human synergy that in our Methodist tradition has modified any tendency to believe that God "does it all."

It is a delightful irony that this new understanding of our claims has helped us recover distinctively Christian teachings that in the recent past were ignored or rejected as being old-fashioned. Whereas thirty years ago our eucharistic liturgy was centered on Jesus' suffering and death for the sins of the world and contained not one word about the resurrection, ascension, or coming again of Christ, our new liturgy treats Jesus' suffering, death, and resurrection as God's giving birth to the community that finds its identity and its salvation as the body of the risen Christ.[13]

Likewise, living through the events of the twentieth century has led us to an eschatology that is more complex and, I believe, truer to the testimony of the early Christians. Thirty years ago our liturgies expressed an almost wholly realized eschatology: the Christ had come. Period. Today our liturgy adds that the Christ is yet to come, and will come, in final victory[14]—which may be interpreted as a literal, personal coming or as the coming of a new age—in confidence that Christians will recognize in that fulfillment the One through whom God gave our community of faith its birth and who as ever-present Word has given it life ever since.

The Reinterpretation of Inclusiveness

There is another understanding that informs our new liturgies and motivates our ongoing process of liturgical reform. This interprets Christian universalistic claims as a call for the Christian community to regard nothing human as alien and to affirm the wholeness of God's creation—not as a strategy for

religious empire building but out of our own need, if the
Christian community is to play the role to which God calls
us. While tensions exist between this understanding and the
previously discussed recovery of our particular peoplehood,
the tension gives evidence of being creative.

This new understanding has led to what is proving so far
to be the hardest struggle in our whole process of liturgical
reform—that of making our liturgies inclusive. Inclusiveness
is an enormously diverse concern with many facets, of which
the following passage describes only a few.

1. In order to be inclusive of women as well as men, our
new liturgies no longer use masculine words to refer to
people in general or to those who perform any particular liturgical function. This is related to the fact that women as
well as men now perform every function that exists in our
worship.

2. With regard to the God-language in our liturgies, our
goal is wholeness and balance rather than the elimination of
the masculine. The use of masculine terms for God like *Father, Lord, King,* and *he* has been substantially reduced; the
use of language that is neither masculine nor feminine has
increased; and some feminine God-language has been cau-
tiously introduced. The Great Thanksgiving, for instance, includes the following reference:

> You *gave birth* to your church
> *delivered us* from slavery to sin and death
> and made with us a new covenant
>   by *water* and the spirit.[15]

Earlier in the passage, God is addressed in the masculine,
"Father," so here we balance the passage with feminine imagery: giving birth, the double entendre of "deliverance/
delivery," and water, which refers most evidently to baptism,
but also to the water of the womb. We are constantly being
reminded how predominantly masculine our God-language
still is, however, so that there is every reason to expect more
inclusive God-language in the book that is being prepared for
adoption in 1992.

3. While the human Jesus was masculine, and while our new liturgies retain such terms for Jesus Christ as *Son, Lord, King,* and *he,* we are continually challenged by those in our midst who claim that more inclusive terms such as Word are more appropriate to the eternal Christ, the second person of the Trinity.

4. Our new liturgies reduce the dominance of clergy, musicians, and choirs in worship by providing for more lay participation and leadership. Baptism is understood as the basic ordination of every Christian to ministry, the term *minister* is no longer used to refer to clergy alone, and ordinations and consecrations following baptism are understood as relating to "the varieties of gifts, service, and working" (1 Corinthians 12:4–6) rather than to a hierarchy of orders. It had also become evident that the use of archaic prayer-book English was reinforcing the dominance of clergy in worship, and the change to more modern English has been a crucial step in democratizing creativity and leadership in our worship.

5. Our liturgies increasingly reflect the variety of ethnic heritages in America and in the world. Notable contributions to our new liturgies have been made by peoples throughout the world and by those in the United States whose heritage is African, Hispanic, Asian, and Native American. Discriminatory language and usages such as identifying black with sin and sorrow is avoided. There is increasing awareness that third-world peoples are rapidly becoming a majority in the worldwide Christian community.

6. We are affirming in a new way the multiplicity of languages in our worship. While Protestants have worshiped in the vernacular since the sixteenth century, and while United Methodist congregations have traditionally been free to worship in whatever language the people feel most at home in, there is a new openness to the use of occasional singing in languages other than the vernacular as a powerful symbol of the multilinguistic, intercultural, historical inclusiveness of the Christian community. For some years it has been increasingly common for choirs to sing anthems in a variety of languages (Latin, for instance). Now in *The United Method-*

ist Hymnal (1989)—which, it is important to note, is for English-speaking congregations—there are a few hymns or hymn stanzas for congregational singing in Spanish, German, French, several Asian and Native American languages (in phonetic transliterations), the biblical languages, and Latin. The continuing use of archaic English in familiar and beloved hymns and prayers side by side with the prevailing use of modern English serves much the same purpose. Also, simultaneous signing of services is increasingly seen as of benefit not only to the deaf but also to hearing persons, who can thereby, at least to some degree, worship in two languages at once.

7. Our new liturgies reflect knowledge from the whole range of ecumenical Christianity and from beyond the Christian community as well. We recognize that wherever Christian communities have flourished they have incorporated and given Christian interpretations to elements from other religions indigenous to the culture.

8. These liturgies reflect our struggle to include persons of all socioeconomic classes, cultural tastes, and degrees of literacy. This includes provision for worship with all degrees of dependence on printed texts.

9. Our announced goal is for congregational worship to unfold so that persons of every age and developmental level can meaningfully participate. This includes involvement of the "child" within each adult. Our new liturgies reflect the beginnings, but only the beginnings, of our journey toward this goal.

10. In these liturgies we struggle to be inclusive of persons with handicaps and to avoid such insensitivities as assuming that everyone can stand or kneel at given points in the service.

11. These liturgies reflect our struggle to worship with our whole being—our bodies and our feelings as well as our intellects, our "right brains" as well as our "left brains," and all our senses.

These facets of inclusiveness are closely interrelated, and of course, the list above is by no means exhaustive.

The Ongoing Task

As we stand back and look at what has been accomplished, it is obvious that we have only begun a radical process of liturgical transformation that appears likely to continue for as far ahead as we can foresee. None of the reforms is completely embodied even in our new official books, let alone in congregational practice. Resistances to these reforms keep appearing as regularly as the rocks that New England farmers must remove from their fields each spring. In the committee meetings that have produced the new liturgies, it has often been said that in years to come, our new books will be seen as having been transitional. Plainly the task of liturgical reform is ongoing. Our new liturgies are waystations on our journey as a pilgrim people.

NOTES

1. To understand United Methodist worship, it is important to see it in the larger context of Christian worship and, more specifically, against the backdrop of the varieties of Protestant worship. James F. White's *Introduction to Christian Worship* (1980), revised ed. (Nashville, 1990), and his *Protestant Worship* (Louisville, 1989) together constitute an excellent introduction to Christian worship and the varieties of Protestant worship as understood by a United Methodist scholar who has played a key role in recent United Methodist liturgical reforms.

2. See *John Wesley's Sunday Service of the Methodists in North America,* with an introduction by James F. White (Nashville, 1984).

3. Ibid., p. iii.

4. *The Rites and Ritual of Episcopal Methodism* (Nashville, 1926).

5. Ph.D. dissertation, University of Notre Dame, 1981.

6. For a brief summary of the history of worship in the traditions represented in the United Methodist Church, see Hoyt L. Hickman, ed., *Companion to the Book of Services* (Nashville, 1988), pp. 34–38. James F. White, at the University of Notre Dame, and Heather Murray Elkins, at Drew University, are cur-

rently engaged in, or supervising, most of the research taking place in this field.

7. *The Book of Discipline* (Nashville, 1968), paragraph 1388.

8. Ibid., paragraph 1385.

9. Hoyt L. Hickman, Don E. Saliers, Laurence Hull Stookey, and James F. White, eds., *Handbook of the Christian Year* (Nashville, 1986), p. 189. Compare the revised version of the Reproaches (pp. 179–80) with the older version found in *The Book of Worship for Church and Home* (Nashville, 1965), pp. 109–10. Liturgies for Holy Week are not included in the *Hymnal* but will appear in the book being prepared for adoption and publication in 1992. *Handbook of the Christian Year* contains a trial version of the proposed official Holy Week services. The reforms mentioned in this paper have been so favorably received that there is little doubt they will be incorporated into the official 1992 volume.

10. See *Handbook of the Christian Year*, pp. 125–52, 170–90.

11. See the common lectionary included throughout *Handbook of the Christian Year*.

12. One such reminder is the Great Thanksgiving for Lent (*Handbook of the Christian Year*, p. 123).

13. See, for instance, these words in our new Great Thanksgiving and in all its seasonal variations: "By the baptism of his [Jesus'] suffering, death, and resurrection, you gave birth to your church, delivered us from slavery to sin and death, and made with us a covenant by water and the Spirit . . . that we might be for the world the body of Christ" (*The United Methodist Hymnal: Book of United Methodist Worship*, pp. 9–10).

14. The words, "Christ will come again," and "until Christ comes in final victory," for instance, are found in the Great Thanksgiving (*The United Methodist Hymnal*, pp. 9–10), and all its seasonal variations.

15. *The United Methodist Hymnal: Book of United Methodist Worship*, pp. 9–10.

Revising the Liturgy for Conservative Jews

JULES HARLOW

CONSERVATIVE PRAYER BOOKS BEFORE THE 1970S

The Conservative movement's first official prayer book in North America appeared in 1927: the *Festival Prayer Book* (for Passover, Shavuot, and Sukkot), published by the United Synagogue of America, the congregational arm of the movement. Before that, and even for many years later, most Conservative congregations used prayer books generally identified as Orthodox,[1] with none of the changes that have come to characterize Conservative liturgy. There are at least three indications that this book broke new ground in presenting a liturgy that would distinguish Conservative Judaism as a distinct movement in the American milieu.

To begin with, it presented minimal, though not insignificant, textual changes. Chief among them was the modification of a passage on sacrifices. In the additional service *(Musaf)* appended on the Sabbath and on festivals, Orthodox prayer books include a petition for the restoration of ritual animal sacrifice in a rebuilt Temple in Jerusalem:

> Because of our sins, we were exiled from our country and banished far from our land. We cannot go up as pilgrims to worship Thee. . . . May it be Your will, Lord our God and God of our fathers . . . to have mercy on us and on Thy sanctuary. Rebuild it speedily and magnify its glory. . . . Bring us to Zion Thy city with ringing song, to Jerusalem Thy sanctuary with ever-

lasting joy. There we will prepare in Thy honor our obligatory offerings.[2] *Animal Sacrifice*

Starting in 1927, Conservative liturgy changed this petition to a recollection. Conservative liturgy continues to pray for the restoration of the Jewish people to the Land of Israel and for the experience of worship there, particularly in Jerusalem, but the liturgy merely recalls with reverence the sacrificial ritual of our ancestors; it does not petition for its restoration: "May it be Your will . . . to lead us in joy to our land and to settle us within our borders. . . . There our ancestors sacrificed to You. . . . "[3]

But in 1927, the editors were still unwilling to insist on the change throughout every synagogue in the movement. Its *Festival Prayer Book* thus appeared in two editions: one presented the change; the other retained the unchanged text with its petition for the restoration of sacrifice. In 1946, however, the next official prayer book of the movement was published in one edition only, and petition had become recollection.[4] Since then, all official Conservative prayer books have maintained the revised text.

By contrast, starting in nineteenth-century Europe, the Reform movements's liturgy generally dealt with the sacrificial cult by eliminating its recollection altogether. The movement's prayer books did not even include the additional service, since that service functions theologically as a replacement for the additional sacrifices offered on the Sabbath and on festivals.

A second long-standing liturgical concern has been the custom of praying for the welfare of the government of the lands in which Jews have dwelt, a practice said to go back to the time of the prophet Jeremiah (Jeremiah 29:7: "Seek the welfare of the city . . . and pray to the Lord on its behalf") but actually attested to no earlier than the fourteenth century.[5] The editors of the 1927 *Festival Prayer Book* mention specifically an American version of the prayer: "A prayer for the Government of the United States has been formulated both in Hebrew and in English, which is not a mere rephrasing of the prayers in the monarchical countries but aims to reflect the spirit of republican institutions and aspirations.''[6]

A third sign that 1927 heralded a modernization of liturgy within the American spirit was the fact that the volume reflects concern with the language of translation and with the aesthetics of layout to help enhance the experience of the worshiper.

The *Festival Prayer Book* was produced by a committee convened by the United Synagogue of America (the lay arm of the movement) but consisting of two faculty members from the Jewish Theological Seminary and three pulpit rabbis. It seems to have proved less than universally satisfying, since in the following years a number of individual rabbis in the Conservative movement published their own prayer books for use in their own congregations and for limited circulation elsewhere. The next official prayer book of the movement was produced by another committee, and it was based upon a manuscript developed by Rabbi Morris Silverman, a pulpit rabbi. It was published in 1946 by the Joint Prayer Book Commission of the Rabbinical Assembly, the rabbinic arm of the movement, and the United Synagogue of America. The commission included six pulpit rabbis and three members of the faculty of the Jewish Theological Seminary of America, the academic institution of the Conservative movement. The professors were chosen because in addition to their academic expertise they had also enjoyed extensive pulpit experience. The 1946 committee maintained the changes of 1927 and introduced additional ones as well.

The chief among the changes introduced in 1946 occurs in three of the blessings included in every morning service. These blessings conventionally praise God "who has not created me (1) a gentile, (2) a slave, or (3) a woman." (From the fourteenth century on, women were instructed to praise God "who has created me according to His will.")[7] These blessings express the sense of privilege that the Jew felt in being able to fulfill the Torah and *mitzvot*, which were not obligatory in full measure for non-Jews, slaves, and

women. However, the negative form in which these blessings
are couched caused Jewish leadership much concern throughout the ages. Supported by the trend of tradition, the commission decided to rephrase the blessings in the positive
form. Thus the blessings were changed to praise God
"who hast (1) made me an Israelite, (2) made me free, and
(3) made me in Thine image" (encompassing women and
men).[8] Other changes and modifications introduced in this
volume are discussed in the foreword to the prayer book.[9]

The Conservative movement's current liturgical renewal
dates from the late 1950s, when the Rabbinical Assembly appointed a committee of pulpit rabbis, chaired by Rabbi Ger-
son Hadas, to prepare a volume for use on weekdays,[10] the
first prayer book to be published under the sole auspices of
the Rabbinical Assembly. It featured a fresh translation into
modern English that replaced *Thee*s and *Thou*s and other ar-
chaisms with vigorous, direct language intended to make the
meaning of the text more readily accessible and thus more
meaningful to contemporary worshipers. The prayer book
would provide those unable to participate in Hebrew with a
devotional text in English that might serve as a vehicle for
both personal and congregational prayer.

Textual changes were introduced in this volume, too. A
major alteration involved the passages dealing with sacrifices
in the *Musaf* services for the first of the month *(Rosh
Chodesh)* and for intermediate days of festivals. Two alternative texts were presented. One follows the approach of the
Sabbath and Festival Prayer Book in recollecting rituals past.
The other returned to the original idea of petition, but only
for the restoration of nonsacrificial worship in Jerusalem:
"Lead us with song to Zion, Your city, and with everlasting
joy to Jerusalem, Your sanctuary. There, as in days of old,
we shall worship You with reverence and with love."[11] To
this, a brief prayer was added on behalf of "Your people Israel, wherever they dwell."

Perhaps the most significant innovation of the Hadas
Weekday Prayer Book is the inclusion of a passage in the *Tefillah* that celebrates Israel's Independence Day. For a stylis-
tic model, the editors looked to traditional expressions of

gratitude for deliverance, which are recited on Purim and on Hanukkah. The received liturgical corpus for those occasions carries prayers that begin, "For the miracles . . . " *(al ha-nissim),* and that then describe the events that those days commemorate. The style and the language of the prayer of gratitude were adapted to produce a passage appropriate for commemorating liturgically Israel's Independence.[12]

A few years later, another Rabbinical Assembly committee was delegated to produce a new edition of the prayer book used on the high holy days of Rosh Hashanah and Yom Kippur.[13] It follows the approach in translation introduced in the *Weekday Prayer Book* but has its own textual innovations as well—some of which we shall describe in what follows. Though based on the earlier Hadas prayer book, this *Machzor* broke new ground and is more properly seen as the first of two major liturgical works for today, the second being a new weekday, Sabbath, and festival prayer book, to which the Rabbinical Assembly turned in the 1970s, *Siddur Sim Shalom.*

SIDDUR SIM SHALOM

Early in the work of the committee appointed for the task of formulating the *Siddur Sim Shalom,* a questionnaire was sent to the entire membership of the Rabbinical Assembly. A very large number of colleagues responded, with some near-unanimous conclusions.

1. The *siddur* should be as comprehensive as possible.
2. It should be published in one volume, not in two, as had been suggested.
3. For purposes of study, the book should contain the complete text of the rabbinic compendium known as *Pirkei Avot* (usually translated as "Teachings of the Sages," or "Ethics of the Fathers").

Other survey results led to our inclusion of texts for various home ceremonies. Though it began only as a project of the

Rabbinical Assembly, which has the responsibility and the authority for making all editorial decisions, *Siddur Sim Shalom* was published in 1985 under the joint aegis of the Rabbinical Assembly and the United Synagogue of America. It was my privilege to serve as editor and translator of that volume, working as a member of the professional staff of the Rabbinical Assembly with a committee of Rabbinical Assembly members.

We followed the approach used for producing the high holy day *Machzor*. The editor and translator prepared the manuscript for a critical reading by each committee member. The committee consisted of (1) rabbis who combined pulpit experience with personal interest and accomplishments in liturgy, rabbinics, and biblical studies, and (2) a seminary faculty member with expertise in Hebrew literature and liturgy. The chair of the committee, Rabbi Max Routtenberg, translated *Pirkei Avot*. Throughout the process, I met with the executive council of the Rabbinical Assembly and with regional rabbinic gatherings to obtain collegial opinion of our work in progress. Finally, the weekday morning service was published in 1983 in the format of a 120-page booklet for trial use at rabbinic and lay conventions as well as in select congregations, whence we received critiques from a wider audience still.

Inevitably, the work of editing prayer books generates tension between tradition and change. Discussions of new prayer books generally emphasize change. Therefore it is important here to stress the great blessing of continuity.

There is far more continuity than change in the Conservative movement's prayer books. Most of their Hebrew texts would be familiar to a Jew from ninth-century Babylonia who knew the Hebrew prayers. Despite the modifications and additions that we made, we saw our major task as simply editing and retranslating the traditional Hebrew text.

The language of prayer in Jewish tradition is Hebrew, the language of revelation. Jewish tradition does permit reciting even the central obligatory prayers in the vernacular, but Conservative Jews have always seen Hebrew as the preferred vehicle for liturgical expression. At the same time, however, we had to unlock the meaning of the Hebrew texts for congregants who do not yet read Hebrew or who do not read it with full comprehension. The purpose of providing a translation of the prayer book is not to help teach the Hebrew language but to produce a devotional text for those who are confined to prayer in English, in the hope that they may have an emotionally satisfying devotional experience to the greatest degree possible, experiencing at least part of what it is to pray in the manner that we call *davening* in Hebrew.

The editorial decisions that went into *Siddur Sim Shalom* were many and varied, but those that give this prayer book its own character can be captured in five basic categories: (1) liturgical responses to the reality of a State of Israel in the Land of Israel; (2) liturgical responses to the Holocaust; (3) the introduction of texts from the past; (4) modifications rooted in the changing role of women; (5) personal prayer and meditation.

Liturgical Responses to the State of Israel

For centuries Jews have prayed for the restoration of Jerusalem and for the reestablishment of a Jewish State in the Land of Israel. Those prayers have been answered, thank God, and the liturgy should not remain unaltered, as if nothing has changed in this regard.

To begin with, the passage for Israel's Independence Day that had already been introduced in the *Weekday Prayer Book* (see above and note 12) was included in *Siddur Sim Shalom* for the *Birkat hamazon* (the grace after meals) of that day as well. In addition, we made every Sabbath and festival liturgy reflect the reality of a State of Israel by adding a phrase to the additional service *(Musaf)*. As we have seen (see above and note 2), the middle blessing of the *Tefillah* on those days already articulates the yearning of the people Israel for restoration to the Land of Israel by asking God "to lead us in joy to our land and to settle our people within our borders." We have added a traditional phrase that refers to God as one "who restores His children to their land." Thus the passage now begins:

> May it be Your will, Lord our God and God of our ancestors who restores His children to their land, to lead us in joy to our land and to settle our people within our borders. There our ancestors sacrificed to You with their daily offerings and with their special offerings, and there may we worship You with love and reverence as in days of old and ancient times.[14]

Finally, in the afternoon service on Tisha Be'av, the day on which Jews mourn the destruction of the First and Second Temples, we altered the following traditional text: "Comfort, Lord our God, the mourners of Zion and those who grieve for Jerusalem, the city so desolate in mourning, like a woman bereft of her children."[15]

That is not the portrait of Jerusalem today. So we changed the tense, leading to the English, "the city which once was so desolate in mourning."[16] The altered version reflects the time in which we live while indicating that we nonetheless continue mourning for the ancient devastation that remains an ineradicable fact of history. On the one hand, we retained the traditional recollection of anguish and sorrow: "For Your people Israel, smitten by the sword, and for her children who gave their lives for her, Zion cries with bitter tears, Jerusalem voices her anguish: 'My heart, my heart goes out for the slain; my entire being mourns for the slain.' "[17] On the other hand, to reflect a Jerusalem partially restored to greatness now, we added the words of Isaiah and Jeremiah, referring to Jerusalem as "rebuilt from destruction and restored from desolation" and praying that "all who mourn Jerusalem of old [and] rejoice with her now . . . [will] hear in the cities of Judah and in the streets of Jerusalem sounds of joy and gladness, voices of bride and groom."[18]

Liturgical Responses to the Holocaust

Particularly in our time, the acknowledgment of evil in God's world is one of the most difficult challenges encountered in putting together a prayer book. The questions of theodicy defy adequate response, but they may not be ignored on that account. It is important even simply to articulate them during a service whose context is faith.

Accordingly, we added an optional reading to the evening service, printed beneath a rule at a part of the service that praises God for redeeming Israel at the Sea of Reeds. Often—not always, but often—when reciting this particular blessing, I have been haunted by the memory of those Jews of the Holocaust who were not redeemed. The following lines that begin the reading articulate this awareness and its bold challenge of God, in a framework of faith:

> We tell of Your love in the morning,
> we recall Your faithfulness at night.
> > *Yet we remember other mornings, other nights*
> > *when love and faithfulness were torn by tragedy.*
> We celebrate miracles of our people's past,
> deliverance from peril into promised land.
> > *Yet we remember slaughter and destruction,*
> > *and questions born from ashes of the undelivered.*
> In spite of Your silence, we reaffirm hope,
> sustained by the certainty born of faith.[19]

I cannot trace here all of the sources of the reading, including the ancient prophets and a modern poet. But I do want to note its last couplet, which mentions God's silence. The idea reflects an ancient rabbinic homily that accuses God of silence during the suffering of God's children. The homily is based on Exodus 15:11, which is included in the text of the blessing for which this reading is an optional supplement.

Siddur Sim Shalom includes passages for supplementing a service on the day that commemorates the Holocaust each year, Yom Hashoah. The mourner's Kaddish designated for that day is a bold modification of the traditional text. It articulates the tension between faith and doubt that the murder of six million Jewish men, women, and children necessarily poses. We preferred a liturgical statement to an essay or a footnote. We recognized that the Jewish statement of faith

par excellence is the mourner's Kaddish, in that precisely
when people may have their strongest reasons for challenging
God—at the death of a loved one—they are asked to declare
God's praise in public. In this special version of the Kaddish,
then, we have interrupted the classic statement of faith-in-
spite-of-it-all with names of places where Jews were brutal-
ized and killed.

> *Yitgadal*
>   Auschwitz
> *ve'yitkadash*
>   Lodz
> *sh'mei raba*
>   Ponar
> *b'alma di v'ra khir'utei*
>   Maidanek
> *b'hayeikhon u-v'yomeikhon*
>   Birkenau.[20]

Yet the tension between faith and doubt is resolved liturgically at the end of this Kaddish, when the concluding words
are recited without interruption.

The Introduction of Texts from the Past

Some of the texts that we have added to the prayer book
appear to be new only because they are so old that most
people are not aware of them. For example, early in the
morning service we have inserted some words that most
printed prayer books omit. The suggestion to include them
comes from the distinguished Rabbi Isaac Luria of sixteenth-
century Palestine: "I hereby accept the obligation of fulfill-
ing my Creator's *mitzvah* in the Torah: 'Love your neighbor
as yourself' (Leviticus 19:18)."[21]

Love is a Jewish value. Not just recommended, it is a
commandment (a *mitzvah*), an obligation. The popular mind
associates commandment with mechanical behavior and ritual
restrictions. But commandments may be moral too. Placing

these words at the beginning of a congregation's morning service makes a statement not only about God's commandments and our obligations but also about our relationships with other people through our relationship to God. We begin our day in prayer with some of those people, so we begin also with a reminder of the *mitzvah* to love them.

Another example of introducing texts from the past (specifically, ninth-century Babylonia and tenth-century Egypt) is presented at the end of the section on personal prayer and meditation below.

The Changing Role of Women in the Synagogue

Siddur Sim Shalom retains the changes in the early morning blessings that were introduced in the *Sabbath and Festival Prayer Book* of 1946, so that both men and women praise God "who has made me in His image."[22] This was the first of a number of liturgical modifications to reflect changes in reality and in perceptions of reality in regard to the role of women.

A related innovation can be found in the Torah service where short prayers are normally recited on behalf of those congregants who are honored by being called up to recite blessings in conjunction with the chanting of Torah. This prayer is normally printed only in the masculine form (in Hebrew, verbs and adjectives are either masculine or feminine), since it has been accepted practice that only men are so honored. Our prayer book assumes that in some congregations women too are called to the Torah, so we printed an alternative prayer in the feminine for them. Further, we added the names of the matriarchs to those of the patriarchs in the texts of these prayers.[23]

On the other hand, we did not include the names of the matriarchs in either the Hebrew or the translation of the central and obligatory *Tefillah*,[24] since its Hebrew formula reflects biblical usage and we felt there was insufficient reason to introduce a change that would break that connection with

our past. However, in the translation of the *Tefillah* and elsewhere, we altered the translation of the Hebrew word *avot.*
Avot generally refers only to the patriarchs. To reflect awareness of the role played by the matriarchs as well, we chose
the more inclusive translation, "ancestors."

People called to the Torah are given the opportunity to
thank God if they have recently recovered from illness or es-
caped other danger. Here too, we altered the grammar of the
traditional congregational response to include women as well
as men; and we specified childbirth as a particular time
of peril.[25]

A prayer on behalf of the congregation is recited at the
end of the Torah service on Shabbat and festivals. The traditional text asks for God's blessing "on the members of this
congregation, them, their wives, their sons and their daugh-
ters," implying that the wives are considered only because of
their marriage to members of the congregation. It was appropriate for a time when women indeed were not active members of congregations. The situation clearly has changed.
Women serve as presidents of congregations and fill many
other important congregational offices. By deleting one
Hebrew word (*unesheihem,* and their wives) we included
women along with men as congregational members in their
own right.[26]

Some women have taken upon themselves the obligation
of wearing a prayer shawl *(tallit)* and phylacteries *(tefillin).*
The reflections composed for recitation before putting them
on originally had only men in mind, and this is reflected
grammatically. We have provided grammatically correct Hebrew texts for women as well.[27]

Perhaps our most significant statement in this area was our
selection of a woman to edit our Passover Haggadah.[28] A
learned and devoted Jew, Rachel Rabinowicz, of blessed
memory (she died in 1987), was, I believe, the first woman
to edit a major Jewish liturgical text. Her appointment as editor, because of her qualifications, declared that liturgical authority is not related to gender.

Personal Prayer and Meditation

By and large the core of Jewish liturgy consists of fixed texts that are obligatory. Too often overlooked, however, is the tradition that calls for an individual's own words or for alternative texts at certain points in the service. Variation in prayer wording can help us to escape from the feeling and the actuality of a fixed routine, which often turns the most beautiful words and the most fervent intentions into mechanical gestures. We have therefore included alternatives to private meditations, and we have tried to encourage the individual to offer prayer or reflections in his or her own words at certain specified times.

An example of such an alternative prayer can be found in the passage following the *Tefillah,* going back to the personal prayer of a fourth-century Babylonian authority, Mar bar Ravina: "My God, keep my tongue from evil, my lips from lies. Help me ignore those who slander me. Let me be humble before all. Open my heart to Your Torah, so that I may pursue Your *mitzvot.*"[29] This meditation appears in almost all versions of the prayer book, but in fact, anything at all may be uttered at this point, including personal spontaneous prayer or silent reflection. We therefore added an alternative passage here, as a model for the many alternatives possible. We want to correct the mistaken view of the service as totally fixed and rigid to the reality of a service that does allow for flexibility and deeply personal prayer at specific points. The weekday *Tefillah* in *Siddur Sim Shalom,* for example, is followed by an optional meditation that is adapted from the extraordinary talmudic claim that even God prays. What is the text of God's prayer? "May it be My will that My love of compassion overwhelm My demand for strict justice." Our alternative begins: "May it be Your will, Lord my God and God of my ancestors, that Your compassion overwhelm Your demand for strict justice; turn to us with Your lovingkindness. Have compassion for me and for my entire family; shield us from all cruelty."[30]

Personal meditations occur elsewhere too: before the open ark at the beginning of the Torah service,[31] or at candlelighting before Shabbat or festivals.[32] But above all, we have altered the supplication rubric (called *Tachanun*) that follows the daily *Tefillah*. Originally the text was not fixed, as worshipers were encouraged to pour out their hearts to God. Over time, however, one particular version of *Tachanun* became virtually canonized by printers. We wanted to restore the sense of the personal here and to delete theological themes, such as self-abasement or the abased condition of Jerusalem, which no longer reflect our reality. Thus we abridged the conventional text but added new material drawn from the ninth-century prayer book of Amram and the tenth-century Egyptian prayer book of Saadiah.[33] We introduced the text with a note pointing out that "any words or thoughts that one cares to offer are appropriate at this point, from a brief reflection to a lengthy expression of deep feelings. Suggested texts follow. You are free to supplement or to replace the texts which are headed by Roman numerals." The roman numerals serve to differentiate each of five sections, with the further suggestion that one might select from among them, legitimizing the possibility of a much shorter text as well.

Critique

The reception of *Siddur Sim Shalom* has been encouraging. Early in 1990 it entered its sixth printing; over 320 congregations have adopted it, and their number is constantly growing. The *siddur* is being accepted as the official prayer book for the Conservative movement.

One guaranteed result in this enterprise of editing prayer books is that you are not going to please everybody with every aspect of the volume. I cannot even completely please myself. Disagreements and compromises are inevitable, particularly with regard to a prayer book published for the Conservative movement, which represents so many viewpoints. Still, I can say that we are proud of this *siddur*, although we are not satisfied.[34]

NOTES

1. For examples of Orthodox texts, see Philip Birnbaum, ed., *Hasiddur Hashalem: Daily Prayer Book* (New York, 1949); and David De Sola Pool, ed., *The Traditional Prayer Book for Sabbath and Festivals* (New York, 1960).

2. Birnbaum, *Hasiddur,* p. 616.

3. Jules Harlow, ed., *Siddur Sim Shalom: A Prayerbook for Shabbat, Festivals, and Weekdays* (New York, 1985), p. 465; cf. the similar sentiment in its predecessor, *Seder Tefillot Yisra'el Lashabbat Uleshelosh Regalim: Sabbath and Festival Prayer Book* (1946), which introduced the change by noting: "It is characteristic of Judaism to recall the sacrificial system which represents a legitimate stage in the evolution of Judaism and religion generally" (foreward, pp. ix–x).

4. *Sabbath and Festival Prayer Book* 1946.

5. Our current traditional prayer was composed in Spain or in the Ottoman Empire, c. fifteenth–sixteenth century. See Barry Schwartz, "*Hanoten Teshua:* The Origin of the Traditional Jewish Prayer for the Government," *HUCA* 57 (1986): 113–120.

6. *Festival Prayer Book* 1927, p. iv.

7. See Birnbaum, *Hasiddur,* pp. 16–18.

8. *Sabbath and Festival Prayer Book* 1946, p. x; pp. 45–46.

9. Composed by the chair of the Joint Prayer Book Commission, Rabbi Robert Gordis. For greater detail, see Robert Gordis, "A Jewish Prayer Book for the Modern Age," *Conservative Judaism* 2/1 (October 1945): 1–20.

10. *Weekday Prayer Book* (New York, 1961).

11. Ibid., pp. 196–99.

12. Ibid., pp. 64–65.

13. Jules Harlow, ed., *Machzor for Rosh Hashanah and Yom Kippur* (New York, 1972).

14. Harlow, *Siddur Sim Shalom,* p. 435.

15. Birnbaum, *Hasiddur,* p. 168.

16. Harlow, *Siddur Sim Shalom,* p. 177.

17. Ibid., p. 177.

18. Ibid., p. 177.

19. Ibid., p. 288.

20. Ibid., pp. 840–84.

21. Ibid., pp. 10–11.

22. Ibid., pp. 10–11.

23. Ibid., pp. 142–45; 402–5.

24. Ibid., p. 107.

25. Ibid., pp. 142–43; 402–3.

26. Ibid., pp. 144–45; 414–15.

27. Ibid., pp. 2–5.

28. Rachel Anne Rabinowicz, ed., *Passover Haggadah: The Feast of Freedom* (New York, 1982).

29. Harlow, *Siddur Sim Shalom,* p. 121.

30. Ibid., p. 122.

31. Ibid., pp. 396 and 397.

32. Ibid., pp. 717–21.

33. Ibid., pp. 128–33. On these early prayer books, see LawrenceA. Hoffman, *The Canonization of the Synagogue Service* (Notre Dame, 1979).

34. For further study, cf. Leslie Brisman, " 'As It Is Written'— in the New Conservative Prayerbook," *Orim: A Jewish Journal at Yale* 1/1 (Spring 1986): 6–22; David Golinkin, "*Siddur Sim Shalom:* A Halakhic Analysis," *Conservative Judaism* 41/1 (Fall 1988): 38–55; Sidney Greenberg, "Reactions to the Rabbinical Assembly *Mahzor,*" *Judaism* 22/4 (Fall 1973): 441–54; Jules Harlow, "A Note on *Siddur Sim Shalom,*" *Rabbinical Assembly Proceedings,* 1984, pp. 105–9; idem, "Highlights of *Siddur Sim Shalom,*" *Rabbinical Assembly Proceedings,* 1986, pp. 21–28; idem, "Faith in Translation," *Moment* (September 1975): 67–71; idem, "A Note on the Rabbinical Assembly High Holy Day *Mahzor* (Reaction to the 1973 Symposium in Judaism)," *Beineinu* 4/1 (January 1974): 3–8; idem, "On Editing a Prayer Book," *Conservative Judaism* (Fall 1971): 61–69; Lawrence A. Hoffman, "Review of *Siddur Sim Shalom, a Prayer Book for Shabbat, Festivals and Weekdays,*" *Worship* 60/6 (November 1986): 555–58; Leonard Levin, "Whither Conservative Liturgy?" *Judaism* 22/4 (Fall 1973): 433–39; Levi Olan, "A New Prayer Book—Conservative Judaism Defines Itself," *Judaism* 22/4 (Fall 1973): 418–25; Jakob J. Petuchowski, "Reflections of a Liturgist," *Rabbinical Assembly Proceedings,* 1986, pp. 4–13; idem, "Review of *Siddur Sim Shalom,*" *Conservative Judaism* 38/2 (Winter 1985/1986): 82–87; idem, "Conservative Liturgy Comes of Age," *Conservative Judaism* 27/1 (Fall 1972): 3–11; Steven Riskin, " 'Modern' Prayer—At What Sacrifice?" *Judaism* 22/4 (Fall 1973): 426–32; Jeffrey Rubenstein, "*Siddur Sim Shalom* and Developing Conservative Theology," *Conservative Judaism* 41/1 (Fall 1988): 21–37.

The *Gates* Liturgies:
Reform Judaism Reforms Its Worship

A. STANLEY DREYFUS

Jewish Liturgy and Reform Judaism's Identity

The framework of the Jewish liturgy[1] and the texts of most of the prayers that comprise it can be traced to the Second Commonwealth and the several centuries immediately following the Destruction in the year 70 C.E. Besides the recitation of Psalms and the reading of scripture, the prime components of the liturgy are two: a credal element, termed the *Shema* and its benedictions; and then the *Tefillah*, or Prayer proper. Of these, the first affirms the divine unity (Deuteronomy 6:4) and is followed by three biblical passages[2] that enjoin the love of God, the study of Torah, and the fulfillment of its commandments, and that also enunciate a doctrine of reward and punishment. These passages are preceded by theological statements on creation and revelation[3] and are followed by the acknowledgment of God as redeemer in history;[4] and, for the evening service, the passages are followed by a supplication against the perils of the night.[5] The second major feature of the liturgy is prayer in the conventional sense, at least for the weekday services.[6] Jews have always felt that petitions for personal, worldly goods mar the solemn joy and detract from the serenity of spirit that the sacred seasons of the year are meant to induce. Consequently, even on weekdays, a goodly part of the Prayer rubric is devoted to praise of God and to expressions of thanksgiving and only limited opportunity is provided the worshiper to give voice to personal supplications within the formal service itself, though extemporaneous private prayer is always encouraged. The content of the regular service is completely prescribed, both for the individual and the congregation, with all the advantages and disadvantages that attach to a fixed liturgy.

The function of a fixed liturgy, according to Moses Maimonides, twelfth-century philosopher and legalist,[7] is to guide people to pray in elegant and grammatically faultless language worthy of the One they address, as well as to teach them how to voice their hearts' desires and the needs of the community in reasonable fashion and logical sequence. Maimonides took it for granted that all Jews pray; his concern was that they should refine their prayer. Nowadays, many Jews, both those who classify themselves as Reform or traditional, and those who are avowedly indifferent, need to be given some understanding of what prayer is and what it is not. In *Gates of Prayer* we include a number of meditations intended to elucidate what prayer achieves. For example: "Prayer invites God to let His presence suffuse our spirits, to let His will prevail in our lives. Prayer cannot bring water to parched fields, nor mend a broken bridge, nor rebuild a ruined city, but prayer can water an arid soul, mend a broken heart, and rebuild a weakened will."[8]

A second purpose of a fixed liturgy is to direct Jews to contemplate the meaning of their history, the miracle of survival.

> In a world torn by violence and pain, a world far from wholeness and peace, a world waiting still to be redeemed, give us, Lord, the courage to say: There is One God in heaven and earth. *The high heavens declare His glory; may earth reveal His justice and His love.*

> From Egypt, the house of bondage, we were delivered; at Sinai, amid peals of thunder, we bound ourselves to His purpose. Inspired by prophets and instructed by sages, we survived oppression and exile, time and again overcoming the forces that would have destroyed us.

Our failings are many—our faults are great—yet it has been our glory to bear witness to our God, and to keep alive in dark ages the vision of a world redeemed.

May this vision never fade; let us continue to work for the day when the nations will be one and at peace.[9]

Again, a fixed liturgy summons Jews, willy-nilly, to attend to *tikkun olam*, literally to the "repair of the world." It compels them to face up to the personal failings that all too often go unrecognized and affirms their obligation to remedy the evils that bedevil humankind, so far as ever mortals can do. The old liturgy spoke in generalities: "We have sinned; we have transgressed; we have done perversely." The new liturgy speaks far more pointedly:

We sin against You when we sin against ourselves. . . .

For passing judgment without knowledge of the facts,
and for distorting facts to fit our theories. . . .

For using the sins of others to excuse our own,
and for denying responsibility for our own misfortunes. . . .

For keeping the poor in the chains of poverty,
and turning a deaf ear to the cry of the oppressed.

For using violence to maintain our power,
and for using violence to bring about change.

For waging aggressive war,
and for the sin of appeasing aggressors.

For obeying criminal orders,
and for the sin of silence and indifference.

For poisoning the air, and polluting land and sea,
and for all the evil means we employ to accomplish good ends. . . .

For using others as a means to gratify our desires,
and as stepping-stones to further our ambitions.

For withholding love to control those we claim to love,
and shunting aside those whose youth or age disturbs us. . . .

Teach us to forgive ourselves for all these sins, O forgiving God,
and help us to overcome them.[10]

Lawrence A. Hoffman has demonstrated that any liturgy should be regarded as not only a systematically constructed and dramatically presented testimonial of faith but also, and even more significantly, as a reflection of the self-image of the religious community, their statement of their perceived identity.[11] On the basis of Hoffman's conclusions (and making allowance for oversimplification), we can see in the 1895 *Union Prayer Book* the self-image of a Jewish community composed in the main of fairly recent immigrants who had found unprecedented acceptance and opportunity on these shores. In consequence, they were of a mind to dispense with many of the traditional practices that had set them apart and sustained them during their age-old struggle for survival, practices that now seemed to hinder their integration into American society and that appeared alien to the American experience. Thus, they undertook to assimilate the style of Jewish worship to the pattern of the dominant culture. They appropriated much in the 1895 prayer book from Protestant churches: rubrics such as *minister* (in place of *rabbi*, or *cantor*, or *leader*, the last representing the German *Vorbeter*, the usual designation for a Jewish officiant), *choir, canticle, hymn, anthem, silent devotion, adoration, benediction*—all previously unknown to the synagogue. So, too, was the introduction of newly composed prayers, which now and then approximate sermons, as adaptations of the pastoral prayers of the church. Furthermore, the traditional prayer book presupposes that public worship will be conducted every morning and evening,[12] and therefore it places the weekday services at the front of the book. The *Union Prayer Book*, following the Protestant practice of concentrating public worship on Sunday, put the Sabbath evening and morning liturgies at the front of the prayer book and relegated the weekday services to the back, thereby signaling that communal worship was no longer required of the Reform Jew and perhaps not even desired.

The 1924 revision of the *Union Prayer Book* was occasioned by widespread insistence that a Reform liturgy should react to the social problems of its age.[13] The community thus had come to regard itself—or at least its spiritual leaders wanted the community to regard itself—as social activists in the prophetic spirit of an Amos or an Isaiah.

Both the 1895 and 1924 prayer books portrayed Reform Jewry's perception of themselves as adherents of a religious faith corresponding to the various Christian denominations, although historically Jews had always considered themselves a distinct people that embraced all those who declare themselves to be Jewish, whether by descent or choice, whether religiously committed or even antagonistic to the Jewish religion. A 1930 critique of the revised prayer book charged that the Judaism it manifested had been reduced to a "drab ethical monotheism, ignoring much of its colorful life and historical associations. . . . Naturally Judaism, being the Jew's way to the Holy One, voices in its prayers the longings and aspirations of the Jewish people. This may be branded by some as *particularism*. Possibly we are a bit too sensitive to what the non-Jewish attendants at our services may say. . . . Most often what is best and noblest in the national is in reality of universal value and significance."[14] And, in reaction to the prayer book's emphasis on social action: "The *Union Prayer Book* conveys the impression that it was especially written for a people composed of retired philanthropists and amateur social workers."[15]

The alarming growth of German antisemitism in the thirties convinced many Jews that assimilation provided no guarantee of acceptance into the larger society, nor even of security. The *Newly Revised* prayer book of 1940 represents the Reform community's new realization that it had jettisoned too many distinctively Jewish practices, and with them some degree of spiritual integrity. The 1940 prayer book restored such ceremonies as the *Kiddush* for the eve of Sabbath and festivals and the memorial service for the seventh day of

Passover.[16] It introduced a ritual for the reading of the Torah
on Friday evenings, in recognition of the fact that many congregants could not leave their offices or places of business to
attend Saturday morning services when the reading of scripture is a regular feature of the liturgy.[17] The 1940 prayer
book substituted *reader* for *minister*, and, because increasing
numbers of Reform Jews had become sympathetic to Zion-
ism, it added a new prayer for the rebuilders of Zion and the
supplication that the Land might be restored not simply as
another state but, rather, "as a living witness to the truth of
Thy word which shall lead the nations to the reign of
peace,"[18] although, in deference to those who remained opposed to Jewish nationalism, the prayer was relegated to a
service read only on the fifth Sabbath of the month!

The enormity of the Holocaust on the one hand, and, on
the other, the establishment of the State of Israel brought a
reawakening of faith and commitment and, for Reform Jewry,
mandated a complete revision of its liturgy. *Gates of Prayer*,
which appeared in 1975, admitted Yom Hashoah, the day of
commemorating the martyrs of the Holocaust, and Yom
Ha'atsma'ut, Israel Independence Day, into the religious calendar. It is a prayer book that speaks to and for a community
comfortable with the open expression of its Jewishness, with
more Hebrew in the service, with devising new ceremonies,
and with reviving old rituals. A token of the latter is to be
seen in the fact that an increasing number of worshipers
cover their heads at prayer and put on a *tallit* (prayer shawl),
practices that Reform Judaism had discarded in its early
years because they were thought to make the Jew appear for-
eign, exotic in non-Jewish eyes. Nowadays most congregants
are eager to play an active role in the synagogue, to demon-
strate their proficiency in reading the Hebrew prayers, and to
sing the responses, where not so long ago they were content
with listening to monologues from the pulpit and to art music
performed by professional choirs. In encouraging lay involvement, *Gates of Prayer* is responding to the popular urge to
recapture the spontaneity and fervor that have traditionally
been characteristic of Jewish worship.

History of the Prayer Book Revisions

In Reform Judaism the publication of liturgy is the responsibility of the Central Conference of American Rabbis, which operates through a standing liturgy committee of six members, plus a chair, who serve for five-year terms.[19] All are rabbis; occasionally laypeople are invited to serve as consultants. An ex officio representative of the American Conference of Cantors provided invaluable assistance in the editing of *Gates of Prayer* and its companion volumes.

The work of liturgical renewal began in 1967, when Rabbi Herbert Bronstein of Glencoe, Illinois, was invited to revise the 1923 edition of the *Union Haggadah*, the home service for the eve of Passover. This Haggadah appeared in 1974. In 1967 the committee also began to revise the 1940 prayer book by commissioning four experimental services for Sabbath eve, each with its own theme. The committee benefited from a series of studies and conferences on worship that were arranged both by Jews and non-Jews, as well as from a number of articles that urged the revision of the 1940 prayer book and from informal communications by members of the Reform community. There was never a dearth of advice!

After having been reworked by the entire committee, the experimental services were printed in pamphlet form and tested in the congregations. The reactions were generally unfavorable. So great was the dissatisfaction of some congregations with the inadequacies that they perceived in the old prayer book and so impatient were they with the progress of the committee that they turned for help to England, where Rabbis John D. Rayner and Chaim Stern had just completed *Service of the Heart* (1967), a prayer book intended for the Union of Liberal and Progressive Synagogues of Great Britain. The North American committee adopted *Service of the Heart* as a model for its own deliberations, and further, appointed Rabbi Stern, who had taken up residence in Chappaqua, New York, as editor. Scholarly liturgist and gifted stylist, Rabbi Stern prepared a manuscript in consultation with the chair of the committee. The draft, which was sensitive to the *Union Prayerbook* tradition, incorporated new materials that Rabbi Stern had himself written, some of them for *Service of the Heart*, or that he had solicited from others, both on the committee and in the Conference at large. Some of the supplementary readings were drawn from non-Jewish sources. The manuscript was carefully reviewed and frequently emended by the committee, often after heated debate. Eventually a trial edition was published and circulated to the membership of the Conference for their comments and criticisms. On the basis of the responses and of further consideration on the part of the editor and the committee, a final draft was sent to the Conference for a mail ballot. Upon receiving overwhelming approval, we prepared the book for publication. A similar procedure was followed with *Gates of Repentance*.

In 1928 Samuel S. Cohon, editor of the 1923 *Union Haggadah* and the 1928 *Rabbi's Manual*, wrote:

> The *Union Prayerbook*, like the other publications of the Central Conference of American Rabbis, is the product of committee endeavor. Committees are, as a rule, composed of men who are not necessarily saints or poets, men of differing minds and of varying viewpoints, which clash on matters which are usually of deep moment. They can, therefore, make progress only through compromise. To this condition we may trace most of the inconsistencies in the *Union Prayerbook*.[20]

The differences in viewpoint that Cohon reported in 1928 fade into insignificance in comparison with the diversity of outlook that prevails in Reform Judaism today. Our constituency runs the theological gamut from traditional theism to religious naturalism, from classical piety to estrangement. To accommodate the various attitudes represented in the community, we had inevitably to sacrifice a degree of unity of content and style, but a book that enunciated a single theology could never have won the ratification of the Conference.

Issues Addressed by the Reforms

Among the most important issues the committee had to consider were these:

1. Reform Jewish liturgy has constantly to strike a balance between the conflicting claims of tradition and modernity. Should prayers hallowed by centuries of pious usage be discarded merely because, literally interpreted, they contradict the scientist? How far can we go in indulging legitimate nostalgia without alienating those who demand that the prayer book speak unequivocal truth? For example, Exodus 31:16f. has traditionally served to justify the observance of the Sabbath. The passage ends, "for in six days the Eternal God made heaven and earth."[21] These words, at odds with scientific hypotheses about the origin of the universe, were omitted from the previous editions of the *Union Prayerbook;* after discussion we agreed to reinstate them as a poetic affirmation that creation stems from the divine will.

2. The classic Hebrew prayers must be made comprehensible to those who have little or no Hebrew. Some of our people clamor for literal translations, as if the prayer book should also serve as a textbook in elementary Hebrew, and as if any one translation could convey all the nuances in the simplest Hebrew sentence. The *Shema* (Deuteronomy 6:4), which liturgically is the confession of Jewish faith, contains only six Hebrew words, but these can be rendered in at least four different ways, all of them faithful to the Hebrew. The *Union Prayerbook* translated the verse, "Hear, O Israel: The Lord our God, the Lord is One."[22] (The original lacks the verb *is*; it must be supplied from the context.) Following Rabbi Samuel ben Meir (1085–1174), we inserted a second *is*, so that the *Shema* as we now read it makes two statements: The Lord is our God, and the Lord is One.[23]

Therefore, because no single translation can be adequate, we have occasionally provided several English versions of important Hebrew texts, some relatively literal, some free and interpretative. In *Gates of Repentance* we marked the paraphrases and interpretative renderings with an asterisk in order to distinguish them from the more literal translations, though at no time did we sacrifice literary grace for a word-for-word translation. Now and then we left untranslated familiar passages that are generally sung. Surprisingly, very few noticed the absence of the English.[24]

3. The English of the earlier prayer books, whether issued for traditional or Reform congregations, almost always imitated the style of the King James Version of the Bible and the *Book of Common Prayer* and, in some cases, the intricate constructions of literary German. Today few people are comfortable with archaic English, nor do they care for the second person singular familiar pronoun *thou* and the obsolete verb forms it commands, much less verbs in the third person that terminate in the syllable *eth*, the bane of children who lisp. Indeed, by eliminating these outworn forms, we are the more faithful to the Hebrew, which addresses the Deity in everyday language rather than reserve a particular (archaic) form for God alone. Our English is unpretentious, yet, we hope, dignified and elegant, a fit vehicle for the exalted sentiments appropriate to worship. True, not all have applauded our decision to use current speech, especially when, for the sake of consistency, we had to rewrite passages as beloved as Psalm 23 and the praise of the woman of valor in Proverbs chapter 31.[25]

4. Now that women have taken their rightful place in the religious community, certain hitherto unquestioned liturgical expressions have become disturbing to many worshipers. Their demand is for gender-inclusive language. *Lord, King, Father, Master* are now *verba non grata*, along with the use of masculine pronouns to refer to God. Most people recognize the justice of these claims, though when the prayer books under discussion were being prepared, it still seemed possible to argue that grammatically speaking, God is not necessarily enrolled as a male, even when God is the antecedent of the masculine singular personal pronoun. Some committee members argued also that some masculine metaphors for the divine are inseparable from the experience of

the Days of Awe—the age-old litany "Our Father, our King," for instance, which points up the paradox of the transcendence and the immanence of God, and which would be diminished by the reduction to the gender-neutral "Our parent, our ruler."

The committee's uncertainties resulted in a compromise position, whereby male-specific references to God were retained. On the other hand, we eliminated many exclusionary references to men rather than to human beings generally, as, for example, in Psalm 15, where the Hebrew has a succession of eleven clauses introduced by *he*. We substitute either *those who*, or *who* alone, turning the masculine singular pronoun into the common gender *they*.[27] Sometimes we translate the Hebrew third person pronoun by an English second person pronoun, without doing violence to the sense of the original.

The women's movement came into its own only after the completion of *Gates of Prayer*. *Gates of Repentance* had the benefit of women's advice on the choice of language, and as a result, it has fewer distressing passages. Without doubt, all future Reform liturgies will be kept free of sexisms with regards to the Deity as well as to human beings.

5. The traditional liturgy, read three times each day throughout the year, remains basically the same for weekdays, Sabbaths, festivals, fast days, Days of Awe. However, in our novelty-hungry generation, repetition very quickly becomes monotonous. Of course that danger was recognized in past generations, and some variety was introduced by means of special melodies for different sacred moments and also by the insertion of *piyyutim,* recondite poetical compositions, generally in acrostic form, which assume that the worshiper is well-versed in rabbinic literature in order to understand the allusions they contain. (For the most part the *piyyutim* have now been eliminated from the prayer books of even the most Orthodox congregations.)

In order to provide variety in our liturgy, we have used more than one version of the classical Hebrew prayers where these have come down to us, and we have reinstated other, long-forgotten prayers. An example is the *Tefillah* of medieval

Palestinian Jewry, which fell into oblivion when the community was destroyed during the First Crusade in 1099. We have introduced it into *Gates of Prayer* in a Sabbath service and, in part, into the service read on Israel Independence Day, when it seems especially appropriate.[28] Furthermore, we have provided fully ten different orders of worship for Sabbath eve, the first quite traditional, two others for occasions when many children are present, and still others on themes of religious naturalism, doubt, estrangement, the mystical search, social justice, covenant, and commandment. Each has new prayers and meditations intended to respond to the situation of today's Reform constituency.[29]

6. As already noted, the twin focal events for the Jews of our day are the Holocaust and the establishment of the state of Israel, both of which have brought Jews to a new self-awareness and a consciousness of mystery. We have tried to see in destruction and rebirth both warning and opportunity, not only for ourselves, but for all God's children.[30]

Critique

The new prayer books have been received with warm approval and some quite strident disapproval.[31] Critics tend to be voluble. Because in our time the Days of Awe speak more compellingly to the Jewish soul than does the Sabbath, *Gates of Repentance* has had a far more positive reception than has *Gates of Prayer*, which has the added task of persuading disparate groups within Reform Jewry that the Sabbath can enhance their lives spiritually, emotionally, even physically, and that Judaism as a whole deserves their attention and support.

Those who worked on *Gates of Prayer* can derive a measure of consolation from the fact that the unfavorable verdicts are often mutually contradictory. What one condemns as pedestrian may well appeal to another as insightful, uplifting, provocative. Again, *Gates of Prayer* is often faulted for being cumbersome. It is indeed a heftier volume that its predecessors, though it weighs less than the contemporary Conservative and Orthodox prayer books, and, for that matter, the

1979 edition of the Episcopal *Book of Common Prayer*. Had *Gates of Prayer* offered fewer services and fewer optional readings, it would be the more easily held, but surely there would have been acrimonious disagreement on the sections to be excised because there is no consensus on what devotional material will most surely touch the hearts and excite the minds of Jews. Furthermore, the prayer book itself is often assigned blame that rightfully belongs to officiants who use it carelessly and even irreverently.

Gates of Prayer is also the victim of unrealistic expectations. It has not effected a religious revival throughout Reform Jewry. No prayer book could achieve that, nor will the revision of *Gates of Prayer* now contemplated meet with greater success. Our next prayer book will do away with the infelicities that mar this one, but very likely others will elude the editors' vigilance. The revision too will be born of controversy and grudging compromise. As those who lived during the era of the Holocaust become older and memories dim, the next generations may become impatient at being reminded of the fate that Jews suffered, just as they will have no immediate acquaintance with the sense of awe and mystery that attended the rebirth of the State of Israel, the sense that the God of the Exodus had entered history again to redeem "this eternal people" (in Leo Baeck's words). Still, it is improbable that many fewer prayers and a more compact book would suffice a people as diverse as ours.

This much we fancy we have accomplished: We have made Reform worship recognizably Jewish in style and mood. No longer is the synagogue service the sole domain of the pulpit and the choir loft, while the faithful are permitted only a minor role in the sacred drama. Nowadays most congregants are not afraid to read aloud, to lift their voices in song, to unite fervently in prayer, in Hebrew as well as English. The new liturgy has enabled at least some Reform Jews to experience firsthand something of the numinous, to come into the presence of the holy, as former generations were privileged to do. And that experience will be shared by increasing numbers as, in the course of time, *Gates of Prayer* ceases to be a novelty and instead becomes familiar. And for those who labored over it, their greatest reward is to discover something unexpected in this prayer or that, something none of its compilers consciously intended, some note that may even have the power to transform a life.

NOTES

1. The traditional Jewish prayer book (*siddur*) is available in many editions. References here are to Philip Birnbaum, ed., *Hasiddur Hashalem: Daily Prayer Book* (New York, 1949). The *siddur* (order [of worship]) comprises the statutory prayers for weekdays and Sabbaths. The *Machzor* (cycle) contains the liturgy for the three festivals and the Days of Awe. The major prayer books of Reform Judaism, which will be discussed here, are these:

1. *The Union Prayer Book for Jewish Worship,* part 1 [*UPB* 1]: prayers for the Sabbath, the three festivals, and the weekdays (New York, 1895); part 2 [*UPB* 2]: New Year's Day and Day of Atonement (New York, 1894)
2. *The Union Prayer Book,* revised ed., part 1 (1924), and part 2 (1922)
3. *The Union Prayer Book,* newly revised ed., part 1 (1940), and part 2 (1945)
4. *Haggadah shel Pesach: A Passover Haggadah* (New York, 1974); revised ed. (1975)
5. *Shaarei Tefillah: Gates of Prayer* [*GOP*] (New York, 1975): liturgy for weekdays, Sabbath, and festivals
6. *Shaarei Habayit: Gates of the House* [*GOH*] (New York, 1977): occasional prayers, largely for the home
7. *Shaarei Teshuvah: Gates of Repentance* [*GOR*] (New York, 1978): liturgy for Rosh Hashanah and Yom Kippur
8. *Shaarei Selichah: Gates of Forgiveness* [*GOF*] (New York, 1980): liturgy for the *selichot* service preparatory to Rosh Hashanah

For notes to *GOP* and *GOR*, as well as essays regarding the liturgical changes that these volumes represent, see Lawrence A. Hoffman, Chaim Stern, and A. Stanley Dreyfus, eds., *Shaarei Binah: Gates of Understanding,* vol. 1 (New York, 1977), and vol. 2 (New York, 1984).

2. Deuteronomy 6:5–9; 11:13–21; Numbers 15:37–41 in the *siddur*. Cf. Birnbaum, *Hasiddur* (hereafter, *Siddur*), pp. 76–79; and, for Reform liturgy, *GOP*, p. 57. The latter eliminated the second paragraph, with its doctrine of retribution, and most of the third paragraph, which enjoins the wearing of fringes, as theologically unacceptable.

3. *Siddur*, pp. 72–78; *GOP*, pp. 55–56.

4. *Siddur*, pp. 78–82; *GOP*, pp. 58–59.

5. *Siddur*, p. 198; *GOP*, p. 35.

6. *Siddur*, pp. 82–98; *GOP*, pp. 60–71.

7. *Mishneh Torah*, book 2, *Sefer Ahavah, Hilkhot Tefillah* 1:4; in English translation as *Mishneh Torah*, book 2, ed. Moses Hyamson (New York, 1947) p. 98b.

8. *GOP*, p. 52.

9. *GOP*, pp. 149–50. Italics indicate congregational responses.

10. Cf. *GOR*, pp. 327–28 and *UPB* 2, newly revised ed., p. 148.

11. Cf. Hoffman, Stern, and Dreyfus, *Gates of Understanding,* vol. 1, pp. 138–68; and Lawrence A. Hoffman, *Beyond the Text: A Holistic Approach to Liturgy,* Jewish Literature and Culture (Bloomington, Ind., 1987), pp. 57–67.

12. Traditionally there are three daily services: morning, afternoon, and evening; but in practice, the evening service is read immediately after the afternoon service, so that the congregation may assemble only twice, rather than three times, each day.

13. See Lou H. Silberman, *"The Union Prayer Book:* A Study in Liturgical Development," in Bertram W. Korn, ed., *Retrospect and Prospect* (New York, 1965), pp. 64–65.

14. Samuel S. Cohon, "The Religious Ideas of a *Union Prayer Book*," *CCAR Yearbook* 40 (1930): 279, 293.

15. Samuel S. Cohon, "The Theology of the *Union Prayer Book*," *CCAR Yearbook* 38 (1928): 250.

16. *UPB* 1, newly revised ed., pp. 93, 206–8, 268–73.

17. Ibid., pp. 94–97, and (for Sabbath morning), pp. 144–50.

18. Ibid., pp. 68–69.

19. See *CCAR Yearbooks* for reports of the committee's deliberations.

20. *CCAR Yearbook* 38 (1928): 268.

21. *GOP*, pp. 133, 309, and elsewhere.

22. Cf. *UPB* 1, newly revised ed., p. 14.

23. For other acceptable translations, see Israel Abrahams, *A Companion to the Authorized Daily Prayer Book* (London, 1922), p. li.

24. Cf. *GOP*, pp. 208, 210, 214–15.

25. *GOP*, 546; *GOH*, p. 31.

26. *GOR*, pp. 117–18, 280–81, 339–40.

27. *GOP*, p. 177; *GOR*, p. 171.

28. *GOR*, pp. 185–86; *GOP*, pp. 599–600, 602.

29. On the themes of the services, see Hoffman, Stern, and Dreyfus, *Gates of Understanding*, vol. 1, pp 171–76.

30. See, for example, services for Tisha Be'av (the anniversary of the destruction of the First and Second Temples), *GOP*, pp. 573–87; and the service for Yom Ha'atsma'ut (Israel Independence Day), *GOP*, pp. 590–611, and pp. 173, 201, 240–41.

31. Among the significant evaluations of *GOP* and *GOR* are the following, all published in the *Journal of Reform Judaism* (called *CCAR Journal* prior to spring of 1978):

Fields, Harvey J. "We Must Fashion *Keva* and *Kavanah*." Vol. 81 (Spring 1973).

Friedland, Eric. "*Gates of Prayer* in Historical-Critical Perspective." Vol. 99 (Fall 1977).

———. "Historical Notes on the American High Holy Day Liturgy." Vol. 142 (Summer 1988).

"*Gates of Prayer:* Ten Years Later—A Symposium." Vol. 131 (Fall 1985).

Hoffman, Lawrence A. "The Language of Survival in American Reform Liturgy." Vol. 98 (Summer 1977).

———. "Setting Boundaries for Prayerbook Criticism." Vol. 131 (Fall 1985).

Levy, Richard. "Upon Arising: An Affirmation of *Techiyat Hameitim*." Vol. 119 (Fall 1982).

Sonsino, Rifat. "*Gates of the House:* A Review." Vol. 99 (1977).

Stern, Chaim. "Reply to a Hostile Review." Vol. 101 (Spring 1978).

PART 3
Critiquing Liturgical Reforms

Introduction

The decade of the 1970s saw the first flush of liturgical publications in large numbers. By the 1980s, the new worship books were in use around the country, and as that decade came to an end, enough time had elapsed for worshipers to evaluate what had been achieved and what had been lost. The critiques that had come at the very outset of the reforms were generally composed by conservatively oriented writers whose passion for the Latin mass, the old *Book of Common Prayer*, the *Union Prayer Book*—or whatever the equivalent was in other traditions—made them doubt aloud the wisdom of any change at all. A series of diatribes were published as editors of the new worship books were taken to task for abandoning archaic styles of English, removing favored rubrics, introducing new hymns, or doing whatever else they and their committees had seen as constituting appropriate liturgical reform in the 1970s.

The critiques that follow, however, differ greatly from those early diatribes. Rather than oppose, the critiques here actually advocate the current reformation of public worship. They wish, however, to move the reforms to a new stage in which we become both more self-critical of what we have done so far and more seriously responsive to specific concerns that have arisen since the onset of the reformation nearly three decades ago.

David N. Power has been Professor of Systematic Theology and Liturgy at the Catholic University of America since 1977 and, before that, at the Gregorian University of Rome. A noted author on liturgical matters, he is charged with coeditorial responsibilities for the liturgy section of the international journal *Concilium*. Power levels a theological critique at both Christian and Jewish liturgical reforms and points to the direction that further reform must take if it is to be theologically responsible.

Michael A. Signer is a professor at the Los Angeles campus of the Hebrew Union College–Jewish Institute of Religion, where he teaches liturgy and medieval studies. His interest in hermeneutics leads him here to challenge liturgical authors and editors with questions that come from a very old, yet (in its current guise) very new, field: poetics.

Since 1980, Janet Walton has been at New York's Union Theological Seminary, where she teaches courses in worship, directs the liturgical preparation of ministers, and oversees daily worship. Her research interests are the relationship between worship and art, and the feminist critique of worship. This latter concern led her to form an interdenominational women's liturgy group to further the development of rituals responsive to women's experience. It is the feminist critique of worship that she presents here.

Worship in a New World:
Some Theological Considerations

David N. Power

To attempt to offer a theological critique of worship in North America today is brash. I must therefore start by disclaiming any virtuosity. How could I pretend to know all the liturgical books and practices of all the Christian churches on the continent, not to mention those of Jewish communities as well? Indeed some may find my knowledge of the practice and theologies even of my own communion, the Roman Catholic church, rather truncated. Even in relatively confined fields, universality of knowledge is impossible today. This acknowledgment sets the context for the modest reflection that follows.

Although a distinctively theological reflection, this essay prefers to ask questions of text and practice rather than look to them for conformity to an already presupposed doctrine. If the questions are well formed, I may be able to offer something even to those who, despite my efforts, find me ignorant or misinformed of their traditions.

I shall first rehearse some of the accomplishments of the renewal of text and practice in synagogue and church over the last twenty-five years. Second, I shall ask what challenge the phenomenon that has aptly been named *reversionism* puts to our renewal. Third, I shall take up three specific liturgical issues that appear to me to be central to the next stage of liturgical renewal in all Jewish and Christian traditions.

RENEWAL: EVER ANCIENT, EVER NEW

Recovery of Tradition

In considering what has been achieved through renewal, a theological model of liturgical development emerges. What we have seen happen is not always what was put in motion by the first efforts at change or by the ideas behind them. Development gathered its own momentum, influenced by forces and intuitions that were not always easy to name.

Both church and synagogue have seen enormous productivity in the revision of books for worship and a strong heightening of communal awareness through liturgical participation. What has gone on in the effort to meet modern needs has been in great part a creative retrieval of traditions. At least in the Roman Catholic church, the initial attempt spawned by the Second Vatican Council was to remove the encrustations of the ages and to rediscover the pristine liturgical forms and texts of earlier centuries, so as to come to a purer liturgical perception and celebration. Even while that program was enunciated, however, it was attenuated by a recognition of the need for adaptation and inculturation within the pluriformity of the contemporary world.[1] What was discovered—by Catholics and non-Catholics alike—was tradition's diversity and versatility. In composing rituals for eucharist and baptism especially, we have been drinking from rich wells, so that liturgical books reflect a plurality of ancient traditions, resounding with the echoes of such forebears as Hippolytus and Basil. Our liturgies are furthermore far richer than before in the proclamation of the scriptures. Within this very diversity, a certain ecumenical convergence has developed, and one finds that it is now also affecting such practices as rituals for the sick and rituals for the burial of the dead. From the work of Hoffman[2] and Reif,[3] to name but two recent writers on the subject, one gets the sense that a similar discovery of the richness and fluidity of the traditions that preceded a period of canonization has been of advantage to Jewish communities, enriching the work of liturgical reform and producing greater mutuality among the different "Judaisms" that have developed on the North American continent.

The Dangers of Modernity and Doctrine

This creative evolution that derives from a better grasp of both the content and the nature of tradition faces two particular difficulties that tempt committees to impose their own ideological solutions. The word *committee* may already conjure up these problems, for we are an age of planners and North America excels in a planned approach to change. Liturgical diversity of the past owed much to the insights of creative local pastors and to popular reaction to, and reception of, what they did. The localized act of pastor and people preceded the book. Today, by contrast, it is a common tendency to come to praise from knowledge rather than to knowledge from praise. The mind defines before the heart exults.

The two concerns that I have in mind are modernity and doctrine. As an example of the desire for modernity, note the calculated use of the face-to-face format in many rituals; as an example of doctrinal concern note how a number of churches have tampered with ancient eucharistic prayers in order to set them right on sacrifice and on epiclesis.[4] Or note the way in which Jewish books are very conscious of the doctrinal implications of attitudes towards the State of Israel.[5]

Jewish-Christian Relations

For Christian communities, this retrieval of tradition has led to a better grasp of the Jewish background of Christian liturgy and of the continuing affinity between Jewish worship and Christian worship. Overenthusiastic scholarship, such as a tendency to settle questions about the Passover seder observed by Jesus, or the text of the *Birkat hamazon* (the grace after meals) of the first century of the common era, or an

insensitive zest, such as appears in the writing of Christian
Passover seders, can blunt the edge of this discovery. But by
and large, it has been beneficial to Christian prayer and to
Jewish-Christian relations. For Jewish congregations, the parallel may be the perception that Jews and Christians arrived
at self-definition in relation to each other, attending too often
to the different rather than to the shared.[6] This historical perception can allow now for more attention to the shared.

Congregational Participation and Diversity

It is remarkable to note the degree to which we have called
forth congregational participation and diversity so that the
nature of God's assembly is more fully expressed. This has
long-term repercussions on the evolution of liturgy, as
shown, for example, in the evolution of a musical repertory
that is determined by the interaction of church musician and
parish liturgy committee, or between cantor and rabbi and
people.[7] Participation does not simply mean that all stand
and sing, but that a body actually brings liturgy into being.
Often, this development clashes with more established no-
tions of ministry and hierarchy, though on the positive side it
raises important questions of inclusivity.

The Cultural Side of Ritual

Through the process of change we have come to a sharper
grasp of the anthropological and cultural side of ritual. Early
scientific attempts at ritual study were based on the data of
field trips to Africa, Samoa, or Bali, but many of us have
now become observer/participants in the working-out of balance between the old and the new in our own congregations.
Through the experience, we have grown more sensitive to
how ritual formulates and shapes identity and belief. Without
yielding to the temptation to overlook the mystery of the divine that is at work in it, we can see that an important aspect
of ritual is that it defines a corporate body in relation to the

ethical and the political and hence affects its way of belonging in the society outside the walls of its places of assembly.[8]

Pluralism in Church and Synagogue

The overriding concern with the ritual that is intended to be central to the life of synagogue or church has made our respective bodies more aware of what is going on at the fringe. Popular devotions cannot be set aside as of no account. The black and Hispanic members of our religious groups are developing their own ways of celebrating in a fashion that goes beyond a difference in the use of language or body rhythm. Most striking of all, however, is the development of women-church at worship with a whole set of texts and rituals that many of the mainstream find jarring. Rather than simply dismissing such developments as gnostic or heterodox, there is a growing—if at times begrudging— recognition that mainstream worship has to be affected in important ways by communion with these fringes. What in the terms of cultural anthropology is called *antiritual* or *liminal*[9] cannot be allowed simply as an outlet of energy that in the long run bolsters the established order. It has to be integrated as a factor of change.

Defining Worship Renewal

The comments above allow us to posit a model of worship's renewal. It is (1) the work of congregations, (2) which face contemporary ethical and political questions, and therefore, (3) turn to God and to the recovery of their heritage, (4) through the interaction of all their parts and with specific attention to their marginal members, (5) in order to find an expression of faith and of communion with God that will give them a distinctive identity and a distinctive way of participating in the life and purpose of humanity.

REVERSIONISM

Symptom of the Crisis

Within twenty years however, even while new books are still being printed and the projected forms of liturgical committees are being brought to light, there has come a sense that this very work has occasioned a fresh crisis, or that the crisis that the work of renewal was intended to confront has been in the meantime compounded. The symptom of this discontent can be described by a word borrowed from Jacob Neusner: *reversionism*.[10] This is not the resistance of the elderly or the middle-aged to change, their pertinacity in clinging to old forms of devotion, or their yearning to return to Latin masses, Sunday services without eucharist, or the old ways of marking the Sabbath. Nor is it simply the cultural resistance to women rabbis or bishops. It is rather the tendency, particularly among the young, to reclaim the ways of their ancestors that the generation of their parents or grandparents abandoned. Sometimes this actually takes the form of a change of allegiance: a Reform Jew joins a Hasidic synagogue, an Episcopalian joins the Roman Catholic church, a Methodist embraces the Anglican way of worship, a Roman Catholic becomes a follower of Maurice Lefebre. More often it is an attempt to search out and win back what elders seem to have abandoned. For Jew and Christian alike, it is a search after numinous expressions that appear to have been beclouded by too much babbling and by a preoccupation with the human.

This reversionism is not to be lightly dismissed or labeled as the enemy of liturgical renewal, but neither is it to be simply accommodated as a way of keeping the young among us. It needs to be considered in terms of what it says about key factors in religious expression. At least the more important of these are the need for a clear religious identity, the sense of living out of a tradition even in the face of social and historical flux, and reverent symbolism of the holy. It may well in fact be possible to grasp the religious crisis unveiled by reversionism if we see it in the context of a more common social crisis.

The Manner of the Crisis

In effect, the crisis of Jewish and Christian worship in the United States is nothing other than the immersion of these religious bodies in this nation's manifold crisis of our time. Since the United States and Canada were founded on the very principles of modernity, one could say that their forms and practices of worship are engulfed in the crisis of modernity that affects the entire northern hemisphere and North America in particular.

This crisis is considered here under five headings (with no pretensions to complete analysis), the intention being to see liturgy in relation to it. First, there is a *crisis of the human*, created by the new enterprises and new worlds spawned by modernity around the time of the French Revolution and the founding of the United States of America, with its Declaration of Independence and its populist Constitution. Second, there is a *crisis of the historical* for a people sometimes described as "living between the holocausts" and, as a result, having little confidence in the continuities of history or in its force for good. Third, there is a *crisis of the democratic forms* that appeared to engage all the people in their responsible shaping of a common future and that have formed a constant challenge to hierarchical conceptions of religion. Fourth, there is a *crisis of the aesthetic* affecting the forms of expression intended to keep a people attuned to fundamental meaning, in touch with its aspirations to the good and the beautiful, and conscious of the world of the divine, in whatever way imagined or conceived. Fifth, there is the *crisis of tradition*, the critical question of whether the past carries aught for our comfort at all. To the extent that during the period of renewal our liturgies have opened more fully to the human, to the historical, to horizontal forms of participation, to attention to forms of the holy other than the *tremendum*, and to a creative working of traditions, they are affected by this multiple cultural crisis.

Religious bodies are caught in the middle of this crisis. Their very identity and power of expression are called into question. As far as worship is concerned, the key questions are whether it succeeds in expressing faith, hope, value, and identity in the midst of this crisis and whether it empowers worshipers to engage creatively in the larger human enterprise.

THREE QUESTIONS

We know from historical precedent that as we move from the stage of new texts to communal enactment of the rites to which those texts refer, our texts will not necessarily be dealt with kindly. First, how may the nature of Jewish or Christian worship as remembrance enable us to form a faith-identity that relates to present actuality? Second, does the model of the circle rather than hierarchy serve to reveal the actuality of the holy? Third, how may the holy be named in face of the discontinuous that affects even our religious traditions?

Remembering the Broken Chain of History

It is almost superfluous to recall that the United States of America was built on trust in human rationality and in the confidence that a new humanity could be forged in freedom from the gods and the prejudices of the Old World. A belief in a Deity and a destiny was built into the soul of the nation, but it was a belief that professed a profound optimism in the human capacity to create a new future and that exalted the human virtues of rationality, equality in opportunity, and free expression. Freedom of religion was built into the very conception of the people, but in effect religious communities strove long to achieve the fusion between their own particular identities and the fundamental beliefs of the American nation of which they desired to be fully a part. Often enough in this endeavor they found themselves at odds with both the nation and the parent bodies of the ancient world, but few of them ceased to engage in the endeavor to be both American and Jew, American and Catholic, or American and Protestant. The image of the wandering Aramean or of the Exodus to the land of promise seemed to be readily adopted by both Jew and Christian to express their sense of the destiny of the American people in this New World in which they or their forebears had found refuge from harsher days, or to which they had come in search of new possibilities for human creativity and commonwealth.

Time and tragedy, however, seem to have eroded our confidence, hampering our capacity to be hospitable to the new or to live up to the welcome inscribed on the base of the Statue of Liberty. We still honor Old Glory and sing "America the Beautiful," when our festive spirits prompt us to recall the nation's benefits, but it is increasingly common today to analyze the American character in terms of its defects,[11] or for faith congregations to give more than due time to excoriating the political and military structures of the nation and the selfish wealth-centered hearts of its people encrusted in a rank individualism.[12] The desire to be believers in a nation whose birth and destiny we continue to wish to celebrate is still present, but now it is accompanied by more diffidence in regard to the powers of the human. Perhaps the humanistic deism of the founding fathers is yielding to the need for a faith in redeeming forces, but liturgies are finding it hard to express both a love for the country and its democratic virtues and a desire for a future that is the fruit of redemption.

Our faith in America's historical destiny seems to have been corroded in different ways by two forces: the attempt in Europe to exterminate the Jewish people as a people; and America's own emergence as a world power, faced all too quickly by the specter of its failure.

The first of these corrosive forces, for which a name is next to impossible to find and for which *Holocaust* or, in other circumstances, *Shoah* is often used, affects Jews more immediately than Christians, but both faiths are inevitably bound up in its remembrance. Looking at new Jewish liturgical books one sees its omnipresence.[13] In Christian books an almost total silence obtains and the images of Israel as a people are still all too easily invoked as images of church: This is actually shocking in face of the attempt to reduce that people to *nonpeople* and seems to include an unconscious complicity in the act, by the very fact of seeing Israel replaced in God's economy by the church.

Coming to America, Reform and Conservative Jews had resolved the issue of being both Jewish and American by absorbing some of the young nation's individualism. They took their Jewish faith as an expression of personal belief, value, and ethic that could guide them in their personal and family lives but leave them open to being fully participant in the ideals and pursuits of the American people. German Jews particularly set aside the interest in Israel as a people and translated their messianism into something other than expectations for the restoration of Israel. When they became witnesses of the efforts in Europe, chief and most appalling among them in Nazi Germany, to obliterate Israel and all memory of it from the face of the earth, and when they were joined by those who were the pained survivors of this Holocaust, American Jews were forced to consider again their sense of identity as one people across many lands and to flesh out their spiritual hope in a distinctive cultural and political embodiment. Sometimes of course this was given a strictly secular interpretation, but even religious-minded Jews had to ask in faith whether the remembrance of Exodus and Israel and the oft-repeated assurance of divine promises did not include a cultural and political hope. Worship has to include the question in anguished remembrance while projecting a hope that defies the very possibility of such extinction. Specific answers leading to specific ethical and political decisions are not of course provided in books and acts of worship, but the religious identity, the remembrance of Israel and its God, and the belief in God that are central to these questions cannot be neglected. Of its very nature ritual has to do with the religious identity, the memory, and the belief in

God that shape a corporate body in relation to the ethical and the political.

Christian worship might perhaps begin to embrace the remembrance of the Shoah only when, as Americans, Christians feel the dislodging of America's secular historical identity. This is not to confuse one with the other but to be awakened to one by a sensitivity to the other. Does not the loss of a secular hope, a trust in the human, sharpen the awe with which we perceive the threat to a divine promise? Can it not translate horror at the mere fact of the slaughter of millions into dread at the attempted extermination of a people? Does not the remembrance and hope of Jesus Christ have to include an abiding hope for Israel as a people?

It will hardly be possible to come to this unless American Christians find a way of including their own history in the remembrance of Christ. Christian Liturgy professes to include events of church in the remembrance of Christ: it remembers martyrs and holy people, for instance. But it includes the historical circumstances of their martyrdom only timidly, as a mere occasion for faith's witness. It seldom makes a braver attempt to include the historical as such and to see it in the light of Christ and of this Christian witness. Yet the martyrs are very historical people: they were first honored for their significance in pointing to a power other than the imperial. What alternative power is celebrated in more modern martyrs, such as Martin Luther King and Oscar Romero, or the Uganda martyrs? The Uganda martyrs are given a feast in the Roman calendar and Martin Luther King figures on the calendar of the *Lutheran Book of Worship*, but how are they celebrated?

For centuries, the Catholic church has been more comfortable in celebrating historical deeds that confirm Christianity or that are seen as confirmed by God's grace and intervention. The Battle of Lepanto found place for a long time on the Catholic calendar and we are not unaware of the practice of the Te Deum, or of the Red Mass at the beginning of assizes. In general, American churches that celebrate Independence Day or Thanksgiving Day do include thanksgiving for the benefits given to the American people. But they ask only common gratitude for the blessings of the people and a common belief in a beneficent God. Bidding prayers upon such days undoubtedly include pleas for the homeless, the sick, the drug addict, and maybe for the victims of war. They thus embrace a sense of the common evil that lurks in things human, reminiscent of the denunciations of such social evils as the quest for power and military might that one hears in the scrutinies of the revised catechumenate of the Catholic confession. Neither plea nor denunciation, however, deals with the *historical* failure that lies behind such evil. True, a loss of confidence in the human and in the achievements of the nation does find its way in some small measure into corporate worship, but never in a manner that one could describe as bold.

The dilemma is that to be bold, worship has to be hopeful; to be part of a common history, it has to include the affirmation of a nation; and to deal with historical event, it has to be confession of lamentation in order to allow for a confession of praise. The American failure in Vietnam appears to have done the most to call the mythology of the nation into question, defying the image of a people that always stood for the good and that could influence a global history by the pursuit of its own ideologies. On the war's heels, there followed lesser failures but ones now more sharply felt, including the failure to build a country that is home to all and that assures the well-being of all its citizens, and the growing realization that the raping of the earth has rendered air and soil inhospitable to human living. The fear of nuclear warfare as final obliteration has given rise in some circles to the expression that we live "between the holocausts." Failure in a present time spawns revisionist history and allows for a recognition of past failure, but looking soberly at one's failures is a very difficult challenge, not easily embraced either by citizen or by country. The American people, however, cannot go forward without remembering as an integral part of their history the slavery of black people, the forced annexation of Hispanic peoples, and the attempts to subjugate the interests of other peoples and the earth itself to our own. The very recognition of their real achievements requires this American coming-to-terms with history.

Despite the alliance of the church with the body politic since the time of Constantine, an alliance protracted in fresh ways by the churches of the Reformation, it seems very hard for Christian communities to remember secular history in the context of Christian remembrance or to see a connection between historical failures and the church's own presence in the world and its hopes for the future. Christians are too secure in the resurrection of Christ and in its assurance of grace and salvation to see it as a challenge to the deeply human or to recognize its social and political implications. They readily enough speak of the ethical imperatives of justice and peace, or of a social gospel, but they are afraid of allowing human failure to challenge the liturgical celebration either of God and of Christ or of the human hope that these images appear to consolidate. It is easier to confess that the only impediment to divine providence and promise is the sin in the human heart than to admit that an ideally conceived political or economic order might in fact embody its measure of evil, or that Christ's promise might not have much to do with economic stability. Might God have been absent from the mainstream of the human enterprise and present only in the struggles of its victims?

Inasmuch as the fear of total failure is embodied in the image of nuclear extinction, perhaps it is from that standpoint that Christians may be able to remember the Holocaust of the Jewish people. This would mean that the violence enacted against the Jews could not be simply counted as one more outrage against the weak, numbering them along with Ukrainians and Poles, or that Jewish genocide could not be listed along with other attempts at genocide. That is not to gloss over the fact that these, too, are abominations, but it is to plead for the particular religious and historical significance of the Shoah that actually casts light on the rest and that holds up hope in the midst of evil. It was possible in an easy-going kind of way to expect the end of Israel until we witnessed the actual attempt to end it, to eliminate not only a certain number of persons but to do away with the people and its culture as a people and a culture. At that moment, we are forced to ask whether the human that comes out of a Christian history or a modern confidence in the human as such is truly human.[14] At that moment, we are forced to ask before God whether God is not more deeply involved with the fate of this people than we had allowed. At that moment we are forced to ask whether the Jesus of Jewish history is not too easily replaced by a universal human or a cosmic savior, in effect obliterating all cosmic significance from the event of the Cross. The Holocaust interrupts history, not only because it shows us where the modern can lead, but also because it implicates the belief in the presence of a redeeming God in human history. It may well be that the passionate stance of Christian communities on behalf of history's victims can become a reality only through the medium of their faith in the enduring place of Israel as a people in the divine economy. What that says to the existence of the State of Israel or to the Palestinian question is not at all clear, but the seeds of a just approach have to be planted in a remembrance of Jesus Christ that does not simply accommodate the remembrance of Israel to the image of the church.

Naturally these ruminations will be ignored if not accompanied by something more concretely affecting liturgy. First and foremost, the common lectionary of Christian churches has to deal more adequately and sensitively with the Hebrew scriptures.[15] Second, the Days of Remembrance ought to become an integral component of the Christian calendar. Third, lamentation needs to play a bigger part at the very heart of Christian remembrance.[16] Fourth, the language of history's victims has to become teacher to the churches as a whole. From recognizing the Jewish people as those whom history has made victim, we have to think also of others, lest they too be forgotten or omitted from both past and future. Without being able to elaborate on the matter here, one must wonder how black language and women's rituals will affect all liturgical expression, beyond simply liking Gospel music and being attentive to inclusive language. Fifth and finally, the products of the earth necessary to rituals have to lead us to a perception that either earth and humanity share a common history and hope, or they will be subject to a common destruction.

The Elect and the Holy

The democracy espoused and promoted by the United States has a universal appeal and is one of the principal benefits that the nation has promoted around the world. Democracy assumes that interaction between people fosters the discovery of truth and power. In several ways now, liturgies have embraced this concept, but still with some hesitation about what it does to the mediating structures of the holy. In Jewish synagogues, rabbis have to work as partners with cantors when it comes to building a repertory of liturgical music. In Catholic churches, there is face-to-face eucharist and confession. In Lutheran and Episcopal churches, ordained ministry is open to women. In all religious groups, small gatherings sit on the ground in a circle—a new symbol of communion and of the quest for the holy.

How curious that religious people embrace the sacred circle and tamper with the mediation of the divine just when voices within the nation raise questions about the illusion of democratic participation! Even while being asked to elect their representatives and to give their opinion on every subject, the American people are beginning to find that they are not in fact in control of their own lives. Still less can they effectively sway the march of the nation. What is being questioned, however, is not the ideal of communications and participation but the subject matter and the link between what is shared among the people and the life of the people.[17]

Religious groups risk adopting the circle or the face-to-face with some naïveté, partly because they have been late in discovering it as a religious mode of participation. Facing one another in ritual does not of itself imply listening for the voice of the Spirit and being attentive to its power wherever it is at work. Including women in the naming of the people or even including the feminine in the naming of God does not of itself mean that women are recognized as ministers and mediators of grace. Like democratic structures that allow for many voices but little communication of worth, the sacred circle can turn out to be only the illusion of the holy. As with democratic action that turns out to be void of power sharing, the religious circle that breeds good feeling can all too soon turn out to be void of the holy and to be simply another motive for reversionism for those who sense this.

The important thing is not the circle but what is being discovered in the circle. If that is the locus of the holy, how is the holy being named? What are the arrows pointing into and out of the circle? Whence comes the divine lightning bolt? Is this circle a conformist ritual full of nostalgia for the populism of the nation? Or is it an antiritual, made up of the wrong people? Who are the people who are called holy and in what matter is communion celebrated?

Some years ago, I wrote of households of faith in the coming church and of their importance in the recognition of God's presence in the world.[18] I did not wish to say, however, that the mere appearance of intentional communities was a sign of the Spirit or that it is enough to make people face each other in an effort at communication. I was rather pointing to the fact that it is in certain kinds of household that there appears to be a greater receptivity to the manifestations of the Spirit. Too often, these households are circles of the wrong people. We know enough about the place of the household in developing the structures of the early church to know that it could also be the locus for the maintenance of an elite or for the preservation of the church's social conformity. On the other hand, it would be equally naive to think that in later centuries, the replacement of the household by other social structures was due simply to the church's adoption of prevailing social symbols and modes of power, in place of the more evangelical. It was often charismatics, the ascetics, and the monks who were a challenge to the episcopacy derived from the household structure, for the very reason that they seemed to point to a holy and a divine not accounted for by episcopal governance.[19]

It is a time for both Christian and Jewish communities to focus more in their liturgical development on the antiritual and the liminal, not as acts and places of containment or even as manifestations of what is the real communality of organized communties, but as challenges that generate different types of power, symbol, and prayer. Victor Turner's theory of structure and *communitas* is actually quite deceptive and certainly not in the long run helpful to communities of divine revelation, for the simple reason that he sees liminality and antiritual as a corroboration of structure and formal ritual. For people of the Word, they ought more properly to be a source of power that challenges and undoes the structural, or at least they ought to unmask its relativity. Some religious communities like to talk of themselves as liminal and marginal just because they are religious and claim to profess an alternative set of values. Their liminality is, however, a grand illusion if they have not learned to be dominated by the power of the weak and to recognize who the greatest is in the kingdom of God.[20]

In asking how this affects liturgical celebration, we can start by looking at the places in our revised books that open the door to a creative integration of the marginal. Fortunately, both Christian and Jewish liturgical books allow for more communal prayer and ritual outside church and synagogue buildings. It was unfortunate for Christianity that quite early on in its history the connection between eucharist and table prayer was obscured, and that in time the only table prayer that was recognized as an expression of church was that said in monasteries. The family meal or the shared meal might be prefaced by some prayer, but its ecclesial nature was forgotten. From the Jewish side of things, in more recent times the lighting of Sabbath candles in the synagogue appears to have resulted in the secondary importance of the Sabbath meal at home. In both cases, the power that emanates from the common table is lost. Happily, the new books of both Conservative and Reform Judaism make room for the table blessing in homes and smaller groups, so that its inclusion as one of the important places of the holy may with proper polity become possible. The new book of blessings of the Roman Catholic church includes meal blessings, but unfortunately blessings still seem rather on the fringe of the church's worship as such. Yet it is in the domestic setting that the lesser voices of the church are heard and it is from there that their greatness in the kingdom can come to be recognized. Not incidentally, it is there, too, that there is most potential for generating reverence for the things of earth.

Two ritual revisions, found in different ways in Christian churches, that are of great potential for the holy are those having to do with the sick and with the dead. These rituals are located not in churches but in homes, where sickness and healing are found, and in the places allotted to the dead. Much of the ritual is such that it does not require the presence of clergy but is quite effectively the prayer of the faithful, in communion with its sick and its dead.[21] This has much to say about the places in which God is present and about the human realities that are revelatory of the divine. The rituals are such that they do not merely invite prayer for the sick and the dead; to be complete, they must actually ask and hear their witness to the sorrow of the world and to the living God in whose hope times present and times past are bound together.

Jewish messianic hope has always kept the dead very much in mind and this has taken on new force in how the victims of the Holocaust are remembered, for example, in the *Gates of Prayer* [22] and in *Siddur Sim Shalom*.[23] This is not the expression of a bland messianic expectation but a plea for the revelation of God in this tragedy and in the remembrance of its victims. If the promise of God's life embraces even such as these, how then is God to be named?

The question for all Americans in the experience of the discontinuous or of historical failure is the question of the holy. Is God present among us in our frailty and failure?

What forms does this saving presence take and what are its names and symbols?

Naming the Holy

The issue of naming is not as simple as having a designation for God or for divine manifestations. It is a matter of naming God out of an experience, of turning to God in the midst of, and even despite, certain experiences. The problem with naming God in contemporary worship occasionally looks like a quarrel over the right word, as in some discussions of inclusive language. However, it is much deeper and relates to being able to recognize the presence of God's love and compassion in the midst of life and death, and of recognizing the experiences out of which the cry is made or the naming done. What I have suggested above is that for us today the presence of the holy is to be found in the remembrance of the Holocaust, in incorporating the discontinuities of history and the failure of the human into our corporate consciousness. It is to be found precisely among the victims of history and among the marginal, or in the cry of the earth itself. This is a more awesome manifestation of God than that found in a shrine or in symbols that point to a transcendent, above and beyond the world and its suffering. The image of God as rock and foundation seems particularly apt as an expression of the holy to which the present invites us. Edward Schillebeeckx puts it well:

> To be aware of a religious foundation in God provides the strength constantly to begin again in working for man and for the world and carrying on the struggle, because in that case no single historical event is the eschatological final event, and by the same token a fiasco is not ultimately failure. . . . We need a liturgy in which we transcend both personal and individual intimacy, and also critical, socio-political concerns, from within (that is, not through an alienating rejection). . . . This awareness of being grounded in God, of persisting when every empirical

foundation and every guarantee have been removed and one
weeps over the fiasco of one's life is the mystical power
of faith.[24]

Addressing God in faith and praise is a matter of doing so
from within the memory of the event and in the midst of the
experience whence the holy comes. Such naming invites us
to transcend our own idealized view of the holy, to accept
God's coming in tragedy, in the poor and the lowly, in the
humanly marginal, in humanity's community with earth, yea
even among the dead. The naming of liturgy, like the naming
of biblical revelation, is a transfer of names that disorients
and uproots in order to redescribe and reorient. As the Almighty was named for the nomadic tribes of the Exodus, or
for the people of the kingdom brought into captivity, for the
lowly maiden of Nazareth, or for the disciples of the Crucified, so God continues to be named for those who perished
in the Holocaust and for those who survived the Holocaust,
for those who fell victim to the nation's failure in Vietnam
and for those who survived it, for the slaves who furnished
the labor for a new democratic nation and for those who now
know the weakness of building on the exploited, for the
women who survived by Sophia and for those born of these
women, for the earth exploited by human audacity and for
those who lament it. The Blessed One is the one blessed by
the sick and the suffering, by the liminal and the forgotten,
and by the compassionate who are not fearful of the invitation into such circles. We do not need so much to find new
names as to know where to utter them and to what to relate
them. The sacred circle has a tremendous power to reveal for
those who dance.

Conclusion: The Poetics of Worship

In the end, the theology of worship engages our traditions
in the poetics of worship, and it is on this basis that we can
make a positive critique of their current evolution. This poet-

ics has a threefold reference, in keeping with the three questions asked earlier.

The first reference is to remembrance, its content, and its modes. It involves the texts and rituals of past traditions and includes the retrieval of some that have been neglected or discarded as liminal. Even today, these are the traditions that remind us of the living God and the sounds in which God's voice echoes, but they have to be transposed into the new discourse brought about by tragedy.

The second reference is to the circle of our praxis, to our involvement as believers in human history. We bring into worship our commitments to persons, to communities, to earth itself and have them questioned and reshaped in that action. The metaphor of living between the holocausts expresses in some measure the nature and anxiety of our involvement. Representing the resounding of new voices, the circle may also express our hope that, free from alienation, we may still commit ourselves to God in trust, with our eyes newly open to the circles of God's manifestation.

The third reference is to the power of refiguration in the naming of the holy. Through its multiple acts of worship, a people interprets its memories and refigures its own life in the hope of life for all, the living and the dead. It imbues past, present, and future with covenant remembrance. It is in worship, that supreme act of memorial, that we find the power and the grace to overcome despair and courageously and wisely to redescribe the world that lies subject to the threat of holocaust, in the confidence that the All-Holy has not abandoned humanity and earth.

NOTES

1. Compare Vatican II, Constitution on the Sacred Liturgy, nos. 33–36 with nos. 37–40.

2. Lawrence A. Hoffman, *The Canonization of the Synagogue Service* (Notre Dame, 1979); *Beyond the Test: A Holistic Approach to Liturgy*, Jewish Literature and Culture, (Bloomington, 1987).

3. Stefan C. Reif, "Jewish Liturgical Research: Past, Present, and Future," *Journal of Jewish Studies* 34 (1983): 161–70.

4. Compare the adaptations of the prayer from *The Apostolic Tradition* in eucharistic prayer 2 of the Roman sacramentary and eucharistic prayer 4 in the *Lutheran Book of Worship*.

5. On this, see Hoffman, *Beyond the Text*, 139–43.

6. Jacob Neusner summarizes much of his work on this point in *Death and Rebirth of Judaism: The Impact of Christianity, Secularism, and the Holocaust on Jewish Faith* (New York, 1987), pp. 33–72.

7. For an interesting reflection on the future of music in the synagogue, see Lawrence A. Hoffman, "Musical Traditions and Tensions in the American Synagogue," in David Power, Mary Collins, and Mellonee Burnim, eds., *Music and the Experience of God, Concilium* 202 (Edinburgh, 1989): 30–38.

8. On this point, I would recommend the concluding reflections of Hoffman, *Beyond the Text*, pp. 172–82.

9. Commonplace distinctions now among liturgical scholars, following Victor Turner, *The Ritual Process: Structure and Anti-Structure* (London, 1969).

10. Neusner, *Death and Rebirth*, pp. 301–31.

11. Exemplified in Robert N. Bellah, et al., *Habits of the Heart: Individuals and Commitment in American Life* (Berkeley, 1985).

12. See James Dunning, "Confronting the Demons: The Social Dimensions of Conversion," in Robert Duggan, ed., *Conversion and the Catechumenate* (New York, 1984), pp. 23–42.

13. For reference to Holocaust and the State of Israel in the Passover Haggadah of both Reform and Conservative Judaism, see Hoffman, *Beyond the Text*, pp. 138–43.

14. For Christian reflections, cf. essays in Elisabeth Schüssler Fiorenza and David Tracy, eds., *The Holocaust as Interruption, Concilium* 175 (Edinburgh, 1984).

15. For a critique of present lectionary use of Hebrew Scriptures, see Gerard Sloyan, "The Lectionary as a Context for Interpretation," *Interpretation* 31 (1977): 331–38.

16. I have proposed this even for the eucharistic prayer in "The Eucharistic Prayer: Another Look," in Frank C. Senn, ed., *New Eucharistic Prayers: An Ecumenical Study of Their Development and Structure* (New York and Mahwah, 1987), pp. 239–57.

17. For how such observations touch on worship, see Michael A. Cowan, "Sacramental Moments: Appreciative Moments in the

Iron Cage,'' in Regis A. Duffy, ed., *Alternative Futures for Worship: General Introduction* (Collegeville, 1987), pp. 35–61.

18. David N. Power, ''Households of Faith in the Coming Church,'' *Worship* 57 (1983): 237–55.

19. For reflections on this phenomenon and its inherent ambiguities, see Peter Brown, *The World of Late Antiquity, AD 150–750* (Singapore, 1980). pp. 96–110.

20. In comments on greatness in the kingdom of heaven recorded in Matthew's Gospel, Jesus asks his followers to humble themselves like children and then to be always ready to receive them. Cf. Matthew 18:1–6 and 19:13–15.

21. The Roman rite has published quite complex revised rituals both for the pastoral care of the sick and for the burial of the dead. See also the sections in the *Occasional Services* of the Evangelical Lutheran Churches, and in the Episcopal *Book of Common Prayer*, and the service of death and resurrection in *The Book of Services* of the United Methodist Church.

22. See the service for Tisha Be'av and Yom Hashoah in *Shaarei Tefillah: Gates of Prayer* (New York, 1975), pp. 573–89.

23. See the service for Yom Hashoah in Jules Harlow, ed., *Siddur Sim Shalom: A Prayerbook for Shabbat, Festivals, and Weekdays* (New York, 1985), pp. 828–43, with its awesome concluding litany of places of death and resistance. See also above, Harlow's essay, ''Revising the Liturgy for Conservative Jews,'' note 20 and related text (a portion of the litany).

24. Edward Schillebeeckx, *Christ: The Experience of Jesus as Lord* (New York, 1980), p. 814.

The Poetics of Liturgy

Michael A. Signer

The Personal Dimension of the Liturgical Text

Jews and Christians have experienced significant changes
in their liturgies over the past twenty-five years. In Judaism,
Reform and Conservative worshipers have new prayer books
for Sabbath, festivals, and holy days. In addition, a trial Re-
constructionist volume for the Sabbath has just been issued,
and new Conservative and Reform Haggadahs have been
composed as well. The appearance of *The Torah: A Modern
Commentary* and *The Five Scrolls* indicate a new attention to
the study of scripture in the worship environment. The equivalent situation among Christians should be evident from the
various editorial statements earlier in this book. The new
United Methodist Hymnal, for example, is described in its
preface as "the first substantial revision of content and format since the 1870's."[1] And from a Catholic perspective, the
changes after Vatican II to vernacular worship have occasioned far more than a linguistic shift; as Kathleen Hughes
makes clear (see her essay above, "The Changing Face of
Roman Catholic Worship") translations were accompanied
by the composition of new texts for the eucharist as well as
for other sacramental occasions.

Not all these shifts have produced unalloyed joy for Jews
or for Christians, whether clergy or laity. Some discomfort is
inherent in any liturgical change, even if it be the alteration
of a simple melody, let alone the introduction of new texts.
Ironically, we are witnessing liturgical renewal that promises
"innovation through tradition," in that communities reappro-

priate ancient rites with the claim that antiquity provides religious authenticity. The reaction of many who come to worship, however, has ranged from indifference to hostility.

If we are to develop a critical stance toward liturgy, we will have to account for the worshiper as part of the process of worship itself. In that regard, it becomes clear that we should attend to the many Jews and Christians who fail to exhibit enthusiasm for our liturgical accomplishments and whose plight should evoke our empathy. Our pride in the recovery and restoration of a long-lost but authentic text may be academically interesting, but totally beside the point, in that experience of liturgical satisfaction often has more to do with nostalgia than with the rite's historical accuracy. The liturgy of our childhood is part of our emotional formation, if not our theological education.

Two illustrations may help us understand this childhood-based resistance to liturgical change. The first example derives from my own experience. One of my students sat next to me during a synagogue service at the Hebrew Union College where I teach. On this particular day the text of the morning service was the *Union Prayer Book,* the prayer book of my childhood. As the cantor played the opening hymn on the piano rather than the guitar, and the reader intoned the English prose with its elevated vocabulary, I sat dreamily back in my seat. My neighbor, however, merely fidgeted uncomfortably and eventually removed his *tallit* (prayershawl), closed his prayer book, and sat silently through the remainder of the service. When the prayers concluded, I walked out with this young man and inquired why he felt that he could not pray. He claimed, "It was not a Jewish service. I feel at home with *Gates of Prayer*—even with the guitar. But I grew up in the Conservative movement, so the *Union Prayer Book* is simply alien to me." I told him that it was the prayer book of my youth and that I was offended by his inability to share my experience. Even though I know that the *Gates of Prayer* is more authentic by historical criteria, the *Union Prayer Book* is still formative for me. Childhood is still an important prism for my liturgical aesthetics.

My second and parallel example, derived from the Catholic experience, comes from the University of Notre Dame, where a colleague recalled being approached after a eucharistic celebration by an older woman who complimented him on the "lovely liturgy" but confided, "Father, what I really miss is the sweet chanting of the canon of the Mass by the priest." Summoning up his best pastoral tone, my friend informed her that she may indeed have missed the "sweet chanting of the priest," but that it would have been impossible to "hear" the canon of the Mass, for it was always said silently. In contrast to my actual memories of the prayer book of my youth, this woman had conjured up a nostalgia of the service she had once known. I am certain that there is also a considerable gap between this woman and me in theological sophistication. What is the significant common thread is the formative factor of childhood experience.

Our cultural context creates barriers for those who come to worship. Contemporary culture emphasizes individual achievement and competence rather than interdependence and community, whereas worship at its best submerges the individual entrepreneur in the relative anonymity of his or her worshiping group. Moreover, for many Jews and Christians, the liturgical atmosphere of synagogue and church is the direct opposite of their work environment. At work they feel competent and in control, recognized and rewarded for their individual achievement. In church and synagogue, they feel infantilized by the texts of worship where both language and theology deprive them of their sense of control.

In order to comprehend their sense of deprivation at worship, we should contrast the prayer book with a text that many worshipers read more frequently, the *Wall Street Journal*. Contrast the *Journal's* "Daily Diary of the American Dream" with the *Gates of Prayer's* dream of the reign of God. On its front page alone, the *Wall Street Journal* presents a broad sweep of vision. Its many narrow columns of text create an impression of expanse and control. The two center columns summarize world and economic news. A quick scan, then, allows for a maximum comprehension of the current state of affairs, worldwide. From the center columns, the eyes move laterally to take in pithy accounts of complex issues in business and politics. The language of the articles is concise and concrete. The numerical and statistical format of much of the information leaves little opportunity for vagueness or uncertainty. By the time you complete a reading of the *Journal* you have a clear sense of the world and the direction your own affairs should take. The connection between life and the marketplace is immediate and obvious.

What a remarkable contrast to the *Gates of Prayer*, where the reader immediately views a text in two languages, English and Hebrew, the latter of which is apt to prove more baffling than informative. In any given synagogue or home there may be a broad spectrum of competence with the reading of Hebrew, but universal literacy in Hebrew prayer is virtually unknown. The English text, too, presents a challenge. While the style of some services is direct and concrete, others reveal a profound sense of poetry and figural language. It is never entirely clear whether the entire congregation comprehends the service of the day.

Moreover, beyond the visual shape of the *Gates of Prayer's* text there is its message, which contrasts starkly with daily culture. The prayer book reminds people that they are not omnipotent; its texts convey a sense of dependence on God and solidarity with the Jewish people. Individual achievement is subordinated to the community's striving for *tikkun olam* (perfecting the world) and *malkhut shamayim* (the reign of God). Jews and Christians are alike here, in that with respect to the demands in our prayer books, all of us feel vulnerable and in need of support. We argue that these values are the very essence of our religious traditions. They are necessary correctives to the so-called barbarian values in the marketplace. However, we all inhabit both worlds. Is it possible to create bridges between contemporary culture and liturgical expression without violating or distorting the latter? What type of discourse might we create between those who plan worship (and are more at home in one world) and those who come to worship (and are more comfortable in the other)?

A more profound sensitivity to language, texts, and reality might lead us away from the resistance of childhood experiences and the sense of adult infantilization within worship toward a dialogue between liturgy and culture.[2] The two worlds of contemporary culture and worship would seem to find a resonance in the two worlds suggested by Martin Heidegger's "A Dialogue on Language between a Japanese and an Inquirer." The dialogue arises out of the Japanese's search for a sense of European aesthetics, because "aesthetics furnishes us with the concepts to grasp what is of concern to us as art and poetry." When the inquirer asks why there is a need for such concepts in a rich Japanese culture, the Japanese responds, "Since the encounter with European thinking, there has come to light a certain incapacity in our language."[3] Clearly, there is a similar "incapacity" in our discourse about liturgy that moves us to develop a conceptual framework in which to have a "conversation" about what is of "concern" to us.[4] We need an archimedean lever shared by worshipers and liturgists, which will move the former toward an appreciation of the worship they attend and provide a language for the latter to reflect intelligently on the worship that they plan.

Both those who plan liturgy and those who pray would agree that aesthetics or beauty provides one appropriate criterion for a worship experience.[5] We might paraphrase Peter Berger's notion that in the modern world, liturgy is a matter of choice rather than destiny. If that is true, How might we choose what is beautiful in liturgy? More significantly, we might ask, What descriptors should we utilize in such an effort?

In *Portrait of the Artist as a Young Man*, James Joyce paraphrases Thomas Aquinas to describe the aesthetic process of judgment: "Ad pulchritudinem tria requiruntur: integritas, consonantia, claritas" ("Three things are needed for beauty: wholeness, harmony, and radiance"). For Stephen Dedalus, the protagonist, these categories are explained in relationship to the perception of an object. First, the image is luminously apprehended as self-bounded; it is self-contained as one thing in its wholeness (*integritas*). The synthesis of the immediate perception is followed by the analysis of apprehension. You apprehend the image as complex, multiple, divisible, made up of its parts, the result of its parts, and their sum as harmonious (*consonantia*). Finally, having moved through these two steps we can arrive at what the thing is in itself so that it is no other thing. We perceive its clarity (*claritas*).[6]

Joyce's representation of Aquinas's tripartite description of aesthetic perception might be a bit too ambitious for liturgical studies at present. Study of our liturgies as ritual is in its early stages. The relationship between liturgy and theology needs further exploration. Theology and legal literature (*halakhah*) are as significant as visual or intellectual perception for an aesthetic critique of Jewish worship. But in addition, if we are to move toward an aesthetic we need to develop the relationship between language and text, a poetics of worship.

Toward a Poetics of Worship

Traditionally, liturgies of both church and synagogue have recognized that worship combines gesture, oral proclamation, and text. This insight can be discerned by reading any medieval Christian pontifical or Jewish *Machzor*, where we find both texts of prayer and a careful description of the choreography of the rituals in which those texts are embedded. Take, for example, *Machzor Vitry*, originally an eleventh-century work that was expanded to become the standard twelfth- or thirteenth-century liturgical customary of Jews in northern Europe. The circumcision ceremony establishes the appropriate benedictions and prayers, but it also indicates where the infant is to be carried, who carries him, and who pays for the various festive meals. There are also prescriptions for various salves used in the healing process of the boy.[7] By contrast, in the interests of economy, modern prayer books include prayer texts and eliminate their ritual contexts.

Modern studies of Jewish liturgy too have focused almost exclusively on prayer texts and their development. Lawrence A. Hoffman has discussed the ideologies that form the sub-text of these studies.[8] The recovery of multiple texts proved the notion of diversity in the tradition. Furthermore, the discovery of changes in liturgical practice over time offers a justification for further changes. Indeed, change is now presumed; the claim with which I began is that this constant change can be experienced as fragmentation and alienation.

Hoffman claims that these developmental studies need to be augmented by a more interdisciplinary approach. He suggests, therefore, that we need to go "beyond the text" and uncover, not only the text, but also the "people, their meanings, their assumed constructs, and the ritualized patterns that make the world uniquely their own."[9] In other words, we ought to pay as much attention to the pray-ers as to the prayers.

While we may move beyond philological studies, however, we cannot move beyond language. Even as we strive to recover the nature of gesture and ritual, we have no option but to resort to written discourse for our communication. We are caught in Heidegger's "prison house of language."[10] Nevertheless, an expanded concept of language and text can provide insights as yet undisclosed by the texts. If we learn only the morphology of a language, the forms of its declensions and conjugations, we have only the elementary tools. Only when we study syntax, how the linguistic units combine to create meaning, do we reach competence.

As religious communities that revere tradition, Jews and Christians are committed to an investigation of their written liturgical traditions as the basis for contemporary expression. The conceptual model of oral versus textual communities may be helpful. Brian Stock suggests that communities in northern Europe during the eleventh and twelfth centuries that had been oral in their orientation toward authority gradually became textual, in that people adopted a new appreciation for the written word, thinking now of facts not as recorded by texts but as embodied in texts.[11] What had been a reciprocal relationship between oral and written cultures began to tip toward an emphasis on written models as a method of retrieving the past. Seeing ourselves as advanced textual communities allows us to acknowledge that our identities are embedded in texts, which, however, encode an amalgam of orality and gesture, as well as their obvious written content.

If the conceptual model of textual communities best describes our liturgical traditions, then the discipline of poetics may provide us with the fulcrum for our critical lever. Poetics, in antiquity and in some of its modern reappropriations, is grounded in the dialectical relationship of reader and text, performer and audience. I have deliberately chosen poetics over rhetoric because it seems to me that poetics focuses on larger units of meaning than rhetoric does. Poetics examines phrases, paragraphs, or chapters, inquiring about their function rather than their persuasive power. Properly utilized, the poetics of worship would investigate the "poeticity" of liturgy—how the prayers produce meaning in the reader and how the reader produces meaning in the texts that make up prayer. Poetics would not study prayers, in the sense of individual prayers and their histories, but prayerfulness.[12] Our poetic analysis of prayers reveals how the texts of prayers function to make prayer possible.

At this point in the argument it may be asserted that we have entered the abyss of the deconstructionist heresy, a caricature of which avers that the literary text has no central core of meaning save what exists in the perception of the reader. It is important to note here, therefore, that the poetics of liturgy makes assertions about textuality, not about meaning. Jacques Derrida's claim is important in this context: by reminding us that there is nothing at all outside the text, he appropriately erases the arbitrary distinction between text, speech, and experience. Isolating any of these aspects of liturgy, or privileging one of them over another, impoverishes the solidity of our critical stance.[13]

Roland Barthes has expanded the concept of textuality by
asserting that the text "is not an aesthetic product; it is a
signifying practice." We look at the text not in terms of what
it means as it lies before us like some objective thing complete unto itself but in terms of the way it signifies to us in
the act we call worship. It is a dynamic, not a static, locus
for our praying. Only in the context of the service does the
text acquire shading and nuance. Barthes captures this dyna-
mism in his assertion that the text "is not an object, it is a
work and a game." Ultimately, the "text exceeds the old literary work: there is, for example, the text of life." Here Barthes approaches the concept of text that unites the literary
work before us and the life of those who pray it.[14]

Poetics of Worship: Model and Praxis

Liturgical study has itself corroborated this call for an expanded concept of text. Gail Ramshaw claims, "Because
words change in meaning, sacred speech requires careful catechesis; lest the tradition become unrecognizable before our
ears. Always the stories of faith must be retranslated into the
latest vernacular, always, the metaphors explicated anew."[15]
One discerns here the resonance of Barthes's idea that meaning transcends the literary text even as it is embedded in it.
The task of liturgical study is to discover how meanings are
reappropriated and how traditions are mediated through every
era's sensitive translators, who live with contemporary concerns. Lawrence A. Hoffman demonstrates this convergence
of our text, translation, and reappropriation when he shows
how shifts in the narrative structure of the Passover seder,
from the biblical period through our own day, created new
images of Israel redeemed.[16]

As ritualized language, the words of our liturgical texts
convey more than doctrine: they form and mold emotions.[17]
Don E. Saliers, distinguishes between *emotion* and *affect*.
Emotions are subject to mood and impulse. Affects are actual
human traits within us. One might, for example, have an
emotional sensation of thanksgiving. However, the affective

dimension of thanksgiving would be an openness toward giving thanks. These affective categories, then, would constitute a way of our own being-in-the-world. When we address God, we ascribe various affects to God and, at the same time, educate ourselves regarding the specific affects within ourselves on which we should construct emotive states.[18] Prayer not only expresses emotion, it forms and critiques it as well. In order to pray, the worshiper requires certain affective predispositions such as gratitude, humility, awe, or wonder. By providing an opportunity to focus a diffuse set of emotions, prayer opens the individual to the potential for self-transcendence or transformation.[19] Perhaps Abraham Joshua Heschel best expressed the reciprocal relationship between prayer and pray-er when he asserted,

> What, as a rule, makes it possible for us to pray is our ability to affiliate our minds with the pattern of fixed texts, to unlock our hearts to the words and to surrender its meanings. Words stand before us as living entities full of spiritual power, of power which often surpasses the grasp of our minds. The words are often the givers, and we are the recipients. They inspire our minds and awaken our hearts.[20]

A poetics of prayer should, therefore, enable us to discern how affect (within us) and verbal signifiers (within the prayers) operate dialectically. We would be on the road to an aesthetic of liturgy that would enable us to "grasp what is of concern to us." Those who provide liturgical texts would do so only with concern for the way those texts might interact with the affects of the worshipers for whom they are intended.

Heschel takes us further into the affective domain of the worshiper by developing two suggestive categories: (1) prayer as an act of expression; (2) prayer as an act of empathy. In the first category, the worshiper sets forth a personal agenda that develops out of his or her own concerns, moods, and desires. These concerns precede the act of prayer. In the second category, prayer as an act of empathy, there is no conscious prior agenda. Rather, the worshiper imaginatively projects his or her consciousness into the words of the text, formulating an empathy for what is being read. In prayer as an act of empathy the words of the text are formative.[21]

One might be tempted to establish a hierarchy of these categories: to claim, for instance, that prayer as empathy is superior to prayer as expression, on the grounds that expression is less valid than empathy, that prayer as expression is merely a stepping stone to the higher level of prayer as empathy. There is, however, a danger in establishing hierarchies. First hierarchical thinking is not an absolute but a gender-oriented mode of thinking.[22] Second, if we accord the personal search for agenda a lower status, we ignore contemporary culture. We lose an opportunity to acknowledge the reality of individualism and achievement as it relates to the lives of our people. Our model, therefore, should treat expression and empathy as poles of a dialectical tension corresponding to the autonomous wish of the individual and the signifying text of prayer.

A poetics of expression and empathy would raise questions of how one might emphasize rubrics in the traditional service to heighten the participation of all who worship. Each signifying unit of prayer text—rubric, prayer, or individual word—can be investigated with respect to its context in the service as a whole and in the cultural environment of the congregation.

Conclusions and Commencements

What may seem highly theoretical here is actually precisely a critique of the way our prayer texts are assembled. A poetics model offers its own metalanguage for liturgical experience, which editors would do well to consider. Experience/empathy is not simply a rephrasing of the well-known debate in Jewish liturgical theology about *Keva* and *Kavvanah* (fixed prayer vs. spontaneous prayers). Rather, it is a conceptual model that validates both the intuition and agenda of the culture-bound individual and the formative aspects of

language. Poetics may reveal other underemphasized aspects
of liturgy and provide new avenues for enriching worship.

One might consider the potential of the reader/text model
for planning liturgy. Even assemblers of text must recognize
that the reader and the process of reading matter as much as
the text they read; all the more so, those who direct worship
must have both text and reader in mind. Barthes and Derrida
warn against absolutizing the text as a series of concrete
fixed meanings. Text is the structuration of meaning, not
meaning itself. By acknowledging the reciprocity of reader/
text as the creation of meaning, the liturgist can focus on
enriching the moment of encounter. The worship leader
should work from the perspective of Ramshaw's "sacred
rhetoric," Saliers's "affective theology," or Heschel's "experience and empathy" in order to understand how words
produce meanings in readers and readers have impact on
words. Paul Ricoeur describes the personal appropriation of a
text as culminating "in the self-interpretation of a subject."
We should arise from prayer understanding ourselves "better . . . differently . . . or simply beginning to understand"
who we are.[23]

Further, poetics would urge liturgical writers and planners
to explore the liturgical praxis of speech and silence. To what
extent must the meaning of prayer be revealed by explicit oral
commentary from the leader of the service? To what degree
can moments of silence provide for individual commentary
and reflection by the participants? Intensified in Jewish worship where the service provides rabbinic texts for study inter-
laced with more explicit genres of prayer, this problem arises
in any service where the word is proclaimed or encountered
against the backdrop of a traditional body of exegesis.

As this volume demonstrates, our churches and synagogues abound with new prayer texts. They are just the beginning. We can expect new editions to proliferate as our
experience with them clarifies both how well and how poorly
they were put together. A critique from the point of view of
poetics urges us to take the pray-ers as seriously as the
prayers; to grant equal validity both to the contemporary

culture that the reader brings to prayer and to the historical tradition whence we derive the prayer texts that we give the reader. It urges us to see the text in the context of how it signifies in all its textuality—its differing rubrics, its layout and design, the way it is ordered from beginning to end, even its accompanying silences. It leads us to the possibility that worshipers may indeed be transformed by their worship.

NOTES

1. *The United Methodist Hymnal* (Nashville, 1989), p. v.

2. For an excellent discussion of the relationship between language, text, and reality, see David Tracy, *Plurality and Ambiguity: Hermeneutics, Religion, Hope* (San Francisco, 1987), pp. 47–65, which synthesizes the work of linguists, structuralists, and psychoanalytic literary criticism.

3. Martin Heidegger, *On the Way to Language* (San Francisco, 1982), pp. 2–3.

4. The idea of "conversation" is developed by Tracy, *Plurality and Ambiguity,* pp. 1–27. On the relationship between "conversation" and literary texts as "discourse," see Paul Ricoeur, "What Is a Text? Explanation and Understanding," in John B. Thompson, ed., *Hermeneutics and the Human Sciences* (Cambridge, 1984), pp. 145–64.

5. See Lawrence A. Hoffman, *The Art of Public Prayer: Not for Clergy Only* (Washington, 1988), pp. 117–18.

6. James Joyce, *Portrait of the Artist as a Young Man* (New York, Penguin ed., 1976), 211–13. I would like to thank Rev. Michael Himes of the University of Notre Dame, Department of Theology, for calling this reference to my attention.

7. S. A. Hurwitz, ed., *Machzor Vitry* (1923), reprint ed. (Jerusalem, 1963), pp. 616–28.

8. Lawrence A. Hoffman, *Beyond the Text: A Holistic Approach to Liturgy,* Jewish Literature and Culture (Bloomington, Ind., 1987).

9. Ibid., p. 182. Hoffman sets out his critique of the philological paradigm of liturgical research in the introduction (pp. 1–19) and reveals its weaknesses in his conclusion (pp. 172–82).

10. Martin Heidegger, "The Nature of Language," in *On the Way to Language,* pp. 57–108.

11. Brian Stock, *The Implications of Literacy: Written Language and Models of Interpretation in the Eleventh and Twelfth Centuries* (Princeton, 1983), p. 62. Stock's examination of the eucharistic controversies may be of interest to students of liturgical history and theology (see "The Eucharist and Nature," pp. 241–325). Students of medieval literature and culture provide various approaches to a broader concept of textuality. Cf. K. Brownlee and S. Nichols, eds., *Images of Power: Medieval History/Discourse/Literature,* Yale French Studies 70 (1986); R. Howard Bloch, *Etymologies and Genealogies: A Literary Anthropology of the French Middle Ages* (Chicago, 1983).

12. I have paraphrased Tzvetan Todorov, *The Poetics of Prose* (Ithaca, N.Y., 1977), p. 35: "What it [poetics] studies is not poetry or literature, but 'poeticity' or 'literariness.' The individual work is not an ultimate goal for poetics; if it pauses over one work rather than another, it is because such a work reveals more distinctly the properties of literary discourse. Poetics will have to study not the already existing literary forms, but, starting from them, a sum of possible forms: what literature can be rather than what it *is.*"

13. Alan Bloom, *The Closing of the American Mind* (New York, 1987), gives the most popular critique of the deconstructionist argument. However, E. D. Hirsch, Jr., *Validity in Interpretation* (New Haven, 1967), is a much more powerful attack. Derrida's arguments are summarized and explained in Jonathan Culler, *Structuralist Poetics* (London, 1975). Meir Sternberg (*The Poetics of Biblical Narrative: Ideological Literature and the Drama of Reading* [Bloomington, Ind., 1985], pp. 1–57) demonstrates the rich possibilities opened by Derrida and others for utilizing arguments about textuality rather than multiple meaning to develop a poetics approach to biblical literature.

14. Roland Barthes, *The Semiotic Challenge* (New York, 1988), p. 7. Barthes traces his writings through three movements: amazement, science, and text (pp. 1–8). At each stage of development his work becomes more sensitive to the way that structures open possibilities of interpretation, rather than narrowing interpretive horizons. Meaning is anchored by context, more than by single phrases or words within a literary work. Not just any meaning is possible.

15. Gail Ramshaw-Schmidt, *Christ in Sacred Speech* (Philadelphia, 1986), p. 33.

16. Hoffman, *Beyond the Text,* pp. 75–144. Hoffman's structuralist and anthropological approach owes much to poetic textual analysis.

17. On which, generally, see David N. Kertzer, *Ritual, Politics, and Power* (New Haven, 1988), pp. 99–101.

18. Don E. Saliers, *The Soul in Paraphrase* (New York, 1980), p. 29. These affective categories seem to carry the status of "prejudice" or "questions" in Hans Georg Gadamer's hermeneutical system. Cf. Hans Georg Gadamer, "The Universality of the Hermeneutical Problem," in *Philosophical Hermeneutics* (Berkeley, 1976), pp. 3–17.

19. On self-transformation in Jewish ritual, see Jacob Neusner, *The Enchantments of Judaism* (New York, 1987).

20. Abraham Joshua Heschel, *Quest for God* (1954), reprint ed. (New York, 1987), p. 23.

21. Heschel, *Quest for God,* pp. 27–32.

22. Cf. Elisabeth Schüssler Fiorenza, *Bread Not Stone: The Challenge of Feminist Biblical Interpretation* (Boston, 1985); and Carol Gilligan, *In a Different Voice* (Cambridge, Mass., 1983).

23. Ricoeur, "What Is a Text?" p. 158. For the relevance of Ricoeur's hermeneutics to the appropriation and translation of classical texts generally, cf. Werner G. Jeanrond, *Text and Interpretation as Categories of Theological Thinking* (New York, 1988), pp. 37–63; and David Tracy, *The Analogical Imagination: Christian Theology and the Culture of Pluralism* (New York, 1981).

The Missing Element of Women's Experience

JANET WALTON

No one ever told us we had to study our lives,
make of our lives a study. . . .
But there come times—perhaps this is one of them—
when we have to take ourselves more seriously or die;
when we have to pull back from the incantations,
rhythms we've moved to thoughtlessly,
and disenthrall ourselves, bestow
ourselves to silence, or a severer listening . . . [1]

All too often liturgies proceed as if gender, culture, race, class, sexual preference do not affect how the whole community prays. For centuries, an androcentric and sometimes misogynist fixed tradition has dictated the most appropriate and authentic way to pray. As scholars and leaders of worship, men have been the primary preservers and transmitters of this tradition. That liturgy has been based on norms established by men in which male experience is deemed the primary reflection of divine-human relationships comes, therefore, as no surprise. Now feminists, in academic as well as church and synagogue settings, have begun to identify the limitations of this situation and its inherent injustice.

The time has come for many women, in Adrienne Rich's words, "to take ourselves more seriously or die." What will this mean for those of us concerned about prayer and ritual? It requires us to identify the dishonesty of liturgical experiences that reinforce women's inferiority, to acknowledge the distortion of symbols and myths that are intended to sustain us in the search for the holy. Calling for collective, careful scrutiny, change demands a letting go of "incantations, rhythms we've moved to thoughtlessly," and a rediscovery of those symbols that offer genuine moments of transformation and solidarity for everyone. Nothing can be taken for granted in this examination. The architecture of synagogue and church buildings and the furniture in them, the metaphors, graphic images, texts, sounds, movements, and leadership used in our liturgies—all these convey profound understandings about divine-human relationships. What these symbols reveal affects the identity and the faith and ultimately the memory of the whole praying community.

Both through "a severer listening" and through "silence," feminists have come to offer a critique of institutional liturgies. By probing the essence of our own experiences, feminists are uncovering those places where the divine and human meet.[2] This work is being enhanced by recent scholarship in many disciplines, primarily theology, biblical studies, ethics, sociology, anthropology, philosophy, and literary criticism.

A feminist liturgical critique might well be expected to look first at traditional language—for example, the assumption, often made, that masculine nouns and pronouns can be understood as being inclusive of men and women alike (as if *man* or *mankind* denotes all human beings); or the exclusion of our foremothers from our traditions' sacred histories (as if "Abraham, Isaac, and Jacob" implies "Sarah, Rebekah, Rachel, and Leah" too, or, similarly, as if "God of our fathers" means "God of all our ancestors"); or, as a final example, the portrayal of God and God incarnate in exclusively masculine form, masculine metaphor, masculine guise. This central concern of feminists is discussed earlier in this book (see above, the essays in part 2). As those comments by editors and planners of the various worship books indicate, the limitations of exclusive language have at least become a primary agendum for most denominations and movements. But language concerns, important as they are, are merely a literary manifestation of a deeper-seated problem, namely, the

skewing of our worship patterns in form and content to reflect how men, but not women, have experienced reality.
Therefore, the present chapter addresses three other, nonlin-
guistic aspects of feminist liturgical critique, elements of our
worship equally important but sometimes less often acknowledged in churches and synagogues: embodiment, authority;
connection.[3]

EMBODIMENT

In 1973, the publication of the work of a women's collective in Boston signaled a pivotal event for many women and
men. For the first time it put in clear, direct words an emerging awareness of the connection between the ways women
perceive their bodies and the ways they identify themselves.
This group's research, entitled *Our Bodies, Our Selves,* was
read by millions of women, primarily white and middle-class
North Americans. (A second edition, published in 1984, addresses the interests of a much broader sampling of women.)
The popularity of the book attests to the critical need it addressed. How women's bodies have been viewed and abused
in our society influences directly women's ways of perceiving and relating to ourselves and all others, including God.

> For us body education is core education. Our bodies are the
> physical bases from which we move into the world; ignorance,
> uncertainty—even, at worst, shame about our physical selves
> create in us an alienation from ourselves that keeps us from be-
> ing the whole people that we could be.[4]

Women's bodies are a profound source of knowledge. Our
rhythmic cycles and reproductive experiences provide unparalleled understandings of the processes of death, life, and
development that regularly challenge every human being.
Women's bodies reflect the inevitability of death, its uncon-
trollable insistence as well as its necessity as a precursor of
new life. Women's bodies mirror processes of growth and the
pain, anticipation, persistence, and wonder that accompany

it. Yet many religious contexts view these same bodies primarily as sources of evil, as temptations to men. Women's physical functioning, such as menstruation or giving birth, has been considered unclean, a source of contamination. As a result, important expressions of women's embodied experiences have been devalued and the wisdom available therein has been ignored. I refer to experiences of menarche, menstruation, pregnancy, childbirth, and menopause. Even shattering experiences—unwanted pregnancy, abortion, mastectomy, rape, incest, marital rape, and battering—teach their own deep lessons. In a misogynist world, women are often taught to hate their bodies and sometimes even to mutilate them through starvation and other forms of self-abuse. Yet these very same bodies make possible the continuation of the human race.

Feminists challenge common misperceptions about women's bodies. They name the violence inherent in that idealized female form from which advertisers, cosmetic surgeons, diet entrepreneurs, and fashion designers make so much profit. Feminists thus reject the suggestion that an invitation to men's pleasure inheres in how a woman moves or holds her body. But they are equally adamant in their contention that body experience is an integral part of the lived reality of the person whose body it is and, as such, is an invaluable source for the recognition of truth, beauty, and justice.

In the liturgical settings that most of us have inherited, however, we have been taught to restrict what we know about ourselves and others (including God) primarily to verbal language. Embodied knowledge is acknowledged at most in processions, bowing, swaying from side to side (or back and forth, as in traditional Jewish *davening*), shaking each other's hands or embracing at the sharing of peace. Deeply felt embodied emotional involvement is kept to a minimum. Passion, grief, utter joy—in fact, any burst of feeling that liturgy might be expected to evoke—is well controlled.

Deeply moved by the experience of many women's struggles to cherish their own bodies, feminists now challenge church and synagogue to expand their liturgical vocabularies to respect embodied knowledge more fully. Clearly, this means engaging our bodies in more active, sometimes spontaneous, movement within our worship; but it also urges us to acknowledge the divine metaphors inherent in body shape and functioning. What we know about God and ourselves through our bodies is yet another means to the discovery of divine-human relationships.

In such worshiping communities the pencil-thin human form would not be idealized as saintly or beautiful. Rather, all shapes, sizes, and colors would be cherished as precious elements of divine revelation. A Christian community that took enfleshment (incarnation) seriously might reflect on the relationship between women's regular shedding of menstrual blood and the meaning of the shedding of Christ's blood. Menstruation offers a concrete example of the interrelationship of death and life that Jesus' death symbolizes.

Such Christians might also look with fresh consideration at some artists' depictions of crucifixes with female forms nailed to them, seeing therein the connection between the violence employed in the death of Jesus and the physical and emotional abuse that many women know through their bodies.[5] Those bodies are all too often brusied, broken, and twisted for the sake of others' greed and pleasure. Female figures on crosses, although labeled blasphemous by some, can be transforming for both women and men, even for those who are complicit in different ways in the abuse of women's bodies. Such feminine crucifixions expose evil and invite those responsible for its perpetuation to change their ways and ask forgiveness.

Attempts to acknowledge our bodies as significant conveyers of divine/human expression are more and more common in feminist liturgical communities. Noteworthy, for example, is the reclamation of the ancient Jewish new-moon ritual with its inherent symbolic parallelism to women's menstrual cycle. Almost two thousand years ago, the new moon was honored as a women's holy day; now, once again, Jewish feminists are devising new-moon rituals that draw on that almost forgotten tradition and reflect the women's own embodied experience. In this and other ways, feminists ponder specific experiences in women's lives such as menarche, menopause, pregnancy, birth, and even miscarriage, hysterectomy, abortion, and rape. Rather than ignore these events or accept them all as equally inevitable, feminists acknowledge and, in some cases, honor them as opportunities for reflection, invitations to fuller and more just human living.

Conscious of the power of ritual experience, feminists challenge the institutionalized ritual gatherings of church and synagogue to embody a more holistic response to divine-human relationships. They invite liturgical assemblies to cherish human flesh as an unparalleled source of divine and human revelation. Baby Suggs, a character in Toni Morrison's *Beloved* sets an example when she calls people to communal prayer by inviting them to dance, to cry, to laugh. "Here," she says, "in this place, we flesh; flesh that weeps, laughs; flesh that dances on bare feet in grass. Love it. Love it hard."[6] Such love, such respect, for our bodies offers unique access to God and to one another.

AUTHORITY

Determining appropriate symbols for a community's worship is an awesome responsibility, requiring not only a profound theoretical or intuitive grasp of how symbols work and an understanding of the history of their interpretation but also an ability to interact with their multilayered meanings. This ability presumes a capacity to *listen* to symbols in order to hear the significance of their rhythms of silence and speech; demands the willingness to *feel* their emotion so as to experience a total encounter with them; calls for *insistent attention* to the ways symbols disclose connections with the struggles and joys of a community's life.

Throughout much of liturgical history, the right to discern what symbols were appropriate and who could embody them was bestowed through ordination or won through academic expertise. Such people were deemed "the authorities" and

given power over others. Granting this power to selected individuals assumed that preparation for ordination had provided requisite skills. It presupposed as well that scholarship,
sometimes quite isolated from a community's life, nonetheless offered the most important criteria for decision making
about appropriate symbols for public prayer. To be sure, liturgical leaders do have an important perspective and scholars' research may offer significant input, but this twofold
dialogue is not enough. Many feminists argue that such hierarchical decision making is inappropriate in its very essence,
in that it ignores the most significant authoritative partner in
the dialogue: the community itself.

To feminists, authority implies partnership rather than
domination, invites collaboration rather than control,[7] respects difference more than similarity. Thus, it enjoins many,
rather than a few, to cooperate in decision making on the
presumption that each person has power.

The authority of the community is not easy to discern.
Not found in a single person or source, it can be difficult to
identify. It is often not orderly. The expression of people's
experiences does not necessarily follow a linear movement
with easily perceived step-by-step logic. It is not predictable.
People who spend most of their time in activities unrelated to
the study of liturgical practices may change their minds from
week to week about the significance of a particular symbol
for them. The authority of a community may not emerge only
from the most articulate or well-educated people. In the
midst of this welter, persistent listening will be required. Inevitably, moving ahead will be uncomfortable, sometimes
challenging the most cherished traditions. It does not dare to
claim certainty, since certitude so often masks an unwilling-
ness to change or to see things differently.

The practice of delegating to the few, rather than to the
many, the exclusive power to determine the appropriate forms
of worship is inherently flawed: the authority that such a system produces will inevitably respond overwhelmingly to the
desires of dominant groups but pay only minimum attention
to the insights of marginalized persons. The results are

readily predictable. Some of the people whom authority passes over manage to leave their church or synagogue and begin another. Many more feel frustrated but find it difficult to articulate it; concluding that religious rituals are meaningless, they discontinue their participation. Still others struggle to make the changes that are required to reflect the pluralistic nature of the worshiping community.

Feminists follow similar patterns. The formation of women-church and the movement among some women to join covens indicates that withdrawal from Jewish and Christian institutional communities is a viable option, permanently or temporarily. Other feminists do not imagine that liturgy can be different, so they put up with what they have. Some seek structures of meaning in other than the classic religious sources, that is, through artistic expressions, or observances of holidays, or gatherings of friends and families. Still others attempt to rediscover what is lacking in familiar traditions and incorporate the missing element in renewed forms. These feminists believe that the power to create can emanate from every individual.

Feminists in each of these categories are offering significant correctives to traditional conceptions of authority. In the interlacing of threads that weaves each to the other there lies a deep recognition that the need for change is not being met. Some recommend obvious examples of ways to accomplish it. They include suggestions—even demands—about the choice and style of leaders, expansion of the canon, new ways of perceiving divine reality, more variable forms of liturgy. A word now about each of these.

Choice and Style of Leaders

Authority rooted in the whole community is best symbolized by a diversity of leaders. Not only does this principle call forth women as well as men, people from minority races and cultures as well from dominant ones, unlearned as well as well-educated, poor as well as rich, but it implies also multiple leaders of worship during one celebration. Contrary to popular misconceptions, worship that is directed by a single leader does not necessarily insure solidarity among the worshipers. Rather, all too often when there is one leader, especially one representing the dominant class, worshipers of other classes are disenfranchised. Forfeiting their power to influence and to act upon the ritual in which they find themselves, they become passive, doing their best not to think about what they are doing or convincing themselves that they do not care. Either way, dynamic dialogue is limited.

For too many years the articulation of public prayer has reinforced hierarchical divisions. Men pray in the name of women; whites (in other than historically black churches) lead blacks; the rich speak for the poor. Since religious leadership generally demands advanced education or ordination, this tradition of a self-perpetuating elite is difficult to change. However, its very retention denies the especially distinctive moments that true liturgy entails: a liminal space where status is less important than ability to love, where graduate degrees are less important than acting justly, where no person's experience matters more or less than any other's.

Feminism challenges liturgical communities to take their internal diversity seriously and to symbolize it with new patterns of leadership. Designing a model that requires all members of the congregation to function authoritatively in some way would invite a freshness and a respect for individual and cultural differences. In such a model, distinctive experiences would be welcomed and honored. Older women, young children, questioning teenagers, homosexual or lesbian couples, homeless people, refugees, interracial families—none of these would be expected to shut out their lived realities in order to fit in. Rather, they would be called on to share what they know as a significant expression of the unpredictable, multifaceted experience of God's presence. Such mutual reverence would offer an authentic base for solidarity.

An enabling style of leadership is therefore crucial. Since people view their membership in a synagogue or church from a wide spectrum of need—whether from social necessity, "heavenly insurance," revolutionary inspiration, a place of comfort, or a space to work out one's faith in a community—forging a sense of solidarity is no easy task. It requires uncommon stamina and persistence. Shared responsibility renders it possible.

Finally, shared liturgical leadership gives us models for relationships more consistent with today's needs. Our world's problems cannot be solved by an elected or appointed elite. To make decisions from the strength of a diversity of people will demand new skills. Not the least of them is the ability to raise up hitherto silent voices, to hear them, and to work with them. Liturgical leadership nullifies its own distinctive power when it imitates hierarchical leadership determined by majority vote. Feminists, whose voices have long been imprisoned, see that the unearthed riches of mutuality and collaboration in all aspects of liturgical expression would begin with new leadership.

Expansion of the Canon

The use of scripture as an unquestioned authoritative resource central to every liturgical experience is no longer acceptable to some feminists. Since scripture has been inescapably influenced by patriarchal values, the reading of many passages, especially as an honored text, is at best inadequate and, at worst, violent.

Some biblical scholars argue for a feminist interpretation of scripture. The "interpretation of" the Bible's "content is forever changing," says Phyllis Trible; new methods of biblical study regularly uncover neglected traditions that "reveal countervoices within a patriarchal document."[8] Accompanied by an ever-growing body of substantiating scholarship, this position is increasingly respected and, in fact, welcomed. It has opened windows long considered shut. Such investigation has laid bare texts that "show the inferiority, subordination, and abuse of the female in ancient Israel and the early church," while at the same time revealing some biblical passages that offer an internal corrective to the sexism of scripture as a whole. Furthermore, this research reveals rarely encountered texts, "tales of terror" that have been systematically ignored in traditional lectionaries. Yet they echo the experience of female victims of abuse. Raising their stories to the level of public proclamation is nothing less than a theological act that "seeks to redeem the [present] time."[9] Uncovering such missing interpretations and texts is no small gain.

However, the canonizing of scripture as the sole essential reading, the one that best contains the only and the best ideals of religious commitment, the primary source of divine-human revelation, and therefore the source more sacred than any other, is itself a suspicious act. This is "everyone's text," we are told; but how can a text written in a misogynist context be paradigmatic for anyone except the dominant culture that it reinforces? "Surely people recognize the context in which a text is written," comes the reply; "they can discriminate what a text may have meant in its original milieu from what moderns should make of it, as they hear it proclaimed." But again, how is it possible for worshiping communities without advanced education in biblical studies and the culture of late antiquity to recognize the same subtle nuances in the text that the scholars hear? The codes of household duty in Ephesians 5:22–23 offer an example: "Wives, be submissive to your husbands, as to the Lord. For the husband is the head of the wife, as Christ is the head of the church." These verses legitimate wife abuse. No interpretation can override the power conveyed in the hearing of this text. A feminist critique enjoins communities not to eliminate scripture entirely but to use it more judiciously; demands the inclusion in the canon of other narratives that begin with an awareness of our androcentric history and consciously address a correction; calls for stories of women saints in every historical period, including the present one, for such stories would establish the value of women's differences, reject their innate inferiority, and claim their ability to interpret truth. Freed from inherent sexism, these accounts would not need the same corrective interpretations. What is considered sacred or canonical would be expanded to include examples and metaphors with which contemporary women and men can readily identify.[10]

New Ways of Perceiving Divine Reality

At the conclusion of Ntozake Shaange's play "For Colored Girls Who Have Considered Suicide When the Rainbow Is Enuf," a tall black woman cries out, "I found God in myself and I loved her fiercely." For many women, from all ethnic and racial backgrounds, such a declaration has been pivotal in developing our own self-understanding and our relationship with God. For black women, it affirms the uniqueness and beauty of being a black female.[11] For them and for other women it articulates a love of self in a society where too many women and young girls learn to hate themselves or, at best, to distrust themselves, subject as they are to so much emotional and physical violence.

Women's awareness of their own worth is intimately connected to both the naming of God and our images of God. As such it has deep implications for liturgical communities. Limiting perceptions of the divine reality, partriarchy insures that women and men will identify divine reality solely through male experience and primarily through the word *Father.* For some women, the father image is useful. It allows them to transcend the weaknesses of unreliable fathers and even their crimes of incest and neglect.[12] For others the image is connected with the comfort, love, and support that they have experienced from their fathers. For these women, the image discloses some important aspects of divine reality.

Other women though—and men too—have experienced the unreliability, at best, and cruelty, at worst, of human fathers; for them to pray to their "Father" is not only not helpful but even unbelievable, connoting disdain, neglect, and violence. However, as if oblivious to the experience of actual worshipers, divine reality in our inherited Christian and Jewish traditions has always been expressed by male imagery. No women's experience of any kind has been similarly examined for its authenticity and appropriateness as an expression of the divine. Therefore, knowingly or not, women have internalized the distorted notion that men more perfectly image God. Such implicit claims of male chosenness legitimate women's second-class status.

Similarly, some black women have imaged God only through white experience. In *The Color Purple,* Alice Walker points to this reality through a conversation between Shug Avery (a wise friend) and Celie (the primary character of the book). "Tell me what your God look like, Celie. . . . Okay I say. He big and old and tall and graybearded and white. . . . "[13] What human beings see in a dominant white male culture influences how they subsequently conceive of God. Just as white males are authoritative and powerful in our human experiences, so too must God be the best of white males. To image God white and male implies the subordination of blacks and especially black women.

Many feminists thus strive to change perceptions of divine reality, skewed by white male assertions about it, by working with the principle of diversity as more consistent with a God who cannot be captured in a single title. Relational images of God as Mother, Lover, and Friend, as well as multiple experiences of goddess traditions are helpful here.[14] Divine unity need not be threatened by such diversity. Unilateral dominance is more likely to shatter unity, rendering people invisible and passive rather than articulate and involved. As Elizabeth Johnson points out (paraphrasing Karl Rahner), "The truth of the mystery of God and liberation of human beings grow in direct and not inverse proportion."[15]

Variable Forms of Liturgy

Hierarchical forms insure dominance. One leader, or a group of leaders positioned hierarchically, symbolizes a line or stratification of power and in some cases implies that these persons are endowed with a special holiness. Though some may hold that hierarchical forms contribute significantly to an experience of solidarity, feminists counter with the claim that solidarity actually suffers when active participation declines. While many define liturgy as the "work of the people" (indeed, that is its etymological meaning), in actual practice only lip service is paid to this principle.

Liturgical leaders argue further that most people do not know enough about worship since they are not educated in the disciplines that affect liturgical expression. Therefore, they say, the planning, leading, and evaluating belong to those who have studied the issues involved. This attitude has motivated some feminists to experiment with forms of worship that have no hierarchical control or, at least, not the kind of power that derives from education or ordination. Forms are chosen to suit the occasion. The primary goal is to provide opportunity for everyone's involvement. Indeed the guiding presumption is that the meaning of the experience is mediated through each member moving interdependently with the group. Over periods of time, patterns emerge. However, these patterns do not become authoritative or normative; they are simply informative. They suggest helpful rhythms and methods for engagement. They make clear what to avoid. Neither chaos nor discomfort characterizes nonhierarchical forms. Rather, most participants find them engaging, fresh, and evocative. No one can count on any other person to do something for her or to express his experience. That responsibility belongs to each person. What results from this kind of liturgy is interdependence, solidarity, compassion, and authenticity at a profound level.

CONNECTION

Within feminist scholarship much attention is being focused on *connection*. Metaphors like circles, webs, and spinning are common. In contrast to hierarchy, separation, and subsequent alienation, bonding images suggest models of sharing and mutual respect. Experiences of connection can inspire people who have enjoyed less privilege to develop a sense of self-respect and confidence. They can offer a context for challenging unjust distribution of power and an incentive to continue struggling against it. Connection, then, implies the presumption that all women bond with each other by virtue of their shared femaleness.

However, a word of caution is in order here. Trying to establish deeper connection can lead to yet other forms of domination, e.g., the privilege of white women over ethnic women or women of color, or of the middle class over the poor. Susan Thistlethwaite argues convincingly that white feminist theology has often assumed similarities among women that do not exist. "The class bias of white feminism" undervalues the experiences of other women. "The route of selfhood," Thistlethwaite maintains, "must lie both in claiming the truths of" black women's "lived experience and in being deeply suspicious of their connections to the dominant American culture and its class and race biases."[16]

Discussion of connection continues nonetheless to characterize feminist liturgical critique. What has been missing from many Jewish and Christian liturgies is not only opportunity for connection (with healthy suspicions of what this bonding requires and implies) but also evidence of how the symbols of liturgy connect to the lived realities of women's lives.

Liturgy is an act. It is not simply idle talk or even inspiring talk but genuine dialogue and an active expression of relationships. To engage in such activity requires a perspective freed from dominant cultural biases. In this place, for this brief time, we see each other differently. We see each other, so to speak, as God sees us, quite apart from status, gender, level of education, or other societal marks of success. Seeing is not all. We also ask something of each other. We ask each other to express the reality of the covenanting God by building tangible relationships marked first and foremost by love and justice. We ask each other to change, and to dare to challenge any values contrary to change that society affirms.

A feminist liturgical critique calls attention to the fact that churches and synagogues have perpetuated, albeit unwittingly, a system that has denied women's memory and

identity and thus women's connections through its use of androcentric language and symbols. This system has also ne-
gated our potential to act. How often one hears in women's
gatherings, "If I had ever known I wasn't the only one who
felt so inadequate . . . who was victimized sexually as a
child . . . who hated her body . . . who was confused about
priorities between family and job . . . " If we are going to
ask people to live out a loving relationship, we have to presume some experience of it. All too often liturgy has reinforced women's worst fears about themselves. Marjorie
Procter-Smith asks: "Is liturgy one of the 'forms created' to
reorganize victimization? Does the liturgy 'translate violence'
into beautiful forms, disguising its danger for women?"[17]

Liturgy that is safe and ultimately transforming for women
requires an examination of every word, every gesture, every
shape, every sound, and every image. Of each we ask the
question: Is it true for us?[18] One poignant illustration
emerges from a further analysis of the Father language for
God. Procter-Smith points out that women abused by fathers
or husbands identify this violence as divinely sanctioned.
"The effect of Father-God language, then, given our patriarchal social and familial structures, is to legitimate male dominance and violence and to inhibit women's legitimate anger
and protest against such treatment."[19] It is as if to say that
such male behavior is not only natural but even Godlike; that
to act differently would imply a willingness to challenge God.
Like it or not, a truth must be faced: for many abused
women, the official divine metaphor of *Father* as one who is
compassionate, just, and loving is simply not true. Bowing or
kneeling cease to be suitable gestures for these women and
many others to express their awe of God's care and presence,
since such submissive postures merely reaffirm the disem-
powerment of servitude. Worse still, bowing and kneeling before another are also highly symbolic and even precisely
reminiscent of postures that abused women are forced to assume. They portray women as being at everyone's beck and
call, too often at the expense of their own lives, and give the
impression that this slavish subordination of women (even if

they are trained to go along with it) is somehow divinely sanctioned.

Feminists challenge synagogues and churches to recognize that the vision of the divine-human relationships symbolized in our liturgies is not just incomplete: it is too often untrue and demeaning. To know the divine and human power disclosed in liturgy and to feel the liberation that accompanies such an encounter requires change, the acquiring of new skills. Adrienne Rich offers this suggestion: "We should try the simple exercises first and slowly go on trying the hard ones, practicing till strength and accuracy become one with the daring leap into transcendence."[20]

Communities might begin by naming our differences, relishing the mystery of God unfolding uniquely in them. From there we will be led to leap more confidently, daring to trust that the Holy One is known through a much broader spectrum of experience than previously imagined. We will discover that "the study of our lives" opens us to a whole new journey with its free-falls, its pain, its limitless demands.

> No one who survives to speak
> new language, has avoided this:
> the cutting-away of an old force that held her
> rooted to an old ground. . . . [21]

Yet our survival as vital liturgical communities requires no less than this: letting go of "the [old] incantations" and discovering what is right before our eyes.

NOTES

1. Adrienne Rich, "Transcendental Etude," in *The Dream of a Common Language* (New York, 1978), pp. 73–75.

2. At one time I took for granted that the word *feminist* was an inclusive term. However, I am clear now that it presumes a universal understanding that does not respect the diversity of women's experiences and needs, especially those shaped by race, class, culture, and sexual preference. For this reason, I qualify my use of the word *women* by suggesting "some" rather than "all." I write here from my experience as a white, middle-class woman, informed generously by the experiences of other women from a variety of

backgrounds—especially by Ann Patrick Ware and others with whom I regularly gather for liturgy.

3. This chapter reflects collaborative work between me and Rabbi Margaret Moers Wenig, Instructor in Liturgy and Homiletics at the Hebrew Union College–Jewish Institute of Religion, New York School, in preparation for a presentation on this topic at the 1988 Notre Dame conference, Two Liturgical Traditions.

4. The Boston Women's Health Book Collective, *The New Our Bodies, Ourselves* (New York, 1984), p. xix.

5. For further discussion, see Janet Walton, *Art and Worship: A Vital Connection* (Wilmington, 1988), pp. 105–7.

6. Toni Morrison, *Beloved* (New York, 1987), p. 88.

7. A full treatment of "Authority" from a feminist perspective is found in Letty M. Russell, *Household of Freedom* (Philadelphia, 1987).

8. Phyllis Trible, *God and the Rhetoric of Sexuality* (Philadelphia, 1978), p. 202.

9. Phyllis Trible, *Texts of Terror* (Philadelphia, 1984), p. 3.

10. Resources abound for such literature: fiction and nonfiction, poetry as well as prose. For a substantial beginning, see Sandra M. Gilbert and Susan Gubar, eds., *The Norton Anthology of Literature by Women* (New York, 1985).

11. See Carol Christ, *Diving Deep and Surfacing* (Boston, 1980), pp. 97–117.

12. A provocative discussion of the metaphors *Father, Mother,* and *the Goddess* as they refer to the divine reality in the emerging understandings of black and white women may be found in Susan Thistlethwaite, *Sex, Race, and God* (New York, 1989), pp. 109–25. For abused children as well as for adults who were abused as children, images of God as Father—or Mother, or Parent—must truly be problematic. The issue of the impact that our choices of metaphors for the divine reality have on persons who have been the victims of abuse becomes very concrete when we consider the staggering statistic—wrenching reality—that "one in three girls, and one out of seven boys, are sexually abused by the time they reach the age of eighteen" (Ellen Bass and Laura Davis, *The Courage to Heal: A Guide for Women Survivors of Child Sexual Abuse* [New York, 1988], p. 20). Males are most often, but by no means exclusively, the perpetrators (for further information on the incidence and effects of incest and other forms of child sexual abuse, see especially the following studies: D. E. H. Russell, *The Secret*

Trauma: Incest in the Lives of Girls and Women [New York, 1986]; Christine A. Courtois, *Healing the Incest Wound: Adult Survivors in Therapy* [New York, 1988], pp. 16–17; Kathryn Quina and Nancy L. Carlson, *Rape, Incest, and Sexual Harassment: A Guide for Helping Survivors* [New York, 1989]; Mike Lew, *Victims No Longer: Men Recovering from Incest and Other Sexual Child Abuse* [New York, 1988], p. 40). Add in other forms of abuse and neglect and the numbers of men and women who have been victimized by one or both parents increases further still. In simple, crass, demographic terms, avoidance and even outright denial of this issue by church and synagogue mean the neglect of well over one-half of any congregation (a much higher percentage obtains if we take into account the families, friends, and partners of the abused). Should we consider this neglect—revealed especially in chosen images of God—as one more way that victims are revictimized? 13. Alice Walker, *The Color Purple* (New York, 1982), p. 165.

14. Cf. Sallie McFague, *Models of God* (Philadelphia, 1987); and Carol Christ, *Laughter of Aphrodite* (New York, 1987).

15. Elizabeth Johnson, "The Incomprehensibility of God and the Image of God Male and Female," in Joan Wolski Conn, ed., *Women's Spirituality: Resources for Christian Development* (New York, 1986), pp. 243–60.

16. Thistlethwaite, *Sex, Race, and God,* p. 91.

17. Marjorie Procter-Smith, *In Her Own Rite: Constructing Feminist Liturgical Tradition* (Nashville, 1990), p. 13.

18. Ibid., p. 13.

19. Marjorie Procter-Smith, " 'Reorganizing Victimization': The Intersection between Liturgy and Domestic Violence," *Perkins Journal* (October 1987): 21.

20. Rich, "Transcendental Etude," p. 73.

21. Ibid., p. 74.

Conclusion

Mark Searle is Associate Professor of Liturgy at the University of Notre Dame. His interests are broad, ranging from the pastoral to the historical, from theology to semiotics. His conclusion to this volume returns us to its starting point, the question, What is a liturgical tradition? And what, therefore, should its future be some day? Aware as few people are of the changes in worship chronicled in part 2, and conscious of the critiques developed in part 3, Searle develops here his own vision of the promise and the pitfalls that may await liturgical planners intent on carrying our liturgical reformation into the twenty-first century.

Two Liturgical Traditions: Looking to the Future:

MARK SEARLE

> Things hidden belong to the Lord our God, but things
> revealed are ours and our children's for all time, so that
> we may observe all the words of this Law.
>
> Deuteronomy 29:28–29

Perhaps not the least interesting dimension of looking to the future of our two liturgical traditions is the fact that the matter should be raised at all. For most generations before us, the only question worth asking about the future was the question of when the end time would arrive. Today, however, the question concerns the future of our traditions. Of old, the question was motivated by hope; today, I suspect, our question is prompted by anxiety. Can what has survived so long survive much longer? Can it survive in its present form? The question of the future arises out of the uncertainties of the present, uncomfortably aware as we are of how little exists in the wider culture to sustain and support the crucial process of transmission against the fallibilities of both ourselves and our children, and how much there is in contemporary experience that undermines our confidence that what we now have deserves to be passed on.

Looking to the future, then, means looking to the present and to how the present already conditions the future. Besides, since things hidden belong to God, our only window onto the future is the present: for us, neither the future nor the past exists except as tensed dimensions, syntactic variants, of the present. Moreover, just as past and future exist only as dimensions of the present, so too does tradition exist only in the lives of people living in the present. Sedimentations of tradition surely seep into books and monuments, but books do not become bearers of the tradition unless they are read by those who are already heirs of that tradition; and monuments, unless they are inhabited by practitioners of the tradition, preserve only memories. Tradition is something alive, past and future meeting in the living present. Liturgy is now or not at all. If we cannot predict the shape it will assume, we must at least assume responsibility for the shape it now has, the shape in which it will be passed on for another generation to live by and to be responsible for.

In reflecting, then, on our present responsibilities to the future, three issues remain to be explored: first, the place of ritual in sustaining tradition; second, some broad characteristics of contemporary American culture that impinge upon liturgical traditions of all kinds; third, some intimations of how our liturgical traditions might have to develop if they are to sustain the next generation in walking in the way of the Lord.

RITUAL AND TRADITION

The first question to be asked concerning the future of our liturgical traditions concerns the connection between liturgy and tradition. Is liturgy essential to the survival of tradition, or is it simply an aspect of tradition that can be taken or left?

At the outset let us clear up an important misunderstanding about the relationship between ritual and tradition. Christians of all stripes share a tendency to concede priority to faith over practice, doctrine over ritual. They take as almost axiomatic that an authentic religious life is the external expression of prior religious convictions. The truth, of course, is rather more complex: a symbiotic relationship exists between belief and practice such that, as studies of conversion have shown, it is often practice that gives rise to faith, rather than vice versa. Isaac Bashevis Singer makes this very point in his novel *The Penitent,* as Joseph Shapiro, a returned Jew, explains:

> Long after I had become a Jew with beard and earlocks, I still lacked faith. But faith gradually grew within me. The deeds must come first. Long before the child knows that it has a stomach, it wants to eat. Long before you reach total faith, you must act in a Jewish way. Jewishness leads to faith. I know now that there is a God.[1]

Tradition is the continuity of such knowing-by-doing from generation to generation. To become a believer is not so much to be instructed in what believers believe as to be inducted into what believers do, into the patterns of interaction and communication that give the community its specific identity, its characteristic ethos. Entering the community, one enters a world of meanings, communicated symbolically rather than discursively, by which one learns to make sense of the world and adopts appropriate attitudes and commitments in light of the founding religious experience from which the tradition sprang.

The priority of symbolic over discursive modes of knowing is captured in Clifford Geertz's well-known definition of religion as

> a system of symbols which acts to establish powerful, pervasive, and long-lasting moods and motivations in men [and women] by formulating conceptions of a general order of existence and clothing these conceptions with such an aura of factuality that the moods and motivations seem uniquely realistic.[2]

The means whereby such "conceptions of a general order of existence" together with their appropriate "moods and motivations" are sustained and passed on are, of course, as many as the ways in which believers associate together. The tradition takes forms as disparate as architectural styles and folktales, as far-flung as cookery and philosophy, but it is ritual as a whole, and religious ritual in particular, that is the kernel of the tradition. As Geertz goes on to point out,

It is in ritual—i.e. consecrated behavior—that this conviction that religious conceptions are veridical and that religious directives are sound is somehow generated. It is in some sort of ceremonial form that the moods and motivations which sacred symbols induce . . . and the general conceptions of the order of existence which they formulate . . . meet and reinforce one another. In a ritual, the world as lived and the world as imagined, fused under the agency of a single set of symbolic forms, turns out to be the same world.[3]

Two things make ritual so central to religious tradition: ritual presents the essential core of the tradition; it is enacted. Ritual participation is an entirely different way of relating to a religious tradition from, say, studying that tradition by reading about it or listening to lectures about it. Ritual does not merely make one think about religion. It makes one religious, in that it leads one of necessity to behave religiously, so that over time, and in company with the community, one gradually becomes formed as a religious person. It does not merely present the tradition; it enacts it. It claims not merely one's attention but one's commitment. It is self-involving. In participating, one gives oneself over to the conventions of a given community, adopting and appropriating the values, the myth, the *Weltanschauung* embodied in the rite. In ritual, above all, one appropriates the tradition in condensed, symbolic form and is socialized into the religious consciousness that is what ultimately constitutes the tradition. In ritual, the tradition formed and developed over a long span of time becomes present in the concreteness of the here and now to catch the participants up into a life larger than their own lives, into a world more real than their own world. The here and now is validated by being caught up into what is always and everywhere. The lives of the participants are given new value by being integrated into the larger, mythic history that reaches back through generations to the beginning of known time and forward through generations to come to the end of time, while the world of their own joys, griefs, and preoccupations is fitted into place in the great cosmic scheme of things. The world of daily life is reinterpreted through the symbols of the rite in what Peter Berger calls "an inner antiphony" between subjective experience and the authority of the tradition.[4]

Tradition will always exist because human beings, unlike other animals, live in, indeed are born into, a world that is already a world of meaning. If we would contribute to it, we must first become part of it, must draw from the tradition. But it is ritual above all that grafts us onto the larger life of the tradition, giving meaning to our lives even as we give life to the tradition.

But precisely here we run into the present crisis of our traditions. Among Christians, approximately 40 percent of mainline Protestants and 55 percent of Roman Catholics regularly take part in the rituals of their churches, while regular synagogue attendance among Jews is as low as 13 percent (though Jews show stronger loyalty to their religious community than do liberal and moderate Protestants, matching that shown by Roman Catholics).[5] This, of course, corroborates the view that not ritual alone but a more diffuse sense of family belonging as well enables people to continue to identify with their tradition. But if, as I have argued, ritual practice is what finally assures the survival of a tradition, only those who continue to observe the tradition's rituals can be relied on to maintain that tradition into the future.

This is particularly a problem for Roman Catholics today, as the Notre Dame Study of Catholic Parish Life revealed. The study found strong confirmation for Andrew Greeley's "communal Catholic," the Catholic who remains Catholic, but on his or her own terms, practicing and believing selectively. What is most interesting, I think, from our perspective, is that even among practicing Catholics, 50 percent felt that regular attendance at Mass was not essential to being "a good Catholic,"[6] despite the long history of defining "active" and "lapsed" Catholics in terms of the regularity with which they frequented the sacraments. This sense of there being a large number of Catholics living off the past tradition but insufficiently literate and committed to be able to pass it

on is shared by John Deedy, who speaks of the crucial role of
the present generation of what he calls "bridge Catholics,"
people shaped by the past but unsure of what they want to
hand on to the future.

> For those who want the past to carry forward, it is not exactly
> easy to be optimistic. In the old days, faith and culture were
> handed on from generation to generation like a cloned unit of
> heredity. The faith is not being handed on in the same way these
> days. Thus the link to the church and its culture weakens.[7]

What I am suggesting, then, is that the connection between liturgy and tradition is such that religious traditions
survive and nourish the lives of their adherents chiefly
through ritual practice or liturgy, so that where the importance of the liturgy is diminished, the survival of the tradition
is in doubt. Those socialized in their youth into the tradition
but neglecting its ritual practice later in life will themselves
continue to live off the tradition, identifying themselves in
some sense as Christians or Jews, but they are unlikely to be
effective transmitters of that tradition to the next generation.
This perennial problem has reached new proportions in our
own time. Why?

THE AMERICAN CULTURAL CONTEXT

It is a commonplace among historians of Judaism and Catholicism in America to say that each tradition has "come of
age" and has finally entered the American mainstream.
American Jews, it is said, are now *American* Jews in a more
profound sense than Jews in Europe might be said to be German, French, or English Jews, for they have come to a stage
where Jewish tradition and American culture have combined
to create a new kind of Jew. Among Christians, it is particularly the Roman Catholics who in the past have tended
to look back, as Jews looked back, to their European roots,
who lived in ethnic enclaves but have now finally "made
it" in America and are in the process of developing a genu-

inely American Catholicism. What this means is that, in Lawrence A. Hoffman's terms, Jews and Christians are experiencing a growing convergence in the style of their religiosity as they assimilate elements of the larger American culture. Moreover, there is every reason to believe that the "American experiment," as it is called, has probably set the stage for how the world will evolve in the near future. In other words, the way religious traditions come to terms with modernity in America will undoubtedly influence the ways in which the same confrontation will be handled in other parts of the world.

This confrontation with modernity is not exactly new. It began with the Reformation, took off with the Enlightenment, and has shaped American life from the beginning. The term *modernity* refers particularly to two related phenomena: the break with tradition and the shifting of authority from external sources to personal experience. These phenomena have in turn given birth to two cultural characteristics that typify the western world but that have found their most explicit affirmation and celebration in America: the myth of progress and the experience of pluralism.

The Myth of Progress

The American experiment is a product of the Enlightenment and of the break with the past and with tradition that the Enlightenment represented. Here there arose a reliance upon rationality, efficiency, development, and progress that gloried in freeing itself from the shackles of superstition and authoritarianism that in the past had held humanity in bondage. As Edward Shils put it:

> In nearly every Western country, an increasing proportion of educated and enlightened persons has for a long time thought that a great many of the beliefs, practices, and institutions prevailing in their societies need to be changed, replaced, or discarded in favor of new ones, which would invariably be better ones. . . . Even with the slight recent turn in the fortunes of the

inheritance and of the past from which it comes, the accent of intellectual and political discourse still remains on a movement forward from the recent and remote past. The emphasis is on improvement.[8]

Despite a rather superficial interest in family roots and an equally meaningless fancy for collecting antiques, Americans by and large feel little attachment to the past. Impatient with the outdated, intolerant of inherited constraints, eager to try out the new, the more advanced, the more enlightened, this country is predicated on breaking with the past and pushing ever forward to new frontiers. Old ways of doing things are assumed to be no longer viable.

The religious dimensions of this break with the authority of tradition were integral to it from the beginning. In the sixteenth century, *sola scriptura* challenged the authority of tradition, and *sola fide* the authority of the church, so that, in Peter Berger's words, "the history of Protestant theology is a paradigm for the confrontation with modernity."[9] Modernity exploded upon Judaism in the nineteenth century with such impact that all three major movements of contemporary Judaism—Reform, Conservative, and Orthodox—are defined essentially by their response to it. Today modernity is a particular problem for Roman Catholics simply because the Roman church, after ignoring it for so long, has only in this century, and particularly in the last thirty years or so, come to grapple with it. In each tradition, the issues have been essentially the same: the challenge to traditional authority mounted by the appeal to experience on the one hand and to historical consciousness on the other. In the nineteenth and twentieth centuries particularly, the study of history became the tool by which moderns could be liberated from the burdens of tradition, rendering it an epiphenomenon of historical circumstance. But, having discredited tradition, historical criticism had to provide its own myth of continuity. As Franz Rosenzweig has written,

> Since the simple acceptance of tradition was no longer admissible, it was necessary to discover a new principle according to

which those *disjecta membra* of the tradition which the critique
had left in its wake could again be fused into one vital whole.
This principle was found in the idea of "progress" of
humanity.[10]

While this new myth, and the whole phenomenon of modernity itself, has fallen somewhat into discredit among many
thinkers today, it still exercises a powerful influence over the
popular mind, while in the university the reduction of tradition to history "as it really was" continues to dominate the
academic study of the Bible and theology.

Pluralism

With the debunking of tradition, the individual is left with
the freedom to choose in matters of religion, as in all else. It
was to protect such freedom that dissenters, recusants, and
nonconformists came to America in the first place, looking
for what they could not find in Europe: a space to live out
their religious convictions. Despite some early forms of establishment, America self-consciously nurtured religious tolerance, which meant religious pluralism. Not one church
binding the nation together in a single religious community,
but a growing multiplicity of churches, sects, and free-
thinkers gave every citizen the freedom to worship—or not to
worship—in accordance with his or her individual conscience. For Christian churches, this has meant coming to
terms with disestablishment and with the religious marketplace; for Jews it has meant coming to terms with emancipation and finding ways of defining identity when an op-
pressive Christian majority no longer defines their identity
for them. For both Christians and Jews, it has been a novel
experience of finding their particular religious communities
to be for the first time a more or less voluntary association
of believers.

The general effect of this experiment has been to situate
religion as belonging more properly to the private, than to
the public, realm. In rejecting any establishment of religion,

the only alternative seemed to be its confinement to the private spheres of domestic life and individual conscience. For a long time, the full implications of such a shift were disguised by the continuance of older forms of community, but they became more apparent in recent decades with the advent of the technological revolution and the creation of mass society. Whereas the industrial revolution began the process by drawing people off the land and out of small, more homogeneous rural communities into the new cities, it also left intact many characteristics of the preindustrial world: the small business; the family farm; the ethnic enclaves where traditional forms of association, and traditional forms of religion, continued to survive. But the second revolution, the revolution in the means of communication—the introduction of telephone and radio and television, the replacement of railroads by interstate highways and of ships by air transportation—has finally swept away most remnants of older forms of community.[11]

These changes link up with and reinforce the myth of progress mentioned earlier, but the further fragmentation of traditional forms of community has meant that pluralism, from being a characteristic of national life, has become also an inescapable fact of local life, where religious beliefs and practices have become so much a matter of personal preference that they are no longer necessarily shared even within the same family. What support had existed for religious traditions in homogeneous local communities has been progressively whittled away, to the point where, in matters of religion, everyone stands alone.

Individualism

So much do we take for granted the enormous split that has opened up between public and private selves and the removal of questions of ultimate concern from the public to the private forum, that we seldom recognize how eccentric our civilization is in the history of humanity, or what extraordinary capacity for adaptation it takes to live with it. We know we live in a world very different from the world in which our liturgical traditions developed. It is not difficult to see that a major source of contemporary alienation from our liturgy lies in the fact that the attitudes we need to survive in our culture are profoundly at odds with the attitudes presupposed and fostered by our liturgical traditions.

One of the attitudes most commonly noted today as characteristic of our society is individualism, described by Edward Shils as "the metaphysical dread of being encumbered by something alien to oneself."[12] Robert Bellah, who, with his colleagues, has done more than anyone to bring the phenomenon to our attention, describes it as the radical freedom to choose our own values and priorities without reference to any wider framework of common purpose or beliefs: "We believe in the dignity, indeed the sacredness, of the individual. Anything that would violate our right to think for ourselves, make our own decisions, live our lives as we see fit, is not only morally wrong, it is sacrilegious."[13] The result is a view of society that sees it as merely a conglomeration of individuals, rather than seeing the individual as the product of an historical community; a tendency to prefer one's own judgment over the judgment of tradition or authority; the quest for self-realization rather than service of the common good; the relinquishment of responsibility for public affairs to managers and technocrats; the valuing of personal freedom over social responsibility. Such radical individualism is a survival response to the conditions of modern living, but where it prevails it undermines our confidence in tradition and renders ritual suspect. In short, it creates a radical incapacity for community.

The Ideology of Intimacy

Such incapacity for community living, however, does not destroy our need for it. In face of the breakdown of older forms of community, there has developed what Francis Mannion has called "intimization: the process by which social complexity is eschewed in favor of a model of human coexistence that puts ultimate value on bonds of intimacy, personal closeness, and radical familiarity."[14] This cult of intimacy manifests itself in the psychologization of religion, in the cult of immediacy, spontaneity, and joyous mutual affirmation. This cult of intimacy is not without its virtues. Some would even go so far as to say that it represents for modern people a new mode of access to the numinous.[15] Max Sennet, however, calls it an "ideology" and argues that it reflects disillusionment with the complex nature of social existence and further contributes to the unwitting loss of those ritual codes and systems that facilitate the negotiation of relations and commitments in the public world.[16]

The religious impact of the ideology of intimacy is visible in the preference for an experiential-expressive approach to religion, an approach that gives priority to personal and interpersonal experience and sees traditional rites and doctrines as so many symbolic expressions thereof. As George Lindbeck puts it, "The structures of modernity press individuals to meet God in the depth of their souls and then, perhaps, if they find something personally congenial, to become part of a tradition, or join a church."[17] The result is the kind of religious group of community that Bellah has identified as a "life-style enclave," where "community and attachment come not from the demands of a tradition, but from the empathetic sharing of feelings among therapeutically attuned selves."[18] Thus, while inherited tradition is stripped of its authority, any and all traditions can be selectively drawn upon if they are found meaningful, to the point where couples write their own marriage rites and Christians who feel so inclined have no misgivings about pirating the Passover seder for their own use on Holy Thursday.

The characteristic elements of American culture all too baldly described here clearly overlap as interrelated dimensions of a new cultural synthesis. This synthesis is new, for while it has its roots in earlier times it represents a genuine break with previous human experience in its accentuation of the autonomy of the individual and in how the implications of such autonomy have been allowed to work themselves out.[19] Obviously, this has brought with it enormous gains that cannot conceivably be relinquished, gains in terms of re-spect for the inviolable dignity of the human person and the elaboration and safeguarding of personal rights, as also in terms of the promise it holds for an end to sectarian vio-lence. But at the same time, it is in many respects at odds now with the very traditions from which it sprang.

If we look at the state of our liturgical traditions today, we can see that the impact of our cultural experience manifests itself in different ways, ranging from impersonal, routinized celebrations at one end of the scale to intense, small-group celebrations at the other. As the English sociologist, David Martin, noted a decade ago:

> The Church itself must reflect these varied pressures: the bu-reaucratization and impersonality, and the reaction in the form either of a familistic suburban religion or else in radical celebra-tions of personal authenticity or community. The rationalization of church organizations and liturgy proceeds *pari passu* with cults of encounter, authenticity, and religious excitement, all of which leap over the constricting limits of the contemporary or-ganization of roles.[20]

At one extreme, then, we find more or less listless perfor-mances of the official rites, conducted with a minimum of participation before scattered congregations in half-empty buildings—liturgies that reflect one pole of our culture: its impersonalism, bureaucratization, privatization, consumer-ism, and functionalism. On the other extreme are celebra-tions that have acceded to the ideology of intimacy—celebrations marked by high levels of participation, low levels of formality, sitting loose to the requirements of au-thority and tradition, democratic in spirit, folksy in tone, open to everything but the past.

The question is this: Where do we go from here? To more reforms of liturgical texts, which may or may not be used? Do we persevere with uninspired and uninspiring and unde-manding celebrations for those who continue to want that kind of thing? Do we ride the wave of intimacy, multiplying small-group celebrations for those who have the energy and commitment to organize them? Or is there some alternative?

LOOKING TO THE FUTURE

In looking to the future, the question is, not merely the pragmatic one of how to continue to adapt our liturgical traditions to the culture of our times, but also the theological one of how to determine whether any or all of the features of our culture are compatible with what our traditions tell us concerning the nature and destiny of the human community and the ways in which our religious communities must reflect that. My own judgment would be that pluralism is the fundamental issue in our culture and is not incompatible in itself with what we understand God's will to be. Nor, frankly, is pluralism likely to disappear—short of some global catastrophe—since it is inseparable from the freedom of choice that modern living provides.[21] On the other hand, the myth of progress is at odds with our theological anthropology, since the myth undermines the awareness of human contingency that is at the root of the religious experience and represents a facile dismissal of the problem of sin and evil. There are signs, in any case, that it is no longer the convincing myth that it once was. Individualism and the cult of intimacy seem equally at odds with our traditions, because they run counter to the conviction that God is creating a people, not merely saving individuals. Besides, to the extent that they promote withdrawal from social responsibilities in pursuit of self-realization, they come uncomfortably close to the biblical concept of sin-as-division; while to the extent that they promote the vision of a private and personal God, they deny the essentially public character of our God as God of all the earth. In short, pluralism will not and need not disappear, but there might be a way of living with pluralism that is more consonant with the biblical tradition than what we have developed heretofore.

It is also worth noting, I think, that the impact of modernity has also been to produce a realignment of our religious traditions. As we noted, it was the Jewish response to the Enlightenment in the first place that replaced Judaism with Judaisms: Reform, Conservative, and Orthodox. The impact on Christianity was not as marked, since its unity had already been ruptured in an earlier encounter with modernity in the sixteenth century. Today, however, the confrontation with modernity is creating new alliances and new divisions comparable to those of Judaism, so that it would almost make more sense to speak of orthodox, conservative, and reform Christianity than it does to speak of Orthodox, Catholic, and Protestant. Every denomination, especially the more authoritarian ones such as Roman Catholicism and Southern Baptist, are living through their response to modernity in painful internal struggles in which many adherents are finding to their surprise that they are closer to other believers than they are to their own coreligionists.

The struggle is confusing because it is worked out along so many different axes: historicism vs. abiding truth; authoritarianism vs. popularism; collectivism vs. individualism; orthodoxy vs. authenticity; and so on. Our officially reformed rites often do little more than paper over the cracks, masking the issues rather than confronting them. The question, though, is not whether these dichotomies can be resolved but whether these dialectics can be transcended in a new religious synthesis that can speak to the conditions of modernity and point us beyond its limitations, a synthesis that espouses pluralism yet manages to avoid the privatization of religion.

Looking to the future, then, means looking for some clue as to how such a conjunction and transcendence of opposites might occur. For such a task, one naturally turns to what one finds at hand, so I want to pause briefly to consider a fascinating, though as yet precarious, new development in my own Roman Catholic community.

The past twenty-five years have seen some remarkable things happening in the Roman Catholic church, but few are more remarkable than the transformation that has occurred in Catholic social doctrine. The term *Catholic social doctrine* is used to refer rather specifically to that tradition of social teaching inaugurated by Leo XIII's 1891 encyclical on the condition of the working classes (*Rerum novarum*) and continued by similar statements of consecutive popes and of the Second Vatican Council. Its most recent representatives are John Paul II's two major encyclicals on the nature of work and on the problems of development.

To appreciate the changes that have occurred in this social doctrine and their relevance for our topic, one must realize that, in its classical phase, from Leo XIII to John XXIII, Catholic social doctrine had certain well-defined characteristics.[22]

First of all, while it represented a major step in the church's coming to terms with the modern world, social doctrine was marked by a certain nostalgia for the era of Christendom. This was never made explicit after the early years, but talk of "restoring" or "reconstructing" a Christian social order represented a hankering after the simpler times of preindustrial Christendom and a vision of society in conformity with the church's model of what a just society would look like. This corresponded to a vision of the parish in the liturgical movement that was modeled on the medieval village. The nostalgia of Jewish immigrants for the *shtetl* of eastern Europe was, perhaps, a similar phenomenon.

Second, Catholic social teaching in its early phase generally accepted existing social structures, which meant existing European social structures; and it advocated a social ethic that worked within those structures rather than challenging them. The emphasis was on a change of heart on the part of both industrialists and workers, where the rich and powerful would be kind to the poor, and inferiors would respect their superiors.

Third, the source of this social teaching was to be found in a purportedly timeless social philosophy that was thought to transcend history and culture and to be equally applicable all over the world, though it was in fact a European creation and represented the ideology of European bourgeois society.[23]

The Second Vatican Council, especially in its Constitution on the Church in the Modern World (*Gaudium et spes*, 1965), represented the beginning of a profound change of focus and method in the tradition of Catholic social doctrine. The very title of the constitution reflects a significant alteration of perspective: the church *in* the world, rather than the church seeing itself somehow apart from the world or above the world. Again using very broad strokes, we can summarize the main characteristics of this new direction as follows:

First, there is a newly present acceptance of history and of historical processes, resulting in the abandonment of supposedly universal social principles and in a newfound willingness to read the signs of the times.

Second, there is a corresponding willingness to engage in dialogue within the church itself, with other believers, and with people of good will everywhere, in order to determine the problems of specific situations and what changes might need to be worked for. The word that has emerged to characterize this new attitude, especially in the letters of John Paul II, is *solidarity,* a term that expresses both the need for the church to engage in the social process and the kind of relationships that need to be developed between groups, nations, and blocs in resolving the problems of poverty, powerlessness, and underdevelopment.

Third, the focus of Catholic social teaching has shifted from justice issues within individual nations to global issues of economic, political, and cultural interdependence, as well as to what Paul VI called the new issues of the postindustrial world, such as the role of women, the development of new forms of social organization, the strengthening of international bodies, and so forth.

Fourth, in accepting the reality of pluralism and the historicity of human societies and cultures, the church has redefined its own role. From claiming the right to teach all nations timeless principles of social equity, the church has shifted into a more prophetic role, speaking in more explicitly religious terms and referring more directly to its own resources in scripture and in the Christian tradition. The present pope, in particular, brings a strongly theological angle to the evaluation and analysis of contemporary problems.

Interestingly enough, the recent encyclical of John Paul II is the first in this whole tradition to refer to the liturgy in support of its presentation of Catholic social doctrine, seeing in the eucharist an embodiment of those "consensual values" that must guide Christian life and action in the world.[24]

How do such developments serve as a guide for the way forward?

The key to the relationship between liturgical tradition, on the one hand, and the broader culture, on the other, is to be found in the way the *ecclesia*—using that term to refer to any religious community—sees itself. In its recent social doctrine, the Roman Catholic church seems to be doing more than issuing a different kind of social teaching: it is in the process of redefining its role in the world in relation to culture. Instead of being the unwitting accomplice of nineteenth- and early twentieth-century European culture, it has come to appreciate that it is now no longer a European church but a world church. In so doing, it has at the same time explicitly reexamined its vocation, its place in the divine plan, in the light of its realization that it lives, not in a Christian world, but in a pluralistic one. It has come to reappropriate its role as a community of memory and a community of hope, a divinely summoned witness to the reality of God and to the promises of salvation. It has come, furthermore, to see that those promises, while not fully to be realized until the end time, are nonetheless valid now and are to be acted upon and worked for in the course of history. As yet, the ramifications of this new public and prophetic role for the church have not been worked out in all areas of its life, yet it would seem to be significant for the future of our liturgical traditions.

For our liturgical traditions to come to terms with the conditions of modernity without yielding to its seductions, it will be necessary for each religious community to come to terms with what it means to be a convenanted people of God. Too often in the past, the claim of election has been a claim of privilege, as if being chosen were for the sake of the chosen and not for the sake of the others. In a pluralistic world, the question is not whether we are a chosen people but what we are chosen *for* and how that is to benefit all God's creation. To be sure, the existence of Israel as a chosen people and the apparent continuing validity of the Mosaic covenant is a problem for Christians, a problem comparable only to the dilemma that Christianity presents for Jews. But the hint given in Catholic social teaching is that to look at the matter this way is to ignore the question of the responsibilities to the larger human community that come with being chosen.

The religious crisis of our time derives not from pluralism itself but from the baneful effects of how we have responded to it hitherto: the privatization of religion, radical individualism, the ideology of intimacy. The cultural crisis that is upon us is the effect of ceasing to believe in, or to be committed to, anything bigger than oneself. The religious crisis is the result of having reshaped our tradition to canonize this error and to reduce the God of all the earth to a convenient deity who meets our spiritual and emotional needs in the wake of our loss of community.

A new sense of *ecclesia* will need to recover three things. First, a sense of the divine vocation of the community, rooted in its history but calling it, as a very particular community with its own historical tradition, into the future. This means each of us undertaking a profound recovery of our own tradition in light of new circumstances. Now and in the future, the term *chosen people* will carry a double entendre: it means a people chosen by God, but also a people constituted by those who have chosen to respond to that call. If traditionalism emphasizes the givenness of our situation, and modernity emphasizes our freedom to choose who we shall be, the only successful outcome to the dialectic is to be found in the recovery of the sense of a particular historical vocation.

Second, the *ecclesia* will need to recognize that its own future is inseparable from the future of humanity as a whole, which is God's creation, made in God's own image. This does not mean, as the relativists have it, that we are all going the same way home. It means that the recovery of particularity will have to be conjoined with a sense of universality, in what Samuel Karff refers to as an *open particularism*.[25] Whatever importance be ascribed to the State of Israel, Judaism is no longer a Mediterranean religion. Nor is Christianity. Catholicism looks to Rome, but it is no longer Roman: it is catholic. Israel is also catholic, and not only in the sense in which Solomon Schechter spoke of "catholic Israel." The challenge is to see our particularity as a form of solidarity with the whole human race whose future we share, for whose *shalom* we are called to work, on behalf of whom we offer up praise and entreaty as a priestly people. Once again we confront a dialectic, between a particularism that emphasizes difference and a universalism that relativizes difference. The only successful outcome must be a contemplative awareness of our common humanity, a humanity that never exists in the universal and abstract but only in the concrete and particular.

Third, the *ecclesia* will seek the numinous not in the frisson of awe and trembling, nor in the intimacies of interpersonal sharing. Not that God is not to be found there, but the way to God is always through self-transcendence, through selflessness, through the exodus into the unknown future into which we are called. Today the *mysterium tremendum* of Rudolph Otto runs the risk of being confused with aesthetic pleasure, while the individual search for religious experience is obviously open to the deceptions of narcissism. Today the commitment to what is larger than ourselves, what transcends and embraces us and reveals us to ourselves in all our contingency and all our dignity, will take us into the public realm to confront us once again with the God of history and with the God of all humanity, with the God who said: "If you are my witnesses, then I am God. If you are not my witnesses, than it is as if I am not God."

Looking to the future, then, I would envisage our liturgical traditions moving on beyond our generation but marked by the struggles we are engaged in. I would see the future of the liturgy as being marked by a common style, whatever our tradition, and I would see that style as having three characteristics:

1. It would be conservative and particularistic, because of our sense of history and our awareness of belonging to a tradition much larger than ourselves.
2. It would be public, in the sense that it would be marked by the self-consciousness of a people that knows itself to be a kingdom of priests and a holy nation, mediating on behalf of all humanity with the God who said: "all the earth is mine" (Exodus 19:5–6).
3. And it would be contemplative, for without contemplation we would not become aware of our common humanity or of the God in whose image it is made and to union with whom all human beings are called.

"Things hidden belong to the Lord our God, but things revealed are ours and our children's for all time, so that we may observe all the words of this Law." In the end, for all our looking to the future, we cannot get much beyond the wisdom of these words. Perhaps that is as well. At least, such seems to be the point of the old hasidic tale told of Rabbi Abraham Yehoshua Heschel of Apt:

> When young Heschel walked across the field, he heard the future in the rustle of growing things; and when he walked through the streets he heard the future in human footsteps. But when he fled from the world and withdrew to the silence of his room, his own limbs told him of the future. Then he began to fear, being uncertain whether he could keep to the true way, now that he knew where his feet were taking him. So he gathered courage and prayed that this knowledge be taken from him. And God in his mercy granted his prayer.[26]

NOTES

1. Isaac Bashevis Singer, *The Penitent* (New York, 1983), p. 161.

2. Clifford Geertz, "Religion as a Cultural System," in Michael Banton, ed., *Anthropological Approaches to Religion* (London, 1965), p. 4.

3. Ibid., p. 28.

4. Peter L. Berger, *The Heretical Imperative: Contemporary Possibilities of Religious Affirmation* (Garden City, N.Y., 1979), p. 66.

5. Wade Clark Roof and William McKinney, *American Mainline Religion: Its Changing Shape and Future* (New Brunswick, N.J., 1987), pp. 83–84.

6. Joseph Gremillion and Jim Castelli, *The Emerging Parish: The Notre Dame Study of Catholic Life since Vatican II* (New York, 1988), p. 50.

7. John G. Deedy, *American Catholicism: And Now Where?* (New York, 1987), p. 173.

8. Edward Shils, *Tradition* (Chicago, 1981), p. 2.

9. Berger, *Heretical Imperative*, p. 57.

10. Franz Rosenzweig, *The Star of Redemption*, 2d ed., trans. by W. W. Hallo (New York, 1970), reprint ed. (Notre Dame, 1985), p. 99.

11. See David Martin, *A General Theory of Secularization* (New York, 1978), p. 87.

12. Shils, *Tradition*, p. 10.

13. Robert Bellah et al, *Habits of the Heart* (Berkeley, Cal., 1984), p. 142.

14. M. Francis Mannion, "Liturgy and the Present Crisis of Culture," *Worship* 62/2 (1988): 108.

15. See Lawrence A. Hoffman, *Beyond the Text: A Holistic Approach to Liturgy,* Jewish Literature and Culture (Bloomington, Ind., 1987), pp. 164–71.

16. Max Sennet, *The Fall of Public Man* (New York, 1977); cited in Mannion, "Liturgy and the Present Crisis of Culture," pp. 108–9.

17. George A. Lindbeck, *The Nature of Doctrine: Religion and Theology in a Postliberal Age* (Philadelphia, 1984), p. 22.

18. Bellah et al., *Habits of the Heart*, p. 232.

19. See Louis Dumont, "A Modified View of Our Origins: The Christian Beginnings of Modern Individualism," *Religion* 12 (1982): 1–27.

20. Martin, *General Theory of Secularization*, p. 89.

21. See Berger, *Heretical Imperative*, pp. 1–31.

22. On the history and character of Catholic social doctrine see M.-D. Chenu, *La "Doctrine sociale" de l'église comme idéologie* (Paris, 1979).

23. Chenu, *Doctrine sociale,* esp. pp. 87–96.

24. John Paul II, *Sollicitudo rei socialis,* p. 48. The term *consensual values* is borrowed from Lawrence A. Hoffman, "Liturgical Basis for Social Policy: A Jewish View," in Daniel F. Polish and Eugene J. Fisher, eds., *Liturgical Foundations of Social Policy in the Catholic and Jewish Traditions* (Notre Dame, 1983), pp. 151–68.

25. See above, Samuel E. Karff's essay, "The Perception of Christians in Jewish Liturgy: Then and Now."

26. Martin Buber, *Tales of the Hasidim,* vol. 2: *The Later Masters* (New York, 1948).

Index

Abortion, 202

Abraham, covenant with, 31, 47

Abraham Joshua Heschel of
Apta, 241

Abrahams, Israel, 156

Abbott, Walter M., 63

Academic Expertise, symbol of
authority, 204–5, 207, 212

Accretion: *See* Addition

Abrogationism, 51, 52

Accommodation, as method of
liturgical reform, 74, 75, 76

Acts, Easter season readings, 60

Addition, as method of liturgical
reform, 74, 75

Advent, defined, 54; *Advent: Relation between the Scriptures*, 53;
Isaiah and Baruch readings in,
54–55; preaching on, 61

Additional Service: *See Musaf*

African-American Christianity,
people of the Exodus, 118

Alienation, 190, 231

Al Hanissim: See For the Miracles

Alenu, 34, 38, 43,

*All glory be to thee, almighty
God*, 111

*All glory be to thee, O Lord our
God*, 111

*All praise O unbegotten
God*, 105

Allegory, as exegesis, 55

Almsgiving, taught by Jesus and
Pharisees, 56

Altar, candles in Anglican church,
7, 13; dedication of in Roman
Catholic church, 74; kneeling
at elevated, 72; missal used
at, 73

Alting von Geusau, L. G. M., 85

Amen, response in Justin Martyr's
day, 71

American Conference of Cantors,
147

American Consultation on Common Texts (Lutheran), 92

American Culture, ambivalence
regarding, 169, 172–73, 226–
34; democracy and the Holy,
175; Enlightenment in, 227;
experiment in religious freedom, 46; individualism, 169,
186–88, 230–31, 234, 235,
239; intimacy (*see also* Circle),
231–34, 239; myth of progress,
227–29, 234; at odds with worship, 186–88; pluralism, 38,
165, 229–30, 234

American Episcopal Church: *See*
Episcopal Church,

American Lutheran Church
(ALC), joins Lutheran Church
in America and Lutheran
Church—Missouri Synod to
work on *Lutheran Book of
Worship*, 89

American Episcopal Church: *See*
Episcopal Church

245